From Partic

TEXT READING PROGRAM

If it were not for these enlightening Text commentaries, we would still be floundering in an intellectual soup. The soup was mighty tasty, but was difficult to get our teeth into without these brilliant observations, comparisons, and analogies. We know this is a vast body of work that has been given us and we are grateful from the bottom of our hearts.
—SYLVIA AND CAP LYONS

A very powerful tool to keep me on track, reading and absorbing just a few pages each day. This process has been an invaluable source of inner peace during this past year.
—CONNIE PORTER

Robert Perry and Greg Mackie are experts at making the sometimes challenging Text not just understandable, but rich with meaning and poignancy. This is a priceless gift to anyone who wants to fully understand the awesome teachings of *A Course in Miracles*. I can think of no better form of support than this!
—JULIA SIMPSON

The Text commentaries offer insights I could not have had alone, because of the deep understanding Robert and Greg have.
—DIETRUN BUCHMAN

An amazing journey into the genius and magnitude of this material. Don't miss this opportunity.
—SHARON EDWARDS

Robert and Greg's insights illuminate Text principles like never before.
—LORETTA M. SIANI, PH.D

I have studied the Text and read it through at least once a year for the last 19 years. I thought I knew it pretty well. However this year has been a real eye-opener. Many of those little question marks I made in the margins have been erased. I shall be forever grateful for this year of Text study.
—WENDY FINNERTY

After 20 years with the Course, I now understand it on a much different level.
—ULLA WALLIN

Robert and Greg's intelligence, insight, and wit, create a fun climate of spiritual scholarship that helps make the Text more intelligible and alive. They're extraordinarily gifted.
—AMY ELLISON

The clear and down-to-earth commentary has helped me connect with the Text as never before.
—NANCY NEVITT

Robert and Greg have a tremendous comprehension of the Course and provide down-to-earth explanations. I know of no better way to learn the message of the Text than this program.
—JAN WORLEY

Translates the beautiful poetry of the Course's Text into everyday common language, making the valuable meaning of each sentence easily understood.
—KATHERINE LATORRACA

Previously, I had never succeeded in completely reading the Text. Participating was the best thing that I did for myself this year.
—DAVID COLWELL

There is nothing else in my years of studying the Course that has helped me so much!
—GEORGE PORTER

I can honestly say I'll finally complete the reading of the entire Text—
and I've been at this for 20 years!
—Barbara Olson

Robert and Greg's insights helped me understand and assimilate the
Course's otherwise complex and difficult passages. I will do this again
next year, and the next, and the next. This program is amazing.
—Jo Chandler

Your program has been a revelation.
—Don De Lene

I would like to say that this year has been too amazing to actually put
into words.
—Kathy Chomitz

Having studied the Course faithfully for 28 years, I never imagined the
insights and miracles I would receive from these commentaries on the
Text!
—Mirkalice Gore

I can truly say that this program has made an incredible difference to
my life. I wholeheartedly recommend it.
—David Fleming

Nothing less than totally inspiring.
—Rev. Jerry Cusimano

THE ILLUMINATED TEXT

Commentaries for Deepening Your Connection with
A Course in Miracles

Robert Perry & Greg Mackie

VOLUME 6

Published by Circle Publishing
A division of the Circle of Atonement
P.O. Box 4238 * West Sedona, AZ 86340
(928) 282-0790 * www.circleofa.org
circleoffice@circleofa.org

Cover design by Thunder Mountain Design and Communications
Design & layout by Phillips Associates UK Ltd
Printed in the USA

ISBN 978-1-886602-37-3

Library of Congress Cataloging-in-Publication Data

Perry, Robert, 1960-
 The illuminated text : commentaries for deepening your connection with A course in miracles / Robert Perry & Greg Mackie.
     p. cm.
 Includes bibliographical references.
 Summary: "Provides in-depth analysis of the Text of A Course in Miracles"--Provided by publisher.
 ISBN 978-1-886602-37-3
 1. Course in Miracles. 2. Spiritual life. I. Mackie, Greg, 1963- II. Title.
 BP605.C68P455 2010
 299'.93--dc22

                        2009039354

CONTENTS

FOREWORD

The Text is the foundation of *A Course in Miracles*. Doing the Course is simply a process of learning and internalizing its thought system, and the Text is where that thought system is laid out. It is an unparalleled spiritual tour de force. Careful study of it will change your outlook in ways that perhaps nothing else can.

Many students, however, find the Text to be very hard going. Many do not finish it, and even those who make it through, perhaps repeatedly, wish they had a deeper grasp of what they were reading.

For this reason, in 2006, the Circle of Atonement offered the Text Reading Program. This was a year-long tour through the Text of *A Course in Miracles* with commentary on each paragraph, written by myself and Greg Mackie, both teachers for the Circle. Before each weekday, we would send out to all the participants via e-mail the reading for that day. This would usually consist of a single section from the Text, accompanied by our commentary as well as practical exercises.

We often supplemented these sections with material from the Urtext, the original typescript of the Course. Our experience was that, especially in the early chapters of the Text, material from the Urtext that was eventually edited out was very helpful and clarifying. So when we felt it was useful, we included this Urtext material in brackets, and let it inform our commentary. We also indicated where a word had been emphasized in the Urtext, as this too often added clarity.

Note: In this volume, words that were originally emphasized in the Urtext are <u>underlined</u>. So when you see an underlined word here, know that that word was emphasized in the Urtext, but that emphasis was not included in the eventual published Course, which included fewer emphasized words. Again, we did this because quite often that emphasis from the Urtext would add clarity.

The reason we developed this program has a bit of history to it. In 2000, we offered a local program in Sedona that included a daily Text class, using a schedule that took us through the entire Text in a year of weekday readings. (On the sixth and seventh days, we rested!) Our friend, student, and colleague John Perry attended that program. When it ended, he began guiding people through the Text using the same schedule, only doing so online. He sent out the Text material for a given day and interspersed it with his own clarifying comments. In fall 2005 he felt guided to suggest we do something similar. Our guidance told us to go ahead, and so that's what we did. Without John's suggestion, however, it is safe to say we never would have done this.

2006, the year of the program, was an intense one. I would write commentaries for three weeks. Then I got a breather for a week while Greg wrote the commentaries. And then the schedule started over. Each day we wrote the commentary that needed to go out the next day. In addition, we led a weekly phone class for participants, in which we summarized the previous week's sections. (The recordings are still available to students who sign up for the online version of the Text Reading Program.)

The response to our program far exceeded our expectations. We have included a few edited comments at the front of the book, but if you want to read the unadulterated student reactions, straight from the various horses' mouths, then go to www.circlepublishing.org and click on the link for the Text Reading Program. During the year of the program, and actually ever since, we have had consistent requests that we put this material into published form.

So here it is, presented in book form as a multi-volume set. We hope you find these commentaries illuminating, and that they do indeed deepen your understanding of the spiritual masterpiece, *A Course in Miracles*.

ROBERT PERRY
SEPTEMBER 2009
SEDONA, ARIZONA

Commentaries on Chapter 22

SALVATION AND THE HOLY RELATIONSHIP

Introduction
Commentary by Robert Perry

1. Take pity on yourself [Ur: yourselves], so long enslaved. Rejoice whom God hath joined have come together and need no longer look on sin apart. No two can look on sin together, for they could never see it in the same place and time. Sin is a strictly individual perception, seen in the other yet believed by each to be within himself. And each one seems to make a different error, and one the other cannot understand. Brother, it is the same, made by the same, and forgiven for its maker in the same way. The holiness of your relationship forgives you and your brother [Ur: you both], undoing the effects of what you both believed and saw. And with their going is the need for sin gone with them.

The first two lines refer back to "Sin as an Adjustment" (T-20.III.9), where Jesus spoke of prisoners not leaping up in joy the instant they are free. To take pity means to show mercy to someone. Jesus, therefore, is saying, "Take pity on these two slaves. Stop whipping them, for having finally found each other, they have been declared free. Show them some mercy, for 'they' happen to be you and your brother. Therefore, stop beating yourselves up and rejoice."

The thing to rejoice about is that you now have the power to see sin for what it is: nothing. Sin says to your brother, "You are the sinner. You have wounded me, and in a way that I find incomprehensible. I would never do anything like that." But then secretly, deep inside, we say, "I'm the sinner. My sinfulness is the real story here." This actually constitutes what we might call a "dual double standard," doesn't it? It says, "You're the sinner; I'm not" and "I'm the sinner; you're not." It says *two* double standards at the *same* time.

Think, then, what happens when two people join. Joining says, "We are one; there is no difference between us." See how this pushes out the statements made by sin. The oneness of joining, then, automatically cancels out the double standards of sin.

2. Who has need for sin? Only the lonely and alone, who see their brothers different from themselves. It is this difference, seen but not

real, that makes the need for sin, not real but seen, seem justified. And all this <u>would</u> be real if sin were so. For an unholy relationship is <u>based</u> on differences, where each one thinks the <u>other</u> has what <u>he</u> has <u>not</u>. They come together, each to complete <u>himself</u> and <u>rob</u> the other. They stay until they think that there is nothing left to steal, and then move on. And so they wander through a world of strangers, <u>unlike</u> themselves, living with their bodies perhaps under a common roof that shelters neither; in the same room and yet a world apart.

Sin involves taking from my brother, and this only makes sense if my brother is different from me. That hidden statement "I'm the sinner; you're not" manifests as the overt statement "I'm lacking; you're not." And this single thought propels us on a lonely search, in which everyone possesses something that we need, something we don't have. This makes us all into con men, and makes our loved ones into our "marks," whose confidence we must gain so that we can steal them blind, before moving on.

That final line is one of the most poignant in the Course. Who of us doesn't know exactly what Jesus is talking about? Who of us hasn't been under that common roof that shelters neither, or in that same room and yet a world apart? But are we prepared to admit what this implies? It implies that

- I secretly believe I'm the sinner, and they are not.
- I then consciously believe that I am lacking, and they are not.
- I therefore enter into relationships to take what they have in order to make myself whole.
- I therefore see everyone as a stranger, unlike myself, selfishly withholding from me what would make me whole.
- It is my life as a con man that makes me so lonely.

3. A holy relationship starts from a different premise. Each one has looked within and seen <u>no</u> lack. <u>Accepting</u> his completion, he would <u>extend</u> it by <u>joining</u> with another, whole as himself. He sees <u>no</u> difference [Ur: *no differences*] between these selves, for differences are <u>only</u> of the body. Therefore, he looks on nothing he would <u>take</u>. He denies <u>not</u> his own reality *because* it is the truth. Just under Heaven does he stand, but close enough <u>not</u> to return to earth. For this relationship <u>has</u> Heaven's holiness. How far from home can a relationship so like to Heaven <u>be</u>?

See how opposite a holy relationship is. (Jesus is talking about a mature or realized holy reltionship here.). The unholy relationship says, "I'm lacking; you're not; hand it over." The holy relationship says, "I'm whole; so are you; let's join."

Application: Think of relationships in your life and ask yourself which mode are you primarily in:

Unholy relationship	Holy relationship
I'm lacking.	I'm whole.
You have what will make me whole.	So are you.
How can I get it from you?	Let's join.

4. Think what a holy relationship can teach! Here is belief in differences undone. Here is the faith in differences shifted to sameness. And here is sight of differences transformed to vision. Reason now can lead you and your brother to the logical conclusion of your union. It must extend, as you extended when you and he joined. It must reach out beyond itself, as you reached out beyond the body, to let you and your brother be joined. And now the sameness that you saw extends and finally removes all sense of differences, so that the sameness that lies beneath them all becomes apparent. Here is the golden circle where you recognize the Son of God. For what is born into a holy relationship can never end.

Something is born into a holy relationship that contains the undoing of the entire separation system. There at the core of the holy relationship is the statement "We are the same." At first, this sameness seems confined to the two partners, but "We are the same; you are different from us" is not real sameness, is it? The logical extension of the sameness at the heart of the holy relationship, then, is for that sameness to spread out. The two partners inevitably become engaged in reaching out beyond their relationship, to give others the message that they, too, are the same. Thus, what was born into their relationship keeps going, keeps rippling out. And as it does, the two partners realize that the sameness they initially saw in each other never ends. And thus they finally recognize that endless, golden circle from "The Forgotten Song" (T-21.I.8). They recognize the endless light, all areas of which are the same, that is the one Son of God.

I. The Message of the Holy Relationship
Commentary by Greg Mackie

1. Let reason take another step. If you attack whom God would heal and hate the one He loves, then you and your Creator have a <u>different</u> will. Yet if you *are* His Will, what you <u>must</u> then believe is that you are <u>not</u> yourself. You can indeed believe this, and you <u>do</u>. And you <u>have</u> faith in this and see much evidence on its behalf. And where, you wonder, does your strange uneasiness, your sense of being disconnected, and your haunting fear of lack of meaning in yourself arise? It is as though you wandered in without a plan of any kind except to wander off, for only that seems certain.

In the previous paragraph, Jesus invited us to let reason lead us to the logical conclusion of our holy relationship: Just as the two of us extended beyond the body and joined one another, so must we now extend together and join with the entire Sonship. Now, we are to let reason take another step: If we refuse to extend and join—if instead we attack and hate whom God loves—we are believing that our will is different from God's. And since we ourselves *are* His Will, this belief alienates us from ourselves. Have you ever said, "I just don't feel like myself today?" The Course claims that this is the case *every* day.

Our physical senses seem to provide incontrovertible evidence that we are not holy Sons of God but solitary hunks of meat wandering aimlessly through a meaningless and chaotic world. Our lives seem so nuts, filled with the alienation and angst and absurdity described so vividly by the existentialists. All of this stems from our decision to attack instead of join.

2. Yet we have heard a very similar description earlier, but it was <u>not</u> of you [see T-20.III.7]. But still this strange idea which it <u>does</u> accurately describe, you *think* is you [Ur: You think *is* you]. Reason would tell you that the world you see through eyes that are not yours <u>must</u> make no sense to you. To whom would seeing [Ur: vision] such as this send <u>back</u> its messages? Surely not you, whose sight is wholly <u>independent</u> of the eyes that look upon the world. If this is <u>not</u> your vision, what can it

show to you? The brain cannot [Ur: can *not*] interpret what your vision sees. This *you* would understand. The brain interprets to the body, of which it is a part. But what it says you cannot understand. Yet you have listened to it. And long and hard you tried to understand its messages.

The previous paragraph's description of alienation is of the false "self" we think we have become: an ego encased in a body. Now, we use the body's eyes to report messages about the ego's world to the body's brain, which then interprets them for the body and the ego it serves. We try desperately to make sense of this crazy world, to find a meaning behind all the madness. But reason tells us we are destined to fail. Why? Because we have closed our *true* eyes—the eyes of Christ—which alone can show us meaning and sanity. The pair of glasses we're wearing is the ego's prescription, not ours. How can we make sense of anything as long as we insist on using eyes that are designed to show us nonsense?

3. You have not realized [Ur: did not realize] it is impossible to understand what fails entirely to reach you. You have received no messages at all you understand [Ur: understood]. For you have listened to what can never communicate at all. Think, then, what happens. Denying what you are, and firm in faith that you are something else, this "something else" that you have made to be yourself becomes [Ur: became] your sight. Yet it must be the "something else" that sees, and as *not* you, explains its sight *to* you. Your vision would, of course, render this quite unnecessary. Yet if your eyes are closed and you have called upon this thing to lead you, asking it to explain to you the world it sees, you have no reason not to listen, nor to suspect that what it tells you is not true. Reason would tell you it cannot be true *because* you do not understand it. God has no secrets. He does not lead you through a world of misery, waiting to tell you, at the journey's end, why He did this to you.

When we deny what we are and identify with "something else"—the ego—we see with its eyes instead of ours. We close our real eyes and let it lead us around. Its eyes are blind to reality so everything it reports to us is incomprehensible nonsense, but we don't question anything it reports to us—what it says must be true. It's as if we put on a blindfold and then hired Stevie Wonder to be our seeing eye dog. Talk about the blind leading the blind!

Reason would tell us that what the ego's eyes report to us can't be true *because* it's incomprehensible. Why? Because God, the Source of truth, never gives us anything incomprehensible. The last line here is a powerful refutation of a common view. When faced with the senseless misery of this world, religious people often tell themselves that while we don't understand all the misery now, "God works in mysterious ways," and someday—perhaps after death—He will make all things known and at last we will understand. But this is not so; "God has no secrets." He gives us only joy, and our true vision would reveal a world that makes perfect sense right now.

Application: Look around at the world you see with your physical eyes. Think of some of the painful things your journey through this world has brought you, and how hard you have tried to make sense of it. Now, say the following:

> *I have wandered through a world of misery.*
> *Long and hard I have tried to understand it.*
> *But reason would tell me that the world I see through eyes that are not mine*
> ***must** make no sense to me.*
> *It is impossible to understand what fails **entirely** to reach me.*
> *Reason would tell me it cannot be true **because** I do not understand it.*
>
> ***My** vision would render this quite unnecessary.*
> ***My** sight is wholly independent of the eyes that look upon the world.*
> *Let me see the world with my true eyes, the eyes of Christ, and find the joy of God that I can understand perfectly right now.*

4. What could be secret from God's Will? Yet you believe that you have secrets. What could your secrets be except another "will" that is your own, apart from His? Reason would tell you that this is no secret that need be hidden as a sin. But a mistake indeed! Let not your fear of sin protect it from correction, for the attraction of guilt is only fear. Here is the one emotion that you made, whatever it may seem to be. This is

8

[Ur: And it *is*] the emotion of secrecy, of private thoughts <u>and of the body</u>. This is the <u>one</u> emotion that opposes love, and <u>always</u> leads to sight of differences and <u>loss</u> of [Ur: sense of] sameness. Here is the <u>one</u> emotion that keeps you blind, dependent on the self you think you made to lead you through the world it made for you.

Not only does God have no secrets; nothing is secret *from* Him. Yet we believe we have made another will that is "secret" from His, and try to *keep* it secret from Him because we believe it is a sin. This belief makes us feel guilty, and thus afraid of God's punishment. Fear—the antithesis of love—is the inevitable outcome of our attempt to make another will apart from Love, and it is to serve the goal of fear that we close the eyes of Christ in us and let the ego use the body's eyes to show us a crazy world of private thoughts, separate bodies, differences, and sin. Yet reason would tell us that all this is ridiculous: Our other "will" is only a mistake to be corrected, not a sin to be punished. There is nothing to fear.

5. <u>Your</u> sight was <u>given</u> you, along with everything that you <u>can</u> understand. You will perceive <u>no</u> difficulty in understanding what this vision tells you, for everyone sees <u>only</u> what he thinks he <u>is</u>. And what <u>your</u> sight would show you, you will understand *because* it is the truth. Only <u>your</u> vision can convey to <u>you</u> what <u>you</u> can see. It reaches you directly, <u>without</u> a need to be <u>interpreted</u> to you. What <u>needs</u> interpretation <u>must</u> be alien. Nor will it <u>ever</u> be made understandable by an interpreter you cannot understand.

Our true sight is entirely different from physical sight. We made physical sight; our true sight was given to us. Physical sight shows us a world we can't understand; our true sight show us everything we *can* understand. We can tell physical sight is not true *because* we cannot understand it; our true sight is perfectly understandable *because* it is the truth. Physical sight conveys what the ego can see; our true sight conveys what *we* can see. Physical sight is interpreted by the ego, an interpreter we cannot understand; our true sight reaches us directly, without the need for any interpreter at all. Wouldn't it be a relief to walk open-eyed through life instead of blindfolding ourselves and following a blind guide?

6. Of all the messages you have received and failed to understand, this course alone is <u>open</u> to your understanding and <u>can</u> be understood.

This is *your* [Ur: This *is* your] language. You do not understand it yet only because your whole communication is like a baby's. The sounds a baby makes and what he hears are highly unreliable, meaning <u>different</u> things to him at different times. Neither the sounds he hears nor sights he sees are stable yet. But what he hears and does not understand <u>will be</u> his native tongue, through which he will communicate with those around him, and they with him. And the strange, shifting ones he sees about him will become to him his comforters, and he will recognize his home and see them there <u>with</u> him.

Who among us hasn't felt that the Course is too hard to understand? Actually, though, this course is the *only* thing we can really understand. It seems so difficult to us only because we've been trying so hard for so long to understand the incomprehensible messages of the ego. We've forgotten our native language, the language of God.

We are now like a baby who hasn't yet learned adult communication. What he hears is gibberish; what he sees is fuzzy and indistinct. The world is an awfully strange place to him. But eventually, the gibberish he hears will become his native language, the shadows he sees will become his loving parents, and his strange surroundings will become his home. In like manner, the message the Course is communicating to us will one day become as clear and understandable—no, *more* understandable—as "See Spot Run" is to us now.

Application: Think of the difficulty you've experienced in understanding the Course. Now, say these words:

> *What's truly not understandable is what my ego has been telling me.*
> *This course alone is open to my understanding and can be understood.*
> *It, not the language of the ego, is **my** language.*
> *It is my native tongue, so I **will** understand it.*

7. So in each holy relationship is the ability to communicate <u>instead</u> of separate reborn. Yet a holy relationship, so recently reborn itself from an unholy relationship, and yet more ancient than the old illusion it has replaced, <u>is</u> like a baby now in its rebirth. Still [Ur: Yet] in this infant is

<u>your</u> vision returned to you, and he will speak the language [Ur: *both* of] you can understand. He is not nurtured by the "something else" you <u>thought</u> was you. He was not <u>given</u> there, nor was received by anything <u>except</u> yourself. For no two brothers [Ur: people] <u>can</u> unite <u>except</u> through Christ, Whose vision sees them one.

Our holy relationship is where we relearn our native tongue: the language of God, the language of oneness. Yet at the beginning, our relationship is like the baby in the last paragraph. We've been speaking the language of unholiness for so long that the language of holiness still sounds like gibberish to us. Yet we will learn it, for in truth our holy relationship is ancient, and it brings our true language and true vision with it. It comes to us from beyond the ego we thought we were. Our holy relationship *must* replace separation with communication, for it comes from Christ, Who sees our oneness.

8. Think what is <u>given</u> you, my holy brother [Ur: brothers]. This child will teach you what you do not understand, and make it plain. For his will be no alien tongue. He will need <u>no</u> interpreter to you, for it was <u>you</u> who taught him what he knows *because* you knew it. He could not come to anyone <u>but</u> you, <u>never</u> to "something else." Where Christ has entered no one is alone, for never could He find a home in separate ones. Yet must He be reborn into His ancient home, so seeming new and yet as old as He, a tiny newcomer, dependent on the holiness of your relationship to let Him live.

Jesus never tires of reminding Helen and Bill just what a momentous occasion their joining really was. When they joined, they became Mary and Joseph, the earthly parents of the Christ. So do all of us who join in holy relationships. As he grows up, He will teach us how to return to God, and we will understand Him because He speaks a language more natural to us than any earthly tongue could ever be. In truth He is not an infant but ancient; however, He *is* an infant in our awareness, reborn into our ancient yet seemingly new holy relationship. Our job now is to nurture Him to adulthood by remembering the holiness of our relationship. Each time we choose to love one another instead of attack, we give Him the sustenance He needs to live.

9. Be certain God did [Ur: does] not entrust His Son to the unworthy.

11

Nothing but what is <u>part</u> of Him is worthy of <u>being</u> joined. Nor is it possible that anything <u>not</u> part of Him *can* join. Communication <u>must</u> have been restored to those who join, for this they <u>could</u> not do through bodies. What, then, <u>has</u> joined them? Reason will tell you that they <u>must</u> have seen each other through a vision <u>not</u> of the body, and communicated in a language the body does not speak. Nor could it be a fearful sight or sound that drew them gently into one. Rather, in each the other saw a perfect shelter where his Self could be reborn in safety and in peace. Such did his reason tell him; such he believed *because* it was [Ur: is] the truth.

We may worry that we're not worthy parents of the Christ child. Our relationship may be so full of attack that we think any day the representative from Children and Family Services will take Him away and put Him into foster care.

But we *are* worthy parents of the Christ child, because we are part of God Himself. We could not have joined otherwise. Moreover, the very fact of our joining shows that deep down, we already know what this Christ child has come to teach us. We joined by temporarily seeing each other with our true vision and communicating with each other in our true native tongue. We set aside our fear of each other and opened the door to love. We briefly listened to reason, and it told us a beautiful thing: "In each the other saw a perfect shelter where his Self could be reborn in safety and in peace." We believed this *because* it is the truth, and our holy relationship began. How could we *not* be worthy? How could our relationship not reach its goal of restoring communication when communication was *already* restored at its beginning?

10. Here is the first <u>direct</u> perception that you can make [Ur: have made]. You make [Ur: made] it through awareness older than perception, and yet reborn in just an instant. For what is time to what was <u>always</u> so? Think what that instant brought; the <u>recognition</u> that the "something else" you thought was you <u>is an illusion</u>. And truth came instantly, to show you where your Self <u>must</u> be. It is denial of <u>illusions</u> that calls on truth, for to deny illusions is to recognize that <u>fear</u> is meaningless. Into the holy home where fear is powerless love enters thankfully, grateful that it is one with you who joined to <u>let</u> it enter.

Jesus continues to celebrate Helen and Bill's original joining. In that holy instant when they joined in seeking a better way, they temporarily saw each other with the direct perception brought by true vision, a reflection of the knowledge they always had. They saw the illusory nature of the ego they had identified with, and accepted their true Self in its place. In denying identification with the ego, they set aside their fear and suspicion of each other and made a home for love. "Think what that instant brought." And think what an instant of joining with another person *can* bring to all of us who seem to be wandering aimlessly, lonely and searching for shelter from the storm of the ego's insane world.

> 11. Christ comes to what is <u>like</u> Himself; the same, <u>not</u> different. For He is <u>always</u> drawn unto Himself. What is as like Him as a holy relationship? And what draws you and your brother [Ur: *you*] together draws <u>Him</u> to you. Here are His sweetness and His gentle innocence <u>protected</u> from attack. And here can He <u>return</u> in confidence, for faith in another [Ur: one another] is <u>always</u> faith in Him. You are indeed correct in looking on your brother [Ur: each other] as His chosen home, for here you will [Ur: willed] <u>with</u> Him and with His Father. This <u>is</u> your Father's Will for you, and yours <u>with</u> His [Ur: Him]. And who is drawn to Christ is drawn to God as surely as Both are drawn to every holy relationship, the home prepared for Them as earth is turned to Heaven.

If someone were to ask you, "What on earth is most like Christ?" what would your answer be? Most people would probably think of a holy person, like St. Francis or Mother Teresa. Certainly these individuals were Christ-like. But who would ever guess that the most Christ-like thing on earth is not a person at all, but *two* people joined in a holy relationship?

When a common purpose draws two of us together, the Christ child is drawn in because He comes to what is like Himself. Our holy relationship now becomes His home. It nurtures Him as He grows up. It protects His sweetness and gentle innocence from attack. He is protected by our faith in each other, because such faith is faith in Him. As we see His home in each other, we throw away the false "will" that led to our feelings of alienation and meaninglessness, and reconnect with the true will for joining we share with Christ and God. This is the Course's recipe for salvation, its path to the pinnacle of spiritual seeking: It is through holy relationships that earth is turned to Heaven.

II. Your Brother's Sinlessness
Commentary by Greg Mackie

1. The <u>opposite</u> of illusions is not disillusionment but truth. Only to the ego, to which <u>truth</u> is meaningless, do they [illusions and disillusionment] <u>appear</u> to be the only alternatives, and <u>different</u> from each other. In truth they are the <u>same</u>. Both bring the same amount of misery, though each one <u>seems</u> to be the way to lose the misery the other brings. <u>Every</u> illusion carries pain and suffering in the dark folds of the heavy garments in which it hides its nothingness. Yet by [Ur: in] these dark and heavy garments are those who <u>seek</u> illusions covered, and hidden from the joy of truth.

This section emphasizes the all-or-nothing nature of truth and illusions. Truth is all the same, illusions are all the same, and truth and illusions are totally different from each other.

We, however, are confused on this issue. For instance, we believe that illusions and disillusionment—which are both illusions—are alternatives, different from each other. Our lives seem to swing between these two "alternatives" do they not?

Think, for example, of a romantic love relationship. In the beginning, we're ecstatically floating in the illusion of being in love. But all too often, once the honeymoon is over, the relationship becomes a living hell and ends with a bitter breakup. We now see what an illusion the "love" really was and are disillusioned. This may be disappointing, but it *does* have a kind of satisfaction to it: "Now I see how miserable that relationship actually was. What a relief!" Eventually, though, disillusionment wears thin and we're tempted again by the illusion of love—"Wow, look at that cute thing over there."

So, each option seems to be an escape from the misery of the other. But both really bring *only* misery, for both are illusions and only truth can bring joy. We don't see the real nature of these illusions because of their "heavy garments": the outer forms they take. These forms hide the full extent of the pain and suffering illusions bring, and the actual nothingness of these illusions. Worst of all, these forms hide *us* from the joy of truth.

2. Truth is the opposite of illusions <u>because</u> it offers joy. What else <u>but</u> joy could be the opposite of misery? To leave one kind of misery and seek another is hardly an <u>escape</u>. To change <u>illusions</u> is to make <u>no</u> change. The search for joy <u>in misery</u> is senseless, for how <u>could</u> joy be found in misery? All that is possible in the dark world of misery is to select some <u>aspects</u> out of it, see them as <u>different</u>, and <u>define</u> the difference as joy. Yet to <u>perceive</u> a difference where none exists will surely fail to <u>make</u> a difference.

Truth is the real alternative to both illusions and disillusionment precisely *because* it offers joy. Whatever their form, all illusions bring misery, so the best we can do when we seek joy in illusions is to find some illusions we prefer (like that romantic love relationship), make them *look* different, and then talk ourselves into believing they're really joyful. A colorful expression I've heard for this is "putting lipstick on a pig." It's still no fun to kiss, no matter how much we dress it up.

3. Illusions carry <u>only</u> guilt and suffering, sickness and death, to their believers. The <u>form</u> in which they are accepted is irrelevant. <u>No</u> form of misery in reason's eyes <u>can</u> be confused with joy. Joy is eternal. You can be sure indeed that any seeming happiness that does not last is really fear. Joy does <u>not</u> turn to sorrow, for the eternal cannot change. But sorrow <u>can</u> be turned to joy, for time gives way to the eternal. Only the timeless must remain unchanged, but everything in time can <u>change</u> with time. Yet if the change be real and not <u>imagined</u>, illusions <u>must</u> give way to truth, and not to other dreams that are but equally unreal. <u>This</u> is no difference.

That's one ugly pig. No matter what the form, illusions bring "*only* guilt and suffering, sickness and death." We've convinced ourselves that *some* illusions—think once more of that romantic love relationship—bring joy, but the way we can tell that we're really putting lipstick on that pig is that our joy doesn't last. All illusions, no matter how "joyful," will lead to the misery of disillusionment, but true joy is eternal so it doesn't turn to misery. However, misery *can* be turned to joy. All we need to do for this to happen is stop running from one fleeting illusion to another and trade all illusions for the eternal joy of truth.

Application: Think of things in your past that you thought brought you joy. Did that joy last? If not, they never brought you real joy at all, for joy is eternal. Look upon these things from your past one at a time and say to yourself:

> *I thought this brought me joy, but the joy didn't last.*
> *Therefore, it was really an illusion that brought me misery.*
> *Real joy is eternal and cannot be turned to misery.*
> *But misery* **can** *be turned to eternal joy,*
> *if I let all of my illusions give way to the eternal truth.*

4. Reason will tell you that the <u>only</u> way to escape from misery is to <u>recognize</u> it *and go the other way.* Truth is the same and misery the same, but they <u>are</u> different from each other in <u>every</u> way, in every <u>instance</u> and <u>without exception</u>. To believe that one exception can exist is to confuse what <u>is</u> the same with what is different. <u>One</u> illusion cherished and defended <u>against</u> the truth makes <u>all</u> truth meaningless, and <u>all</u> illusions real. Such is the power of belief. It <u>cannot</u> compromise. And faith in innocence <u>is</u> faith in sin, if the belief excludes <u>one</u> living thing and holds it out, <u>apart</u> from its forgiveness.

Once again, an appeal to reason: The only way to escape from misery is to stop thinking that some illusions can bring us joy. We need to realize that *all* illusions bring misery without exception. This realization will give us the incentive we need to turn away completely from illusions and find the joy of truth.

Here we see a formula that is central to the Course:

- Truth is the same.
- Illusion (misery) is the same.
- Truth and illusion are completely different from each other.

Our whole problem is that we think there are exceptions to this formula—for instance, the belief that some illusions bring joy, which (since only truth brings joy) is the same thing as believing that some illusions are true. Yet this formula is an inexorable law of mind which works regardless of what we tell ourselves. Thus, thinking one illusion is true leads inevitably to us believing that *all* illusions are true and all truth is illusion.

Jesus then applies this rule to a particular version of truth and illusion: innocence and sin. We may think we have faith in innocence, but if we think *one* living thing is a sinner, we really have faith in sin. If we forgive everyone except Hitler, we haven't truly forgiven anyone.

> 5. Both reason <u>and</u> the ego will tell you this, but what they <u>make</u> of it is <u>not</u> the same. The ego will assure you now that it is <u>impossible</u> for you to see <u>no</u> guilt in anyone. And if <u>this</u> seeing [Ur: vision] is the <u>only</u> means by which <u>escape</u> from guilt can be attained, then the belief in sin must be eternal. Yet reason looks on this another way, for reason sees the <u>source</u> of an idea as what will make it either true or false. This <u>must</u> be so, if the idea is <u>like</u> its source. Therefore, says reason, if escape from guilt was given to the Holy Spirit as His purpose, and by One to Whom <u>nothing</u> He wills <u>can be</u> impossible, the means for its attainment are <u>more</u> than possible. They must be <u>there</u>, and <u>you</u> must <u>have</u> them.

The idea that concluded that last paragraph sounds really daunting, for it means that to free ourselves from guilt we must see *everyone* as totally sinless. How on earth can we do this? It only feels daunting, though, because we're listening to the ego's interpretation of it: "There's no way in a million years you can see *everyone* as sinless, so if this is the only way to escape from guilt, you're doomed."

Application: Reason has a different take on this whole situation. Go through the logic reason presents and really let it sink in. Let it reassure you that you have what it takes to escape from guilt and accomplish the goal of this course:

> *Every idea is like its source.*
> *Therefore, ideas that come from true sources are true.*
> *The idea that escape from guilt is possible comes from a true source, the Holy Spirit.*
> *Indeed, escape from guilt is the Holy Spirit's whole purpose, and nothing He wills can be **impossible.***
> *Therefore, the means for escaping from guilt—seeing no guilt in anyone—are more than possible.*
> *They must be there, and I must have them.*

6. This is a crucial period in this course, for here the separation of you and the ego <u>must</u> be made complete. For if you <u>have</u> the means to let the Holy Spirit's purpose be accomplished, they <u>can</u> be used. And <u>through</u> their use will you gain faith in them. Yet to the ego this [Ur: they] <u>must</u> be impossible, and no one undertakes to do what holds <u>no</u> hope of <u>ever</u> being done. *You* know [Ur: You *know*] what your Creator wills is possible, but what you <u>made</u> believes it is not so. Now <u>must</u> you choose between yourself and an [Ur: the] <u>illusion</u> of yourself. <u>Not</u> both, but <u>one</u>. There is no point in trying to avoid this <u>one</u> decision. It <u>must</u> be made. Faith and belief can fall to either side, but reason tells you misery lies <u>only</u> on one side and joy upon the other.

Application: Jesus gives us a crucial application of the formula that says all truth is the same, all illusions are the same, and truth and illusions are totally different from each other. Let's make the choice in which the separation between us and the ego becomes complete:

I have two options.
One is the illusion of myself, the ego.
It tells me that seeing no guilt in anyone, the means to accomplish the Holy Spirit's purpose, is impossible.
If I listen to it, I won't even attempt the means, because no one attempts what has no hope of ever being done.
Faith and belief in this illusion of myself will bring me misery.

The other is my true self.
*I **know** that what my Creator wills is possible.*
*I **have** the ability to see no guilt in anyone, the means to let the Holy Spirit's purpose be accomplished.*
*The means **can** be used, and using it will help me gain faith in it.*
Faith and belief in my true self will bring me joy.

Now must I choose between my true self and the illusion of myself.
*Not both, but **one**.*
There is no point in trying to avoid this one decision.
*It **must** be made.*
Therefore, right now, I let go of the illusion of myself and choose

my true self.
I set aside misery and choose joy.

7. Forsake not now your brother. [Ur: *Forsake not now each other.*] For you who <u>are</u> the same will <u>not</u> decide alone <u>nor differently</u>. Either you give each other life or death; either you are each other's savior or his judge, offering him sanctuary or condemnation. This course will be believed <u>entirely</u> or not at all. For it is wholly true or wholly false, and <u>cannot</u> be but partially believed. And you will either <u>escape</u> from misery entirely or not at all. Reason will tell you that there <u>is</u> no middle ground where you can pause uncertainly, waiting to choose between the joy of Heaven and the misery of hell. <u>Until</u> you choose Heaven, you *are* in hell and misery.

The decision to see no guilt in anyone begins with the person right in front of us. You can really see Jesus pleading with Helen and Bill to get off the fence and make that one either/or choice. Because they are one, they sink or swim together; as a later passage tells us about the holy relationship, "What one thinks, the other will experience with him" (T-22.VI.14:2). They must see no guilt in *each other*. They must stop finding ways to wriggle out of what Jesus is telling them and realize that the all-or-nothing nature of his course compels their minds to either fully accept what he's telling them or reject it. Until they make a full commitment to the joy of Heaven by totally forgiving each other, they will continue to wallow in hell.

This choice, of course, is the same choice all of us are called to make. Are *we* willing to forgive totally? Are we willing to get off the fence and decide for Heaven once and for all?

8. There is no <u>part</u> of Heaven you can take and weave into illusions. Nor is there <u>one</u> illusion you can enter Heaven <u>with</u>. A savior cannot <u>be</u> a judge, nor mercy condemnation. And vision <u>cannot</u> damn, but <u>only</u> bless. Whose function is to save, <u>will</u> save. *How* He will do it <u>is</u> beyond your understanding, but *when* must be your choice. For time <u>you</u> made, and time you <u>can</u> command. You are no more a slave to time than to the world you made.

Jesus continues hammering home the point that this is an all-or-nothing choice: to enter Heaven completely, we must see no guilt in anyone. But we're still complaining about how impossible this seems. How will the Holy Spirit pull this miracle off? And how long is this all this going to take? It seems that it will take *forever*. It seems that we're doomed to suffer until the world around us has a major shift, which doesn't look too likely anytime soon.

Jesus responds to these concerns by telling us that *how* the Holy Spirit will save us is beyond our understanding, but *when* He does is our choice. We are in command of time and the world we made. We don't have to wait for anything; we can decide to forgive and return to Heaven at any time.

> 9. Let us look closer at the whole illusion that what you made has power to enslave its maker. This is the <u>same</u> belief that <u>caused</u> the separation. It is the meaningless idea that thoughts can <u>leave</u> the thinker's mind, be <u>different</u> from it <u>and in opposition</u> to it. If this were true, thoughts would not be the mind's extensions, but its <u>enemies</u>. And here we see again another form of the same fundamental illusion we have seen many times before. <u>Only</u> if it were possible the Son of God could <u>leave</u> his Father's Mind, make himself <u>different</u> and <u>oppose</u> His Will, would it be possible that the self he made, and all <u>it</u> made, should be his master.

Why does it seem that we are *not* in command of time and the world we made? Why does it seem that we have to wait forever for salvation to be complete? The reason is that we believe ideas can leave their source. Just as the separation began when we believed that we could leave God's Mind and oppose His Will, so the separation is maintained by our belief that our own thoughts can leave *our* mind and oppose *our* will. It appears now that we are at the mercy of the ego and the world we made. But none of this is true; it is pure illusion.

> 10. Behold the great projection, but look on it with the decision that it <u>must be healed</u>, and <u>not</u> with fear. <u>Nothing</u> you made has <u>any</u> power over you unless you still would be <u>apart</u> from your Creator, and with a will <u>opposed</u> to His. For <u>only</u> if you would believe His Son <u>could</u> be His enemy does it <u>seem possible</u> that what <u>you</u> made is <u>yours</u>. <u>You</u> would condemn His joy to misery, and make <u>Him</u> different. And all the misery you made has been your own. Are you not <u>glad</u> to learn it is not true? Is it not welcome news to hear <u>not one</u> of the illusions that you made <u>replaced</u> the truth?

Application: Jesus wants us to "behold the great projection" and decide to heal it, so let's do that now.

I came to believe that what I made has power over me and is my enemy because I wanted to be God's enemy.
I wanted to be apart from my Creator, with a will opposed to His.
I wanted to condemn His joy to misery and make Him different.

*But I don't **really** want any of this, for all the misery I made has been my own.*
I am glad to learn that my misery is not true.
I am glad that not one of the illusions I made has replaced the truth.
I am glad that nothing I made has any power over me.

11. Only *your* thoughts have been impossible. Salvation <u>cannot</u> be. It *is* impossible to look upon your savior as your enemy and <u>recognize</u> him. Yet it <u>is</u> possible to recognize him for what he <u>is</u>, if God would have it so. What God has given to your holy relationship <u>is there</u>. For what He gave the Holy Spirit to give to you *He gave.* Would you not look upon the savior that has been given you? And would you not exchange, in gratitude [Ur: and gladness], the function of an executioner <u>you</u> gave him for the one he has in truth? Receive of him what God has given him for you, <u>not</u> what <u>you</u> tried to give yourself [Urtext omits "yourself"].

Have you noticed how Jesus keeps coming back to our complaint that salvation is impossible? But it *is* possible, because God wills it, and He has given us the perfect means to accomplish it: the holy relationship. It won't happen as long as we're determined to see our partner as our executioner instead of our savior, but we *will* see him as the savior he is if we simply accept what God has already given us. Why wait? Why not gratefully look upon the savior God has given us *right now*?

12. Beyond the body that you interposed between you and your brother [Ur: the bodies that you interposed between you], and shining in the golden light that reaches it from the bright, endless circle that extends forever, is your holy relationship, beloved of God [Ur: and holy as] Himself. How still it rests, in time and yet beyond, immortal yet on

earth. How great the power that lies in it. Time waits upon its will, and earth will be as it would have it be. Here is no separate will, nor the desire that anything be separate. Its will has no exceptions, and what it wills is true. Every illusion brought to its forgiveness is gently overlooked and disappears. For at its center Christ has been reborn, to light His home with vision that overlooks the world. Would you not have this holy home be yours as well? No misery is here, but only joy.

The holy relationship is the cure for every disease this section has been talking about. On the surface, a holy relationship can be full of conflict and difficulty and bodies misbehaving (as Helen and Bill experienced). But underneath all that, within that golden circle of the Son of God (another reference to T-21.I.8), is the fully realized holy relationship, which expresses itself in time through our conscious relationship, yet also rests in eternity.

We think the world we made has power over us, but our relationship has all the power. We think we're the slaves of time, but time waits upon our relationship's will. We're still hooked into the ego and see separation and differences, but our relationship shares God's Will and is beyond separation. We constantly make exceptions and hold some illusions apart from forgiveness, but our relationship forgives all illusions without exception. Christ has made His home at the center of our holy relationship, and as we come to dwell in this home with Him, we will finally let go of misery and find everlasting joy.

> 13. All you need do to dwell in quiet here with Christ is share His vision. Quickly and gladly is His vision given anyone who is but willing to see his brother sinless. And no one can remain beyond this willingness, if you would be released entirely from all effects of sin. Would you have partial forgiveness for yourself? Can you reach Heaven while a single sin still tempts you to remain in misery? Heaven is the home of perfect purity, and God created it for you. Look on your holy brother, sinless as yourself, and let him lead you there.

What do we need to do to dwell with Christ in His home at the heart of our holy relationship? How do we become consciously aware of the realized holy relationship within us that was so beautifully described in the last paragraph? We simply need to be willing to see our partner sinless. Of course, we can't really see him sinless without seeing *everyone* sinless, so our willingness to forgive him must include everyone else. When we offer this willingness, Christ at the heart of our relationship "quickly and gladly" provides the means to accomplish this goal: His vision. Only through total forgiveness of everyone will we find total forgiveness for ourselves. And total forgiveness starts with forgiving that holy savior right next to us, and letting him lead us to the Heaven God created for all of us.

III. Reason and the Forms of Error
Commentary by Greg Mackie

1. The introduction of reason into the ego's thought system is the beginning of its undoing, for reason and the ego are <u>contradictory</u>.2Nor is it possible for them to coexist in your <u>awareness</u>.3For [Ur: And] reason's goal <u>is</u> to make plain, and therefore obvious.4You can *see* reason.5This is not a play on words, for here <u>is</u> the beginning of a vision that has meaning.6Vision is sense, quite literally.7If it is not the body's sight, it *must* be understood.8<u>For it is plain</u>, and what is obvious is <u>not</u> ambiguous.9It <u>can</u> be understood.0And here do reason and the ego separate, to go their separate [Ur: *different*] ways.

As we read earlier (T-21.V.7-8), reason is not something the ego made that was then reinterpreted by the Holy Spirit. Rather, reason is *diametrically opposed* to the ego. It is a virus that infects the ego's thought system and ensures its doom. So, the ego fends off reason by using the body's eyes, which are incapable of seeing meaning.

Reason "is the beginning of a vision that has meaning." The body's eyes are physical senses; true vision is *sense*, as when we say that a person is sensible or reasonable. The body's eyes see form; true vision sees *meaning*. This may sound odd, but it is reflected in our language: One dictionary definition of "see" is "to have a clear understanding of something," as when person who reaches such an understanding says, "Oh, I *see*."

Reason's understanding is "plain," "obvious," and "not ambiguous." This emphasis on obvious and unambiguous meaning runs counter to much of our postmodern culture. In this culture, the idea that things are ambiguous and open to many meanings is celebrated, while the search for a plain, single meaning is often regarded as too "limiting." As Bob Dylan once said, "Definition destroys." But in the Course's view, obscurity and ambiguity are of the ego; lack of definition destroys. A single meaning is what we're after.

2. The ego's whole continuance depends on its belief you cannot learn this course. <u>Share</u> this belief, and reason will be unable to <u>see</u> your

24

errors and make way for their correction. For reason <u>sees through</u> errors, telling you what you <u>thought</u> was real is not. Reason <u>can</u> see the difference between sin and mistakes, because it <u>wants</u> correction. Therefore, it tells you what you thought was uncorrectable <u>can</u> be corrected, and thus it [Ur: and therefore] <u>must</u> have been an error. The ego's <u>opposition</u> to correction leads to its fixed belief in sin and <u>disregard</u> of errors. It looks on <u>nothing</u> that can be corrected. Thus does the ego damn, and reason save.

We often feel like we'll never learn this course—as the last section said, it seems impossible. Why? Because we're listening to the ego, which desperately does not want us to learn this course. It doesn't want correction, so it sees nothing that can *be* corrected. It looks around with the body's eyes and says to us, "Look at all this sin. How can you possibly believe this crazy course that tells you everyone is sinless? You're doomed." Reason, though, doesn't share the ego's agenda. It wants correction, and so it looks straight through all the ego's evidence for sin and tells us, "This is all just a silly mistake. It can be corrected, just as the Course tells you it can. Salvation is yours for the asking."

3. Reason is not salvation in itself, but it <u>makes way</u> for peace and brings you to a state of mind in which salvation can be given you. Sin is a block, set like a heavy gate, locked and without a key, across the road to peace. No one who looks on it <u>without</u> the help of reason would <u>try</u> to pass it. The body's eyes behold it as solid granite, so thick it would be madness to <u>attempt</u> to pass it. Yet reason sees through it easily, <u>because</u> it is an error. 6The <u>form</u> it takes cannot conceal its emptiness from <u>reason's</u> eyes.

The body's eyes look on sin. We see what people's bodies do, and on that basis decide that they're sinners. We may not use the word "sinners," but we decide on the basis of their behavior that there's something fundamentally wrong with them. This perception does feel like a solid block barring the road to peace, does it not? How often have we said in one form or another, "I would love to be at peace, but how can I be at peace in the face of _____ (fill in other person's offending behavior here)?"

Without the vision given us by reason, we'll never get past this block. Sin looks like the *truth*, and we can't see beyond it. But reason sees that it is only an *error*, and therefore sees through it easily. Reason looks past the forms that our body's eyes focus on. Thus it opens the door to peace and opens our minds to salvation.

> 4. Only the form of error attracts the ego. Meaning it does not recognize, and does not see if it is there or not. Everything the body's eyes can see is a mistake, an error in perception, a distorted fragment of the whole without the meaning that the whole would give. And yet mistakes, regardless of their form, can be corrected. Sin is but error in a special form the ego venerates. It would preserve all errors and make them sins. For here is its own stability, its heavy anchor in the shifting world it made; the rock on which its church is built, and where its worshippers are bound to bodies, believing the body's freedom is their own.

Deciding on the basis of people's behavior that they're sinners amounts to seeing a form and giving it the meaning of "sinner." But if all we're seeing is a form, how can we know what it means? This is a classic case of judging a book by its cover. Reason would show us that everything the body's eyes see is a correctible error. But the ego, which is blind to meaning, sends out the body's eyes to search for forms it likes, forms it sees as particularly juicy evidence of sin. It must do this, for finding sin is the guarantee of its survival.

> 5. Reason will tell you that the form of error is not what makes it a mistake [sin]. If what the form conceals is a mistake, the form cannot prevent correction. The body's eyes see only form. They cannot see beyond what they were made to see. And they were made to look on error and not see past it. Theirs is indeed a strange perception, for they can see only illusions, unable to look beyond the granite block of sin, and stopping at the outside form of nothing. To this distorted form of vision the outside of everything, the wall that stands between you and the truth, is wholly true. Yet how can sight that stops at nothingness, as if it were a solid wall, see truly? It is held back by form, having been made to guarantee that nothing else but form will be perceived.

In the ego's view, the form of something is what makes it a sin. This is how our religious moral codes work, right? We have lists of behaviors we're not supposed to do; if we do them, we're "sinners" by definition, and no real correction is possible—we're going to pay the price for what

26

we've done (or we may believe that Jesus paid the price for us). But reason tells us that whatever form our "sin" takes, it is only an error of the mind, which can be easily corrected regardless of its form.

We'll never see this as long as we're looking with the body's eyes, because the body's eyes see *only* form. To them, the surface of everything, an illusory wall which actually stands *between* us and the truth, is all that is true. The ego made them for the very purpose of looking on error and seeing it as real, for the ego wants to see sin, and real error *is* sin. True vision is held back by our faith in the body's eyes. If nothing but form can be perceived, how will we ever see past the block of sin?

> 6. These eyes, made not to see, will never see. For the idea they represent [sin] left not its maker, and it is their maker [the ego] that sees through them. What was its maker's goal but not to see? For this the body's eyes are perfect means, but not for seeing. See how the body's eyes rest on externals and cannot go beyond. Watch how they stop at nothingness, unable to go beyond the form to meaning. Nothing so blinding as perception of form. For sight of form means understanding has been obscured.

As we've seen, the body's eyes were made by the ego, which "sees" through them. They were made *not* to see because that is the ego's goal; real vision would obliterate it. The body's eyes are the perfect means for not seeing, because they can only see form. They cannot get beyond the form to the meaning and understanding that reason would reveal.

Application: Look around and notice "how the body's eyes rest on externals and cannot go beyond. Watch how they stop at nothingness, unable to go beyond the form to meaning." You may find yourself attaching meanings to the forms you see around you, but those meanings are not in the forms themselves. Other people seeing the exact same forms would ascribe different meanings to them. How can these eyes ever reveal meaning?

> 7. Only mistakes have different forms, and so they can deceive. You can change form *because* it is not true. It could not be reality *because* it can be changed. Reason will tell you that if form is not reality it must

be an illusion, and is <u>not there</u> to see. And <u>if</u> you see it you <u>must</u> be mistaken, for you are seeing what can *not* be real as if it were. What cannot see <u>beyond</u> what is not there <u>must</u> be distorted perception, and must perceive illusions <u>as the truth</u>. 7Could it, then, <u>recognize</u> the truth?

Our errors take all sorts of different forms, and as long as we see forms as real—which we will as long as we rely on the body's eyes—we will be deceived into thinking that they're sins. We'll look around at all those bodies doing awful things in so many different forms and conclude that this world is going to hell in a handbasket. But reason tells us that the very fact that errors take so many different and ever-changing forms demonstrates that they are *not* real, since reality is changeless. Because form is not reality, it must be illusion, and seeing it must be a mistake. We may not like hearing how mistaken our usual way of seeing is, but isn't it good news to hear that the sinful world we see isn't the truth?

8. Let not the <u>form</u> of his mistakes keep you from him whose holiness is <u>yours</u>. Let not the vision of his holiness, the sight of which would show you <u>your</u> forgiveness, be kept from you by what the body's eyes <u>can</u> see. Let your awareness of your brother <u>not</u> be blocked by your perception of his sins and of his body. What is there in him that you would attack <u>except</u> what you associate with his body, which <u>you</u> believe can sin? <u>Beyond</u> his errors is his holiness and <u>your</u> salvation. You gave him not his holiness, but tried to see your sins in him to save yourself. And yet, his holiness *is* your forgiveness. Can <u>you</u> be saved by making sinful the one whose holiness *is* your salvation?

Here is a practical application of all we've been talking about. We've projected our sins onto our brother (here, it is our holy relationship partner) in order to escape them at his expense. Now, because of this projection, we use our body's eyes to look at this brother's behavior, and conclude he is a sinner. We must not do this if we want to be saved. Instead, we must use our reason to look beyond his body's behavior and see his holiness instead. Only in this way will we truly escape our "sins," through letting his holiness forgive us and bestow on us the priceless gift of salvation.

Application:

Bring to mind a particular person against whom you hold a
   grievance.
See this person's body engaged in the behaviors that offend you.
Now, see these behaviors transform into a solid block of granite,
   standing between you and this person.
This is the block of sin, set like a heavy gate, locked and without a
   key, across the road to peace.
As long as you see this block, you will not find peace and salvation.

Open your mind now to what reason would tell you.
You don't have to see these behaviors as a solid block of sin.
After all, they are just forms, devoid of meaning.
Reason sees through this block easily, because this person's seeming
   "sins" are only errors.
The form those "sins" take cannot conceal their emptiness from
   reason's eyes.

So now, with reason's help, let go of your perception of this person
   as a sinner.
Let not the form of his mistakes keep you from him whose holiness
   is yours.
Let not the vision of his holiness, the sight of which would show you
   your forgiveness, be kept from you by what the body's eyes can
   see.
Let your awareness of your brother not be blocked by your
   perception of his sins and of his body.
Watch the seemingly solid block of sin fade away, until the person
   behind it is revealed, a being of pure holiness, streaming with
   light and love.
In his holiness is your salvation.
Accept salvation from him now, with gratitude and love.

9. A holy relationship, however newly born, must value holiness above
all else. Unholy values will produce confusion, and in awareness. In an
unholy relationship, each one is valued because he seems to justify the
other's sin. Each [Ur: He] sees within the other what impels him to sin

29

<u>against his will</u>. And thus he lays his sins upon the other, and is <u>attracted</u> to him to <u>perpetuate</u> his sins. And so it <u>must</u> become impossible for each to see <u>himself</u> as causing sin by his <u>desire</u> to have sin real. Yet reason sees a holy relationship as what it <u>is</u>; a common state of mind, where both give errors gladly to correction, that both may happily be healed as one.

In an unholy relationship, we value the other person because he seems to justify our sin. We say, "I was forced to do what I did by that awful thing you did." This is the whole reason we keep the other person around; she is a convenient scapegoat. Actually, the only reason we "sinned" was that we ourselves wanted to make sin real; it's all our doing. But now we've deluded ourselves into thinking that dumping our seeming sins on our partner will set us free of them.

If we want to accomplish the goal of our holy relationship, we need a whole new set of values. Instead of valuing our partner as a dumping ground for our sin, we need to value her holiness above all else. This is the only thing worth valuing, because it is *this* that sets us free. Each of us has tried to free ourselves of sin at the other's expense, but reason tells us that a holy relationship is "a common state of mind" in which we both gain or lose together. The only sane thing to do, then, is for both of us to give our errors over to correction so we can be healed *together*.

IV. The Branching of the Road
Commentary by Greg Mackie

The first two paragraphs here are from one of Jesus' "special messages" to Helen. They were dictated on March 11, 1968, about ten months after the material in the rest of this section. I will indicate insertions from the original version with the initials "SM."

> 1. When you come to the place where the branch in the road is quite apparent, you cannot go ahead. You <u>must</u> go either one way or the other. For now if you go straight ahead, the way you went [SM: were going] before you reached [SM: came to] the branch, <u>you will go nowhere</u>. The whole purpose of coming this far was to decide which branch you will take now [SM: *which branch you will take from here on*]. The way you came no longer matters. <u>It can no longer serve.</u> No one who reaches this far <u>can</u> make the wrong decision, although [SM: but] he <u>can</u> delay. And there is no part of the journey that seems more hopeless and futile than standing where the road branches, and not deciding on which way to go.

The special messages were generally given to Helen to deal with specific situations in her life. However, I can't find any information about the context of this special message, so I don't know what specific situation it is talking about.

In general terms, it is clearly about the spiritual journey. As we walk down the path, we eventually reach a place where the branch in the road becomes obvious. One way is the way of the ego; the other is the way to God. Reaching this place was the whole point of the journey thus far. What will we do now? Will we make the choice for God or will we set up camp at the branch? The good news is that making the choice for God is inevitable—we can only delay it. But why delay it? Why not make the choice now?

> 2. It is but [SM: only] the first few steps along the right way that seem hard, for [SM:because] you <u>have</u> chosen, although [SM:but] you still may think [SM: you still think] you can go back and make the other

31

choice. This is not so. A choice made with the power of Heaven to uphold it cannot <u>be</u> undone. Your way <u>is</u> decided. There will be nothing you will <u>not</u> be told, if you acknowledge this.

When we finally break camp and set out on the road to God, it will seem hard at first. We can still see that other road, and it still looks tempting. Isn't this what the spiritual journey feels like? We're deeply attracted to the promises of God, but that old ego life hasn't totally lost its appeal. Meditating and reading the Course and forgiving are great, but it still seems like it would be fun to deliver that perfect zinger that puts so-and-so in her place. But really, there's no turning back. We've committed to God, and now we need to keep putting one foot in front of another on the right way. It will get easier, because the power of Heaven is behind our choice, and we will be guided every step of the way.

> 3. And so you and your brother stand [Ur: And so you stand], here in this holy place, before the veil of sin that hangs between you and the face of Christ. Let it be lifted! Raise it together with your brother, for it is but a veil that stands between you. Either you or your brother alone [Ur: Either alone] will see it as a solid block, nor realize how thin the drapery that separates you now. Yet it is almost over in your awareness, and peace has reached you even here, before the veil. Think what will happen after. [Ur: Think what will happen after!] The love of Christ will light your face [Ur: faces], and shine from it [Ur: them] into a darkened world that needs the light. And from this holy place He will return with you, not leaving it nor you. <u>You</u> will become His messenger [Ur: messengers], returning Him unto Himself.

This is the beginning of the section proper. Here once again is the culminating image of the obstacles to peace: We and our holy relationship partner are standing before the final veil that covers the face of Christ. To lift it, we must forgive each other. Without this mutual forgiveness, each of us will see the veil as a solid rock of sin (an image from the last section). We will not be able to see beyond each other's bodies doing all those awful things they do. But as we forgive, we will see that the veil is so thin that the peace of God already shines through it to us.

This section then adds an element to the image that wasn't in the earlier references. In the "Obstacles to Peace" section, once the veil is lifted, we disappear into the Love beyond the veil and the journey is over.

But here, after we lift the veil and see the radiant face of Christ, we come back to the world *with* Christ and shine His light "into a darkened world that *needs* the light." We become His messengers.

> 4. Think of the loveliness that <u>you</u> will see, who walk with Him! And think how beautiful will you and your brother look to the other! [Ur: And think how beautiful will each of you look to the other!] How happy you will be to be <u>together</u>, after such a long and lonely journey where you walked alone. The gates of Heaven, open now for you, will you now open to the sorrowful. And none who looks upon the Christ in you but will rejoice. How beautiful the sight you saw beyond the veil, which you will bring to light the tired eyes of those as weary now as once you were. How thankful will they be to see you come among them, offering Christ's forgiveness to dispel their faith in sin.

The rest of this section is a beautiful description of "what will happen after" we lift the veil and look upon the face of Christ. There are essentially two aspects to this: 1) We will see the loveliness of Christ in each other, and 2) We will together extend Christ's vision to the entire world, seeing that same loveliness in everyone.

Application: Jesus really wants us to *think* of this, to try to imagine what this would be like. He wants us to catch a glimpse of the boundless joy this would bring, so we'll have an incentive to forgive each other. So, as John Lennon said, let's imagine:

Think of what will happen when you and your brother forgive each
  other.
Think of how beautiful the sight of Christ beyond the veil will
  be.Think of how beautiful you will look to each other.
Think of how happy you'll be to be together, after such a long and
  lonely journey.
Think of the loveliness of the world you'll see, when both of you are
  walking with Christ.
Think of how joyous it will be to open the gates of Heaven to the
  sorrowful.
Think of how wonderful it will be to bring Christ to light the tired
  eyes of the weary.

Think of their gratitude when they see you come among them,
    offering Christ's forgiveness.
Think of how much those who look upon the Christ in you will
    rejoice.
Could anything else possibly offer more than forgiving each other
    can?

> 5. Every mistake you make, your brother [Ur: the other] will gently have corrected <u>for</u> you. For in his sight your loveliness is <u>his</u> salvation, which he would <u>protect</u> from harm. And you will be your brother's [Ur: And each will be the other's] strong protector from <u>everything</u> that seems to rise between you both. So shall you walk the world with me, whose message has not yet been given everyone. For you are here to let it be <u>received</u>. God's offer still is open, yet it waits acceptance. From you who have accepted it is it received. Into your hand, joined with your brother's, [Ur: Into your joined hands] is it safely given, for you who <u>share</u> it have become its willing guardian and protector [Ur: guardians and protectors].

Even at this advanced stage of the journey, we will still make mistakes. We will still be tempted to see sin in each other and in the world, to let that that block of granite rise between us again. But now, when this happens, each of us will release the other from her mistakes through forgiveness. We will do this gladly, for each of us now sees that the other's sinlessness is *our* salvation, so we have every incentive to protect it from harm. By being guardians to each other, we receive God's gift of forgiveness into our joined hands, and we become *its* guardians. So do we join with Jesus and give this gift to the world.

> 6. To all who share [with each other] the Love of God the grace is given to [Ur: be] the givers [to the world] of what they have received. And so they learn that it is theirs forever. All barriers disappear before their coming, as every obstacle was finally surmounted that seemed to rise and block <u>their</u> way before. This veil you and your brother lift together [Ur: you lift together] opens the way to truth to more than you. Those who would let illusions be lifted from their minds are this world's saviors, walking the world with their Redeemer, and carrying His message of hope and freedom and <u>release</u> from suffering to everyone who <u>needs</u> a miracle to save him.

The first two lines here give us a formula that is frequently repeated in the Course: receive, give, recognize. First, the two of us (in the holy relationship) share the Love of God with each other—we *receive* it. This then enables us to *give* His Love to the world. Finally, this act of giving enables us to *recognize* that God's Love is ours forever. There is no stopping it once the snowball of God's Love gets rolling down the hill: Just as both of us surmounted the obstacles to peace that we imposed between us, so will we together surmount the obstacles to peace that the world seems to impose (see T-19.IV.1:2-3). For when we lifted that final veil, it wasn't just for our benefit. How strange it would be to say, "Well, we've saved ourselves. All you other chumps are on your own." No, our lifting of the veil opens the way to truth for *everyone*. Now we are "this world's saviors."

Notice that in each of the last two paragraphs we are told that we will "walk the world" with Jesus and our Redeemer. Saving others doesn't simply mean that salvation extends from our minds to others without us doing anything, though it definitely includes that. It also includes actually going out into the world and giving to others, being miracle workers just as Jesus was two thousand years ago. We *carry* our Redeemer's message of freedom to those who suffer and need miracles to heal them.

> 7. How <u>easy</u> is it to offer this miracle to everyone! No one who has received it for himself <u>could</u> find it difficult. For <u>by</u> receiving it, he learned it was not given him alone. Such is the function of a holy relationship; to <u>receive</u> together and give as you received. Standing <u>before</u> the veil, it still seems difficult. But hold out your hand, joined with your brother's, [Ur: But hold out your *joined* hands] and touch this heavy-seeming block, and you will learn how easily your fingers slip through its nothingness. It is no solid wall. And only an illusion stands between you and your brother, and the holy Self you share together.

This, then, becomes the function of the holy relationship: "to receive together and give as you received." We who have received the miracle of God's Love into our relationship are now called to offer this miracle to everyone. Before we lift that veil together, this function seems like a daunting prospect. How can the two of *us*, with our dysfunctional relationship (caused mainly, in our eyes, by that partner of ours who keeps dropping the ball) do such a thing? How can *we* become miracle workers like Jesus? But once we join our hands in forgiveness and reach out together to that seeming granite wall of sin, we will see what a thin veil it really is. And then we will know that only an illusion stood between us and our shared Self, and we will see just how easy it actually is to offer the miracle of God's Love to everyone.

Application: Bring to mind a brother with whom you are in conflict and do the following visualization:

See the two of you standing before a solid wall of granite.
This is the wall of sin that seems to block your joining.
But now, the two of you decide to forgive one another.
You join hands and reach out to this heavy-seeming block.
To your surprise, your joined hands slip right through it.
It fades away before your eyes, and you see the face of Christ shining
    before you.
This is the holy Self you share.
You have received the miracle of God's Love.
Now the two of you are free to give the miracle of God's Love to
    everyone.
By doing so, you will recognize that it is yours forever.

V. Weakness and Defensiveness
Commentary by Greg Mackie

1. How does one overcome illusions? Surely not by force or anger, nor by <u>opposing</u> them in <u>any</u> way. Merely by letting reason tell you that they <u>contradict</u> reality. They <u>go against</u> what must be true. The opposition comes from <u>them</u>, and <u>not</u> reality. Reality opposes nothing. What merely is <u>needs</u> no defense, and offers none. Only illusions need defense <u>because of weakness</u>. And how <u>can</u> it be difficult to walk the way of truth when only <u>weakness</u> interferes? *You* are the strong one [Ur: ones] in this seeming conflict. And you need <u>no</u> defense. Everything that needs defense <u>you do not want</u>, for anything that needs defense will <u>weaken</u> you.

Imagine that someone thinks he is Luke Skywalker battling Darth Vader and the evil Empire, and he asks you how to overcome them. Do you say, "Send those X-wing fighters in and destroy the Death Star"? No, you reason with the person, saying, "This is all in your imagination. There is no evil Empire. *You* are the strong one in this seeming conflict." If this person is deeply committed to his delusion, he may resist reason— "Hey, maybe you're an Imperial spy sent to mess with my mind." But this fierce defense of his delusion is a testament to how weak it really is. The truth about him simply *is*, and he has to go to great lengths to fight it off. *It* needs no defense at all.

In the Course's view, *we* are this person. We think we're doing battle against a formidable ego. How do we overcome it? It seems that we're weak and the ego has all the firepower. Instead of fighting it, though, we need to reason with ourselves, saying, "The ego is in my imagination. *I* am the strong one in this seeming conflict." The ego's fierce defenses are a testament to how weak it really is. Therefore, it is actually easy to walk the way of truth, for our "opponent" is a weak illusion. All we need to do is realize that defending this illusion weakens us—who wants that?— and rest in the strength of our reality, which needs no defense.

2. Consider what the ego wants defenses <u>for</u>. <u>Always</u> to justify what <u>goes against</u> the truth, flies in the face of reason <u>and makes no sense</u>.

37

Can this *be* justified? What can this be except an invitation to insanity, to save you <u>from</u> the truth? And what would you be <u>saved</u> from but what you <u>fear</u>? Belief in sin needs <u>great</u> defense, and at <u>enormous</u> cost. All that the Holy Spirit offers must be <u>defended against</u> and <u>sacrificed</u>. For sin is carved into a block out of <u>your</u> peace, and laid <u>between</u> you and its return.

When we defend the ego, we are defending our *belief in sin* against truth itself, insanely justifying what cannot be so. This sounds strange, but we can see it in our resistance to the Course when it tells us to give up our investment in the body, the vehicle of sin. We think the Course is asking us to sacrifice all our goodies for the sake of truth, but the real sacrifice comes from our attempts to justify what goes *against* the truth. To "save" that solid block of sin, we sacrifice the Holy Spirit's gifts and abandon our peace. What could be more insane than to fear the truth and grimly hold on to an illusion that brings us nothing but pain?

3. Yet how can peace <u>be</u> so fragmented? It is <u>still</u> whole, and <u>nothing</u> has been <u>taken from</u> it. See how the means and the material of evil dreams are nothing. In truth you and your brother stand together [Ur: you stand together], with <u>nothing</u> in between. God holds your hands, and what can separate whom He has joined as one with Him? It is your Father Whom you would defend against. Yet it remains impossible to keep love out. God rests with you in quiet, undefended and wholly undefending, for in this quiet state alone is strength and power. Here can <u>no</u> weakness enter, for here is no attack and therefore no illusions. Love rests in <u>certainty</u>. Only <u>uncertainty</u> can <u>be</u> defensive. And <u>all</u> uncertainty is doubt about <u>yourself</u>.

We put a lot of effort into defending the illusion of sin against the truth, but as John Adams once said, "Facts are stubborn things." Our insane belief in sin can't change our reality any more than the guy who believes he's Luke Skywalker can change *his* reality. We still rest in everlasting peace. We still stand together, hand in hand with each other and with God (a reference to the holy relationship). We are right now basking in God's Love, which needs no defense because nothing could possibly oppose it. Even while we're attacking in defense of our tenuous illusions about ourselves, our true Self abides in the certainty of Love.

4. How weak is fear; how little and how meaningless. How insignificant before the quiet strength of those whom love has joined! This is your "enemy,"—a frightened mouse that would attack the universe. How likely is it that it will <u>succeed</u>? Can it be difficult to disregard its feeble squeaks that tell of its omnipotence, and would drown out the hymn of praise to its [every heart's] Creator that every heart throughout the universe forever sings as one? Which <u>is</u> the stronger? Is it this tiny mouse or everything that God created? You and your brother are <u>not</u> [Ur: You are *not*] joined together by this mouse, but by the Will of God. And can a mouse <u>betray</u> whom God has joined?

In our holy relationship, the two of us have joined together, yet we are still holding onto the belief in sin. We still have trouble forgiving each other (as Helen and Bill did). The fear of truth that keeps sin in place seems like an invincible enemy, keeping us from reaching the goal of our union. Yet that dreaded "enemy" is only a frightened mouse that appears to roar.

Application: Bring to mind someone you are close to—your holy relationship partner, or anyone who walks the path to God with you. Consider how your belief in sin—manifested in your grievances and conflicts with each other—has seemed to be a solid block keeping you from truly joining and finding your way to God:

Now, hand in hand with this person, see that solid block transform into a tiny, squeaking mouse.
How insignificant before the quiet strength of you whom love has joined!
All that stands between you is a frightened mouse that would attack the universe.
How likely is it that it will succeed?
Which is stronger: this tiny mouse or everything that God created?
You are *not* joined together by this mouse, but by the Will of God.
And can a mouse betray whom God has joined?

5. If you but <u>recognized</u> how little stands between you and your <u>awareness</u> of your union with your brother! [Ur: *awareness* of your union!] Be not deceived by the illusions it presents of size and thickness,

weight, solidity and firmness of foundation. Yes, to the body's eyes it looks like an enormous solid body, immovable as is a mountain. Yet within you is a Force that no illusions can resist. This body only seems to be immovable; this Force is irresistible in truth. What, then, must happen when they come together? Can the illusion of immovability be long defended from what is quietly passed through and gone beyond?

Again and again, Jesus pleads with us to recognize how weak and little is that which appears to stand between us. Why does it appear to be so huge to us? Because we're still using our body's eyes to tell us what reality is. As long as we do that, we can't help but see sin in our partner and everywhere we look. Instead, to borrow an image from our deluded friend who thinks he's Luke Skywalker, we need to let the Force be with us. This Force is the Will of God, revealed when we look through the eyes of reason. As this Force and the mountain of sin come together, the Force will move the mountain, just as Jesus promised long ago that our faith could do. How could we continue to believe in sin after seeing *this*?

6. Forget not, when you feel the need arise to be defensive about anything, you have identified yourself with an illusion. And therefore feel that you are weak because you are alone. This is the cost of all illusions. Not one but rests on the belief that you are separate. Not one that does not seem to stand, heavy and solid and immovable, between you and your brother. And not one that truth cannot [Ur: can *not*] pass over lightly, and so easily that you must be convinced, in spite of what you thought it was, that it is nothing. If you forgive your brother [Ur: each other], this *must* happen. For it is your unwillingness to overlook what seems to stand between you and your brother [Ur: between you] that makes it look impenetrable, and defends the illusion of its immovability.

Application: To conclude, we are given an application of everything this section has discussed. Again, bring to mind someone who walks the path to God with you, perhaps the same person you used in the last exercise. Think of a current situation with this person which brings up feelings of defensiveness, and apply these words to the situation:

I am defensive because I have identified with an illusion.

V. Weakness and Defensiveness

The illusion of myself is what I am defending.
I therefore feel weak, because I feel separate and alone.
My defensiveness makes this illusion look like a solid block between me and this person.

Holy Spirit, help me let go of my unwillingness to overlook this apparent block between us.
Help me to forgive this person.
When I do so, I will see truth pass over this block so easily, that I will be convinced that it was actually nothing.

VI. The Light of the Holy Relationship
Commentary by Greg Mackie

1. Do you want freedom of the body or of the mind? For both you cannot have. Which do you value? Which is your goal? For one you see as means; the other, end. And one must serve the other and <u>lead</u> to its predominance, increasing <u>its</u> importance by <u>diminishing</u> its own. Means serve the end, and as the end is reached the value of the means decreases, [Ur: and is] eclipsed entirely when they are recognized as functionless. No one but yearns for freedom and tries to find it. Yet he will seek for it where he believes it <u>is</u> and <u>can</u> be found. He will believe it possible of mind <u>or</u> body, and he will make the other <u>serve</u> his choice as means to find it.

"Freedom" means the ability to do what we will. We all yearn for freedom. But what kind of freedom do we seek: freedom of the body or of the mind? Whichever one we choose, we will see the other as a means to it. We will either use the mind to obtain the body's freedom or use the body to obtain the mind's freedom. If we do the former, our life becomes body-centered; if the latter, it becomes mind-centered. Clearly this is a significant choice.

2. Where freedom of the <u>body</u> has been chosen, the mind is used as <u>means</u> whose value lies in its ability to contrive ways to achieve the body's freedom. Yet freedom of the body <u>has</u> no meaning, and so the mind is <u>dedicated</u> to serve illusions. This is a situation <u>so</u> contradictory and <u>so</u> impossible that anyone who chooses this has <u>no</u> idea of what is valuable. Yet even in this confusion, so profound it cannot <u>be</u> described, the Holy Spirit waits in gentle patience, as certain of the outcome as He is sure of His Creator's Love. He knows this mad decision was made by one as dear to His Creator as love is to itself.

If you were to ask people what freedoms they value and seek, they would probably list things like freedom to say and do what they want, to live and work where they want, to be with the people they want, to elect the leaders they want, etc. These are all forms of freedom of the body, are they not? We devote our minds to contriving means to get these freedoms, everything from cutting the apron strings and leaving home to setting the ground rules for our relationship to devising a political system. The mind is now dedicated to securing the body's freedom.

But the freedom of the body means nothing, so the mind has dedicated itself to serving illusions. Seeing the body's freedom as our goal is contradictory and impossible, because seeing the body as an end means we are serving the goal of sin (see T-18.VII.1:1-3), and being enslaved to sin is the very antithesis of freedom. Yet as insane as this is, the Holy Spirit is not distressed, because the outcome is certain. He knows that we are God's Son, so we will inevitably wise up and make the right choice.

> 3. Be not disturbed at all to think how He can change the role of means and end so easily in what God loves, and would have free forever. But be you rather grateful that you can be the means to serve His end. This is the only service that leads to freedom. To serve this end the body must be perceived as sinless, because the goal is sinlessness. The lack of contradiction makes the soft transition from means to end as easy as is the shift from hate to gratitude before forgiving eyes. You will be sanctified by your brother [Ur: one another], using your body [Ur: bodies] only to serve the sinless. And it will be impossible for you to hate what serves whom you would heal.

The only true freedom is freedom of the mind to do what it *really* wills to do: to love without limit, as God does. If we had this, we would feel free even if our bodies were in prison. Therefore, to find true freedom, means and end must be switched so that the body serves the goal of freedom of the mind.

This switch seems impossible to us, but fortunately it's the Holy Spirit's job. We need simply be grateful that *we* can serve *His* end. What is His end? The exact opposite of the goal of sin that we serve when we see the body as an end; His goal is sinlessness, the awakening of everyone to their true sinless nature. To serve this goal, we must see the body as sinless—that is, not inherently sinful. This resolves the contradiction our old goal produced, because now we're using a sinless body to serve the goal of sinlessness. Now we're using the body to serve the mind. Specifically, now we're using the body only as a means to forgive and heal our holy relationship partner—an earthly form of loving without limit. Using the body only for this transforms it from a hateful vehicle for sin to a holy vehicle for healing (see W-pII.5.4).

4. This holy relationship, lovely in its innocence, mighty in strength, and blazing with a light far brighter than the sun that lights the sky <u>you</u> see, is chosen of your Father as a means for His Own plan. Be thankful that it serves yours not at all. Nothing entrusted to it can <u>be</u> misused, and nothing given it but <u>will</u> be used. This holy relationship has the power to heal <u>all</u> pain, <u>regardless</u> of its form. Neither you nor your brother [Ur: Neither of you] alone can serve at all. Only in your <u>joint</u> will does healing lie. For here <u>your</u> healing is, and here will <u>you</u> accept Atonement. And in your healing <u>is</u> the Sonship healed *because* your will and your brother's [Ur: your wills] are joined.

Devoting ourselves to serving the Holy Spirit's goal of sinlessness means (in this context) using our holy relationship as a means of serving God's plan for salvation. Jesus never tires of praising the holy relationship: I wonder what a light far brighter than the sun looks like? When we devote our holy relationship to serving God's plan, everything else—including the body—becomes a means to serve *it*. Nothing used in the service of the holy relationship can be misused, because the holy relationship itself cannot be misused. On the contrary, it is the most powerful means of healing imaginable. Alone we could not heal anything, but together we can heal *everything*. Through our joining, our own healing is assured, and that healing will extend to heal the entire Sonship.

5. Before a holy relationship there <u>is</u> no sin. The <u>form</u> of error is no longer seen, and reason, joined with love, looks quietly on <u>all</u> confusion, observing merely, "This was a mistake." And then the same Atonement <u>you</u> accepted in <u>your</u> relationship <u>corrects</u> the error, and lays a part of Heaven in its place. How blessed are you who let this gift be given! Each part of Heaven that you bring is given <u>you</u>. And every empty place in Heaven that you fill again with the Eternal Light <u>you</u> bring, shines now on <u>you</u>. The means of sinlessness can know no fear because they carry <u>only</u> love with them.

Joining in holy relationship undoes sin. When our holy relationship is fully realized, we no longer look at the world with the body's eyes and see "real" forms that prove the reality of sin. Instead, we look at the world with the eyes of reason and thus see only correctible error (see T-22.III). This enables the gift of healing we received in our holy relationship to be given to the entire world, replacing sin with a reflection of Heaven. This, in turn, blesses *us*, because the gift of Heaven that we gave is returned to us. We used to be afraid because we were seeking the goal of sin, but now there is no fear because we're serving the goal of sinlessness, and thus bring only love to the world.

> 6. Child of peace, the light *has* come to you. The light you bring you do not recognize, and yet you will remember. Who can deny himself the vision that he brings to others? And who would fail to recognize a gift he let be laid in Heaven through himself? The gentle service that you give the Holy Spirit is service to yourself. You who are now His means must love all that He loves. And what you bring is your remembrance of everything that is eternal. No trace of anything in time can long remain in a mind that serves [Ur: minds that serve] the timeless. And no illusion can disturb the peace of a relationship that has become the means of peace.

Once again, we have the "receive, give, recognize" formula. We have received the light, but we don't know it, at least not fully. The only way we can recognize it is to give it to others, using our bodies and ourselves only as means to serve the Holy Spirit's plan of salvation. By giving what we have received to others, by loving all that the Holy Spirit loves, by using our minds to serve the timeless, we will no longer remain in time ourselves. All of the illusions that disturbed our relationship when we were seeking the goal of sin are undone, because our relationship has now become the means of peace.

> 7. When you have looked upon your brother [Ur: each other] with complete forgiveness, from which no error is excluded and nothing kept hidden, what mistake can there be anywhere you cannot [Ur: can *not*] overlook? What form of suffering could block your sight, preventing you from seeing past it? And what illusion could there be you will not recognize as a mistake; a shadow through which you walk completely undismayed? God would let nothing interfere with those whose wills are His, and they will recognize their wills are His, *because* they serve His Will. And serve it willingly. [Ur: How can it *not* be theirs?] And could remembrance of what they are be long delayed?

Once we have forgiven each other completely, we will be able to forgive *everyone* completely. We will have the power to heal anyone anywhere. And by serving God's Will through giving forgiveness to others, we will recognize that our wills are His. This will ultimately enable us to remember who we are.

Application: Think of someone you need to forgive. Use these lines as an incentive to help you forgive this person:

> *When I have looked upon [name] with complete forgiveness,*
> *there will be no mistake anywhere I cannot overlook.*
> *Whether it is the Holocaust, or 9/11,*
> *or the worst thing that happened to me in my own life,*
> *it will be as easy for me to see past and walk through as a shadow.*
> *By serving God's Will for total forgiveness,*
> *I will learn that my will is His,*
> *and thus remember who I really am.*

8. You will see your value through your brother's [each other's] eyes, and each one is released as he beholds his savior in place of the attacker who he thought was there. Through this releasing is the world released. This is your part in bringing peace. For you have asked what is your function here, and have been answered. Seek not to change it, nor to substitute another goal. This one was given you, and only this. Accept this one and serve it willingly, for what the Holy Spirit does with gifts you give your brother [Ur: each other], to whom He offers them, and where and when, is up to Him. He will bestow them where they are received and welcomed. He will use every one of them for peace. Nor will one little smile or willingness to overlook the tiniest mistake be lost to anyone.

Here we see another oft-repeated Course theme: saving our savior. I see my holy relationship partner as the Christ, my savior instead of an attacker. Through my vision of him, he is saved: He sees his value through my eyes. Moreover, he now sees *me* as the Christ, the holy being who saved him, and this saves me: I see my value through his eyes.

Through this exchange, the entire world is saved. This is our only function. If we give the gift of salvation to each other, the Holy Spirit will take care of extending the gift to others. He can do this without our active participation, as in Workbook Lesson 97, where He takes the gifts of our practice periods and brings them to everyone who is open to them: "He will not overlook one open mind that will accept the healing gifts they bring, and He will lay them everywhere He knows they will be welcome" (W-pI.97.5:2). He can also do this *with* our active participation, guiding us to those He wants us to serve.

Either way, smiling at our partner's little mistake instead of giving him "the look" has far greater healing power than we could ever imagine. Something to remember next time he leaves the toilet seat up or she wants to watch figure skating instead of the football game.

> 9. What can it be but universal blessing to look on what your Father loves with charity? <u>Extension</u> of forgiveness is the Holy Spirit's function. Leave this to Him. Let <u>your</u> concern be only that you give <u>to</u> Him that which can <u>be</u> extended. Save no dark secrets that He cannot use, but offer Him the tiny gifts He can extend forever. He will take each one and make of it a potent force for peace. He will withhold no blessing from it, nor limit it in any way. He will join to it <u>all</u> the power that God has given Him, to make each little gift of love a source of healing for everyone. Each little gift you offer to your brother [Ur: to the other] lights up the world. Be not concerned with darkness; look <u>away</u> from it and <u>toward</u> your brother [Ur: each other]. And let the darkness be dispelled by Him Who knows the light, and lays it gently in each quiet smile of faith and confidence with which you bless your brother [Ur: each other].

As we've seen, forgiving each other is not for us alone—it brings universal blessing. Each little gift of forgiveness we give to the Holy Spirit, He will "extend forever." Wow! We needn't be concerned with the darkness in our relationship, the remnant of that goal of sin that pops up in our petty arguments and petulant looks. We just need to look away from darkness and toward each other. As we give each other that quiet smile of faith and confidence, the Holy Spirit will dispel the darkness with His Light and bless the world with the blessing we give each other.

Application: We can never have too much incentive to forgive, so again think of someone you need to forgive—perhaps the same person as last time. With this person in mind, repeat these lines:

If I give the little gift of forgiveness to [name],
the Holy Spirit will take this gift and extend it forever.

He will make it a potent force for peace.
He will withhold no blessing from it, nor limit it in any way.
He will join to it all the power that God has given Him.
He will make this little gift of love a source of healing for everyone.
He will use this little gift to light up the world.

Holy Spirit, let me give the little gift of forgiveness to [name].
Let me bless him with a quiet smile of faith and confidence.
Let me look on what my Father loves with charity,
and by so doing give a universal blessing to the world.

Commentary by Robert Perry

The first half of this section seems quite separable from the second half. Indeed, it was taken down by Helen on a different day—usually an indication of a new discussion. There is, however, a clear connection between the two halves. Both speak of the power that lies in the holy relationship to save the entire world.

> 10. On your learning depends the welfare of the world. And it is only arrogance that would <u>deny</u> the power of your will. Think you the Will of God is power<u>less</u>? Is this <u>humility</u>? You do not see what this belief has done. You see yourself as vulnerable, frail and easily destroyed, and at the mercy of countless attackers more powerful than you. Let us look straight at how this error came about, for here lies buried the heavy anchor that seems to keep the fear of God in place, immovable and solid as a rock. While this remains, so will it seem to be.

Application: Say the following to yourself:

On my learning depends the welfare of the world.

Note your reactions to this line. Does your mind give it full assent, or hold back in cautious skepticism? Then say,

To deny the power I have is nothing but arrogance.
For God has placed His Will in mine.

Do I think the Will of God is powerless?
*Is this **humility**?*

Of course, you have already denied the power you possess. And this is why your daily experience is one of being "vulnerable, frail and easily destroyed, and at the mercy of countless attackers more powerful than you."

The question, then, is: How did we come to deny this power? Jesus promises to give us an answer in the following paragraphs, an answer that will show that this denial of power is intimately linked with our fear of God.

> 11. Who can attack the Son of God and <u>not</u> attack his Father? How can God's Son be weak and frail and easily destroyed <u>unless his Father is</u>? You do <u>not</u> see that <u>every</u> sin and <u>every</u> condemnation that you perceive and justify *is* an attack upon your Father. And that is <u>why</u> it has not happened, nor <u>could</u> be real. You do not see that this is your attempt <u>because</u> you think the Father and the Son are separate. And you <u>must</u> think that They are separate, <u>because of fear</u>. For it <u>seems</u> safer to attack another or yourself than to attack the great Creator of the universe, Whose power you <u>know</u>.

Jesus' answer begins by pointing out that, since Father and Son are joined, every attack on the Son is also an attack on the Father. Imagine that this is true. Imagine that the last time you verbally attacked someone, you were simultaneously tongue-lashing God. It's as if a boy were toying with a lizard on the bank of a river, flipping it around, burning it with a magnifying glass, only to realize that the "lizard" was really a newly hatched crocodile—right as its thirty-foot-long, highly protective mother emerged from the river a few feet away.

There are two ways to go with this. One is to imagine that there is no mama crocodile, to imagine that this person you are attacking is totally disconnected from God. That is what we have done, in order to allow ourselves to attack without fear. The other is to realize that since attack on God cannot be real, attack on the Son cannot be real, either. The deepest implication of this is what the next paragraph says: "[Attack] *is impossible*."

> 12. If you were one with God <u>and recognized this oneness</u>, you would

know His power is <u>yours</u>. But you will <u>not</u> remember this while you believe attack of <u>any</u> kind means <u>anything</u>. It is unjustified in <u>any</u> form, <u>because</u> it has no meaning. The only way it <u>could</u> be justified is if you and your brother [Ur: if each one of you] were <u>separate</u> from the other, and all were separate from your Creator. For <u>only</u> then would it be possible to attack a part of the creation <u>without</u> the whole, the Son <u>without</u> the Father; and to attack another <u>without</u> yourself, or hurt yourself without the other feeling pain. And this belief you <u>want</u>. Yet wherein lies its value, <u>except</u> in the desire to attack in safety? Attack is neither safe nor dangerous. <u>It is impossible</u>. And this is so <u>because</u> the universe [the Sonship] is one. You would not choose attack on its reality if it were not <u>essential</u> to attack to see it separated from its maker [Ur: *separate from its Creator*]. And thus it seems as if love could attack <u>and become fearful</u>.

Application: Attack only makes sense if it can be discrete. Imagine someone, from any point in your life, to whom you would secretly like to give the message, "You are a horrible person. I look forward to seeing you suffer." Now imagine that as you said this to this one person, you literally couldn't stop yourself from saying it to your mother (assuming she wasn't the initial person), then your spouse, then your beloved child, then your best friend, then a perfect stranger on the street, then Jesus, then God, and then finally yourself. What happens to the original attack impulse when you imagine all that?

For myself, I find that the attack impulse evaporates. Even if I want to attack the first person, the last thing I want to do is attack the rest. That would cause me tremendous pain. Yet that is what is happening in every attack. There are no smart bombs. The "obvious" solution to this is to simply deny that this is happening, to imagine that everyone is separate and therefore attack can be discrete. That way I can attack in safety.

But there is a cost to this. By seeing everything as separate, we see ourselves as separate from God and from His power. We therefore see ourselves "as vulnerable, frail and easily destroyed, and at the mercy of countless attackers." This, then, is how we denied our power. We did it so we could shoot our brother without causing collateral damage.

13. Only the <u>different</u> can attack. So you conclude *because* you can attack, you and your brother must be <u>different</u>. Yet does the Holy Spirit explain this differently. *Because* you and your brother are <u>not</u> different,

you <u>cannot attack</u>. Either position is a logical conclusion [Ur: if only the different can attack]. Either could be maintained, <u>but never both</u>. The <u>only</u> question to be answered in order to decide which <u>must</u> be true is whether you and your brother are different [Ur: *whether you are different*]. From the position of what <u>you</u> understand you seem to <u>be</u>, and <u>therefore</u> can attack. Of the alternatives, this <u>seems</u> more natural and more in line with your experience. And therefore it is necessary that you have <u>other</u> experiences, more in line with truth, to teach you what *is* natural and true.

You cannot attack someone else unless you are genuinely separate from each other. How could a pool of water attack itself? As I have said before, attack requires two separate forms that can collide and cause injury to each other.

Again, we can go two ways with this. Our experience has taught us that we *can* attack, and this seems to prove to us that we *are* separate. Think of someone you have attacked. The fact that your will can operate apart from hers, and come from outside of her to bring harm upon her, proves that the two of you must be separate, right?

The Holy Spirit, however, goes the other way with this. He says because you are *not* separate, you *cannot* attack. This, too, makes perfect sense, but it is certainly not in line with our experience. Yet Jesus, undaunted, says, "Therefore it is necessary that you have *other* experiences, more in line with truth, to teach you what *is* natural and true."

> 14. This is the function of your holy relationship. For what <u>one</u> thinks, the <u>other</u> will experience <u>with</u> him. What can this mean <u>except</u> your mind and your brother's [Ur: your minds] are one? Look not with fear upon this happy fact, and think not that it lays a heavy burden on you. For when you have <u>accepted</u> it with gladness, you will realize that your relationship is a reflection of the union of the Creator and His Son. From loving minds there *is* no separation. And every thought in one brings gladness to the other <u>because</u> they are the same. Joy is unlimited, <u>because</u> each shining thought of love <u>extends</u> its being and creates more of itself. There is no difference <u>anywhere</u> in it, for every thought is like itself.

How do we get those other experiences, the ones that teach us we are not separate? That's what a holy relationship is for. In such a relationship, it can be remarkable how thoughts and feelings and states and insights can transfer from one partner to the other, without being physically communicated. Have you ever had this sort of thing happen to you?

If you have, the next step is to realize what it implies. It implies that you and that other person are not separate. You can regard this as an unwelcome burden: "Oh great. Now whatever I think is going to affect him." This is what Jesus was talking about before—seeing lack of separation as threatening, because it means attack cannot be penned in, but will automatically jump the fences and roam free. Or you can take a further step and realize its full implications: "Oh, I get it. If my brother and I are not separate, then attack cannot be real."

The paragraph closes with a beautiful vision of what it really means for minds to be one. It means not that their thoughts of attack will spread out like ink in a bathtub, but that their thoughts of love will shine out like the rising sun, spreading everywhere the radiance of joy.

> 15. The light that joins you and your brother shines throughout the universe, and <u>because</u> it joins you and him, so it makes you and him one with your Creator. And in <u>Him</u> is all creation joined. Would you <u>regret</u> you cannot fear alone, when your relationship can also teach the power of love is there, which makes <u>all</u> fear impossible? Do not attempt to keep a little of the ego with this gift. For it was given you to be <u>used,</u> and <u>not</u> obscured. What teaches you that you <u>cannot</u> separate <u>denies</u> the ego. Let <u>truth</u> decide if you and your brother be different or the same, and <u>teach</u> you which is true.

Again, there are two ways to greet the fact that minds are not separate. You can say, "Let's face it. I am inevitably going to have thoughts of fear and attack. I just wish they didn't have to infect everyone else." It's as if all noses are one, so that as soon as you get a virus, there's no way to keep everyone else from catching it, too.

But hold on. What you are, in essence, saying is this: "Since all minds are one, there are no fences to contain my ego's destructiveness." Do you see what is wrong with that statement? If all minds are one, then *the ego is not real.* If all minds are one, then only love is real. And the love in one mind shines out to all minds, teaching them all that the ego is impossible.

This is what our holy relationship has the power to do—teach all minds that the ego never was. Why are we not rejoicing over this gift? We are like someone who has been given a billion dollars to spend on helping the world, and all he can say is, "I wish I didn't have this burden. What if I screw it up?" He's ignoring the big picture: *He's got a billion dollars with which to help the world.*

Application: Remember a time when you had a loving thought toward another person, some sense of gratitude or appreciation, some little upwelling of genuine love.

Now imagine this thought flowing from your mind directly into this other person's mind, because there is no boundary between them. The body is only an illusion of a boundary. So see this thought bringing instant gladness to your brother because your minds are the same.

Now see this thought of love and joy keep extending. Behind your brother there are a thousand minds into which this thought extends. See it going into all those minds, bringing them joy. Then behind each one of those minds there are a thousand more. See it going into all of those minds, bringing every one of them joy and gladness.

Now see the Holy Spirit take this thought and join to it all the power of God. See Him carry it around this aching world where pain and misery appear to rule. See him shine it into every single mind that is open to this thought. See it shine into the mind of a housewife in India, a starving child in Ethiopia, a gang member in Los Angeles, a dying woman in China, bringing gladness to every one of them. Realize that this is going on countless times all over the world. And every time someone accepts this thought as their own, it increases in healing power.

> Thus will your thought be multiplied a thousandfold and tens of thousands more. And when it is returned to you, it will surpass in might your little thought as much as does the radiance of the sun outshine...a firefly....The steady brilliance of this light remains and leads you out of darkness, nor will you be able to forget the way again (W-pI.97.6).

Commentaries on Chapter 23

THE WAR AGAINST
YOURSELF

Introduction
Commentary by Robert Perry

1. Do you not see the <u>opposite</u> of frailty and weakness is sinlessness? <u>Innocence is strength,</u> and nothing else is strong. The sinless cannot fear, for sin of any kind is weakness. The show of strength attack would use to <u>cover</u> frailty conceals it not, for how can the unreal <u>be</u> hidden? No one is strong who has an enemy, and no one can attack unless he thinks he <u>has</u>. Belief in enemies is therefore the belief in <u>weakness,</u> and what is weak is <u>not</u> the Will of God. Being <u>opposed</u> to it, it is God's "enemy." And God is feared as an <u>opposing</u> will.

We think innocence is weakness. It is beautiful and pure, but easily crushed, which is why most of us abandon innocence for carrying a big stick. Yet Jesus turns this around. Weakness, he says, is carrying the big stick. We wonder if he is kidding. But then he backs this up with reasoned argument.

- You only attack when you think you have an enemy.
- If you have an enemy, someone who can damage you, then you must be vulnerable.
- If you are vulnerable, you cannot be *truly* strong.
- You must be putting on a show of strength to cover up your hidden frailty and vulnerability.
- "Belief in enemies is therefore the belief in weakness."

It seems that he really has a point. In this view, innocence is not the refusal to raise a hand against one's enemies. It is refusal to *see* enemies. And that means refusal to see one's strength as compromised by the existence of a competing power. That's real innocence. And that's real strength.

2. How strange indeed becomes this war against yourself! You will believe that <u>everything</u> you use for sin can hurt you <u>and become your enemy</u>. And you will fight <u>against</u> it, and try to weaken it <u>because</u> of this; and you will think that you succeeded, and attack again. It is as

certain you will fear what you attack as it is sure that you will love what you perceive as sinless. He walks in peace who travels sinlessly along the way love shows him. For love walks <u>with</u> him there, <u>protecting</u> him from fear. And he will see <u>only</u> the sinless, who can <u>not</u> attack.

This is a hard message to grasp. Let's go back to the big stick. What is your version of the big stick, the thing you carry so that people know they better not mess with you? Jesus here suggests that somewhere inside, you see this stick as a constant affirmation that you have enemies, and therefore as a constant reminder that you are weak and vulnerable. This causes you to have a love/hate relationship with the stick itself.

Think of the Samurai swordsman. He knows full well that those who live by the sword die by the sword. And so even while he loves his sword, he must secretly hate it. Now the sword itself becomes a kind of enemy. And sure enough, he keeps trying to put it down. He keeps trying to get out of the swordsmanship business, and keeps getting drawn back in—a theme we see in many stories.

The final lines show us a different way. We can walk sinlessly through life, attacking no one, seeing everyone as our friend. If we do, we will walk in peace and in complete lack of fear, for love will walk with us.

3. Walk you in glory, with your head held high, and fear no evil. The innocent are safe because they <u>share</u> their innocence. Nothing they see is harmful, for their <u>awareness</u> of the truth releases everything from the illusion of harmfulness. And what <u>seemed</u> harmful now stands shining in their innocence, released from sin and fear and happily returned to love. They share the strength of love *because* they looked on innocence. And every error disappeared because they saw it not. Who looks for glory finds it where it <u>is</u>. Where <u>could</u> it be but in the innocent?

That first line is such a wonderful image, isn't it? Imagine walking in glory. Remember that "glory" in the Course usually refers to the radiance surrounding a holy person. So imagine walking surrounded by the light of your holiness, with your head held high, and fearing no evil. You fear no evil because you see innocence everywhere, in everyone. Everything you look on is bathed in the light of your innocence. And so what looks like harmfulness is transmuted into gentleness, its errors corrected because you refused to acknowledge them as real.

Notice that this is designed as a kind of correction of the famous Psalm 23, which says, "Yea, even though I walk through the valley of the shadow of death, I will fear no evil." This says, "I do not walk in shadow; I walk in glory. I do not see myself surrounded by death; I see myself surrounded by innocence. And that is why I fear no evil."

> 4. Let not the little interferers pull you to littleness. There <u>can</u> be no attraction of guilt in innocence. Think what a happy world you walk, with truth beside you! Do not give up this world of freedom for a little sigh of seeming sin, nor for a tiny stirring of guilt's attraction. Would you, for all these meaningless distractions, lay Heaven aside? Your destiny and purpose are far beyond them, in the clean place where littleness does not exist. Your purpose is at variance with littleness of any kind. And so it is at variance with sin.

As you walk in glory, with your head held high, seeing innocence everywhere, you walk through a happy world, a world of freedom. Yet there will be constant temptations to see an enemy, and therefore leave this glorious world and return to littleness. These temptations are "the little interferers," the "meaningless distractions." What do they look like? They look like some little thing that tempts you to see sin again and respond with attack.

Application: Imagine yourself right now walking in glory, with your head held high, and fearing no evil because you see only innocence. Now keep your eye out, for the next several minutes (as you return to reading and after that, to your other activities), for a little interferer—something that tempts you to see sin out there, to see an enemy. When you spot one, ask yourself,

Would I lay Heaven aside for this meaningless distraction?

> 5. Let us not let littleness lead God's Son into temptation. His glory is <u>beyond</u> it, measureless and timeless as eternity. Do not let time intrude upon your sight of him. Leave him not frightened and alone in his temptation, but help him rise above it and perceive the light of which he is a part. <u>Your</u> innocence will light the way to his, and so is <u>yours</u> protected and <u>kept</u> in your awareness. For who can know his glory, and

perceive the little and the weak about him? Who can walk trembling in a fearful world, and realize that Heaven's glory shines on him?

Traditionally, we ask God to not lead us into temptation. Now Jesus is asking *us* to not lead our *brother* into temptation—actually, to not let our littleness lead him into temptation. Our littleness would see him as an enemy, held captive to the pettiness within him and countless dangers around him. If we see him this way, we do lead him into temptation.

But we can instead see the light in him, see his glory. And we need to see his glory, for that is the only way that we can see the glory in ourselves.

Application: Let us pray a new version of the Lord's Prayer:

Our Father, Your holy Name is ours, for we are Your Son.
Reveal to us our innocence, just as we reveal to our brothers their
innocence.
And let us not lead them into temptation by seeing them as our
enemies.
But let us deliver them from evil by seeing their glory.
For theirs is the power and the glory, along with us and with You,
forever and ever.
Amen.

6. Nothing around you but is <u>part</u> of you. Look on it lovingly, and see the light of Heaven in it. So will you come to understand all that is given you. In kind forgiveness will the world sparkle and shine, and everything you once thought sinful now will be reinterpreted as part of Heaven. How beautiful it is to walk, clean and redeemed and happy, through a world in bitter need of the redemption that your innocence bestows upon it! What can you value <u>more</u> than this? For here is <u>your</u> salvation and <u>your</u> freedom. And it <u>must</u> be complete if <u>you</u> would recognize it.

We often do feel like we are walking through the valley of the shadow of death. The world is so full of danger, so full of attack that we can hardly keep from walking through it in fear and trembling. Yet this same fact can be a blessing, for the world needs the redemption that we can bestow on it, by shining our innocence on everything. Thus, rather than lamenting all the sin out there, we can think this way:

> *How beautiful it is to walk, clean and redeemed and happy, through a world in bitter need of the redemption that my innocence bestows upon it!*

Try to imagine walking through the world this way. Imagine this being the thought that fills your mind as you walk through the supermarket or down the street or through your own kitchen.

If you really take this attitude to heart, the shadowy valley of death that you see will transform before your eyes into a landscape of glory, in which everything sparkles and shines with the light of Heaven. And then you will understand that *you* shine with the light of Heaven, and that Heaven is where you belong.

I. The Irreconcilable Beliefs
Commentary by Robert Perry

1. The memory of God comes to the quiet mind. It <u>cannot</u> come where there is conflict, for a mind at war against itself remembers not eternal gentleness. The means of war are <u>not</u> the means of peace, and what the warlike would remember is <u>not</u> love. War is impossible unless belief in <u>victory</u> is cherished. Conflict <u>within</u> you <u>must</u> imply that you believe the ego has the power <u>to be victorious</u>. Why else would you identify with it? Surely you realize the ego <u>is</u> at war with God. Certain it is it <u>has</u> no enemy. Yet just as certain is its fixed belief it has an enemy that it <u>must</u> overcome and <u>will succeed</u>.

The memory of God can only come into a mind that is like itself—quiet, gentle, and peaceful. A mind that is not quiet is a mind that contains conflict. And think what that means. If the mind contains conflict, then one part of it is in conflict with another part of it. The mind is at war with itself. How can the Love of God enter such a battlefield?

It gets worse. For the war is being waged by your ego on *you*, the real you, the part of you that is at one with God. The ego, in other words, is trying to defeat both you and God. Unless you thought it could succeed, there would be no reason to identify with it. Yet how can it succeed?

2. Do you not realize a war against yourself would <u>be</u> a war on God? Is victory <u>conceivable</u>? And if it were, is this a victory that you would <u>want</u>? The death of God, if it were possible, would be <u>your</u> death. Is this a <u>victory</u>? The ego <u>always</u> marches to defeat, <u>because</u> it thinks that triumph over you is possible. And God thinks otherwise. This is no war; only the mad belief the Will of God can be attacked and overthrown. You may <u>identify</u> with this belief, but never will it be more than madness. And fear will reign in madness, and will <u>seem</u> to have replaced love there. This is the conflict's <u>purpose</u>. And to those who think that it is possible, the means seem real.

Somewhere inside, we have allied ourselves with the ego in an attempt to defeat both God and ourselves—or rather, our Self. Yet what a hopeless endeavor! Even if we could defeat God, we would be wiping ourselves out of existence. And yet God knows that not only can He not be defeated, *we* cannot be defeated either. This is not a war; it is madness. It is a little boy dreaming that he, singlehandedly, is going to defeat the greatest army on earth. As long as we identify with the ego, this is the madness we believe. And this is why we are afraid, for fear reigns in madness.

> 3. Be certain that it is impossible God and the ego, or yourself and it, will <u>ever</u> meet. You <u>seem</u> to meet, and make your strange alliances on grounds that have no meaning. For your beliefs converge upon the body, the ego's chosen home, which you believe is <u>yours</u> [your chosen home]. You meet at a mistake; an error in your self-appraisal. The ego joins with an <u>illusion</u> of yourself you <u>share</u> with it. And yet illusions cannot join. They <u>are</u> the same, and they are nothing. Their joining lies in nothingness; two are as meaningless as one or as a thousand. The ego joins with nothing, <u>being</u> nothing. The victory it seeks is meaningless as is itself.

It seems that we have joined with the ego, but have we really? Our joining with the ego is like us joining with a cartoon. I've seen movies where people actually interact with cartoons, but that only happens in movies. In real life, we can no more meet with our ego than we can interact with a cartoon. We and the ego are completely different orders of reality—we are real and the ego is not.

How, then, do we *seem* to meet? Through the body. It is the common ground on which we have made our strange alliance with the ego. Yet, oddly enough, the body is yet another cartoon, another illusion, just like the ego. And it doesn't matter how many illusions join forces. It's like adding up zeroes. No matter how many you add up, you still get zero.

> 4. Brother [Ur: Brothers], the war against yourself is almost over. The journey's end is at the place of peace. Would you not now <u>accept</u> the peace offered you here? This "enemy" you fought as an <u>intruder</u> on your peace is here transformed, before your sight, into the <u>giver</u> of your peace. Your "enemy" was God Himself, to Whom all conflict, triumph and attack of <u>any</u> kind are all unknown. He loves you perfectly, completely and eternally. The Son of God at war with his Creator is a condition as ridiculous as nature roaring at the wind in anger,

proclaiming it is part of itself no more. Could nature possibly establish this, and make it true? Nor is it up to you to say what shall be part of you and what is kept apart.

I believe that the opening lines are a reference to the holy relationship, and that they mean this: The two of you stand together in the place of peace, the very end of the journey, which is where you visit in the holy instant. Here in this holy place, you see this person who seemed to be an intruder on your peace revealed to be the *giver* of your peace. You fought him, but now you realize that in fighting him, you were fighting God Himself. Yet God doesn't even know what war and conflict are. He's never heard of them. All He knows is love. All He does is love you, you who are part of Him. Trying to fight your Creator is like nature roaring at the wind, or like your finger trying to injure your hand. Does this make any sense?

> 5. The war against yourself was undertaken to teach the Son of God that he is not himself, and *not* his Father's Son. For this, the memory of his Father must be forgotten. It *is* forgotten in the body's life, and if you think you are a body, you will believe you have forgotten it. Yet truth can never be forgotten by itself, and you have not forgotten what you are. Only a strange illusion of yourself, a wish to triumph over what you are, remembers not.

The whole point of your war on yourself is to cause yourself to forget who you are, to forget that you are God's Son. This means forgetting the memory of God (the full awareness of God). The way you do this is to identify with things that do not have this memory. You identify with the body, which only remembers meaningless sensations. And you identify with the ego, which does not have a clue what God is.

But this does not mean that *you* have forgotten. You are like an actor who, for a brief time, so completely identifies with his character that he is not thinking about his real life, which will resume immediately after the performance. Has he really forgotten his real identity? Or has he just momentarily identified with something else?

> 6. The war against yourself is but the battle of two illusions, struggling to make them different from each other, in the belief the one that conquers will be true. There *is* no conflict between them and the truth. Nor are

they different from each other. Both are <u>not</u> true. And so it matters not what form they take. What made them is insane, and they remain part of what made them. Madness holds out no menace to reality, and has no influence upon it. Illusions <u>cannot</u> triumph over truth, nor can they threaten it in any way. And the reality that they deny is <u>not</u> a part of them.

I must confess that I find this paragraph difficult to puzzle out. We have two illusions that seem different, that are battling each other for supremacy, but which are really the same. Further, they were both made by a *third* illusion, which happens to be insane.

My best guess (based on 8:3-4 and 4:1-4) is that the two illusions are my brother and myself—or rather, my *image* of my brother and my *image* of myself. I'm hoping that once these two illusions duke it out, my illusion of myself will emerge as the victor, as the one that is really true.

In this interpretation, the third illusion would be my ego, which made both illusions (of my brother and of myself). The point is that none of these illusions has any connection to reality. They are not more true or less true. They are simply *un*true.

A great symbol for all this is Shakespeare's story of Othello. There, Iago conspires to bring down Othello, by convincing him that his wife, Desdemona, has been unfaithful to him. This turns the noble Othello into a violent and angry man, not at all the person he was before. Iago, then, has manufactured two illusions—one of Desdemona and one of Othello. In the same way, the ego manufactures two illusions—one of us and one of our brother—in order to pit them against each other.

> 7. What *you* remember *is* a part of you. For you <u>must</u> be as God created you. Truth does not fight against illusions, nor do illusions fight against the truth. Illusions battle <u>only</u> with themselves. Being fragmented, they fragment. But truth is indivisible, and <u>far</u> beyond their little reach. You will remember what you know when you have learned you <u>cannot</u> be in conflict. One <u>illusion</u> about yourself can battle with another, yet the war of two illusions is a state where <u>nothing happens</u>. There is no victor and there is no victory. And truth stands radiant, <u>apart</u> from conflict, untouched and quiet in the peace of God.
>
> 8. Conflict must be between two <u>forces</u>. It can<u>not</u> exist between one power and nothingness.

Truth and illusions have no meeting ground. All truth is one within itself. And all illusions are the same as each other. Yet since the essence of illusions is fragmentation, they fragment; they splinter into warring factions. Yet this war has several important characteristics: First, the opponents are not actually different; they are just the same illusory stuff wearing different uniforms. Second, nothing actually happens, since the opponents are illusory. No one either wins or loses. Third, none of this touches the truth, which "stands radiant, apart from conflict, untouched and quiet in the peace of God."

Only when this senseless, nonexistent war leaves your mind will you remember what you have known all along: your eternal oneness with God.

Application: Think about a conflict you are having with someone else. Now realize that the two of you are not really in conflict. An illusion of you is in conflict with an illusion of the other person. These illusions only *seem* different. In truth, they are two vials filled with the same fog. Further, realize that in this war, nothing is really happening. Can a game be real in which neither team exists? Now say to yourself the following:

> *The truth of who I am and who [name] is stands radiant, apart from conflict, untouched and quiet in the peace of God.*

There is nothing you <u>could</u> attack that is not part of you. And *by* attacking it you make two illusions of yourself, <u>in conflict</u> with each other. And this occurs whenever you look on <u>anything</u> that God created with anything but love. Conflict is fearful, for it is the birth of fear. Yet what is born of nothing cannot <u>win</u> reality through battle. Why would you fill your world with conflicts with yourself? Let all this madness be undone for you, and turn in peace to the remembrance of God, still shining in your quiet mind.

This paragraph confirms, I feel, the direction I have gone with this section. The two illusions that are battling each other are our illusion of ourselves and our illusion of someone else. Since that other person *is* ourselves, our illusion of him is also an illusion of ourselves. The picture communicated here is sobering: Our made-up image of self is in perpetual conflict with made-up images of everyone else. And while these images wage ceaseless war, behind each one is the very same Self, serene and untouched. In this light, let us ask ourselves Jesus' question:

Why would I fill my world with conflicts with myself?

9. See how the conflict of illusions disappears when it is brought to truth! For it seems real <u>only</u> as long as it is seen as war between <u>conflicting</u> truths; the conqueror to be the truer, the <u>more</u> real, and the <u>vanquisher</u> of the illusion that was less real, <u>made</u> an illusion by defeat. Thus, conflict is the choice <u>between</u> illusions, one to be crowned as real, the other vanquished and despised. Here will the Father <u>never</u> be remembered. Yet <u>no</u> illusion can invade His home and drive Him out of what He loves forever. And what He loves <u>must</u> be forever quiet and at peace *because* it is His home.

We think the little personal wars we wage are wars between conflicting *truths*. We are hoping that our truth emerges "the truer, the *more* real, and the *vanquisher* of the illusion that was less real, *made* an illusion by defeat." Yet if our truth is at war, then it is not the truth; it is an illusion. And if this is our life, this ceaseless war in which every combatant is an illusion, then how can we ever remember the truth? How can we remember the infinite grandeur of Heaven while we are engrossed in a titanic, tabletop struggle between plastic army men that only we can see?

We need to remind ourselves that what is battling here are two *illusions*. Then we will simultaneously realize that the battle is meaningless. And then it will vanish.

10. [Ur: And] You who are beloved of Him are no illusion, being as true and holy as Himself. The stillness of your certainty of Him and of yourself is home to both of You, Who dwell as one and <u>not</u> apart. Open the door of His most holy home, and let forgiveness sweep away all trace of the belief in sin that keeps God homeless and His Son with Him. You are not a stranger in the house of God. Welcome your brother to the home where God has set him in serenity and peace, and dwells with him. Illusions have no place where love abides, protecting you from <u>everything</u> that is not true. You dwell in peace as limitless as its Creator, and <u>everything</u> is given those who would remember Him.

Over His home the Holy Spirit watches, sure that its peace can never <u>be</u> disturbed.

This section's vision of life as we know it reminds me of computer games my older son has played, called MMORPG. Here is an entry on them from Wikipedia:

> A **Massively-Multiplayer Online Role-Playing Game** (MMORPG) is an online computer role-playing game (RPG) in which a large number of players interact with one another in a virtual world. As in all RPGs, players assume the role of a fictional character (traditionally in a fantasy setting) and take control over many of that character's actions. MMORPGs are distinguished from single-player or small multi-player RPGs by the game's persistent world, usually hosted by the game's publisher, which continues to exist and evolve while the player is away from the game.

In other words, you show up as an illusory character, with a collection of deadly powers, on this virtual battleground. And everyone else does, too. So they all see (and do battle with) the character you control. But they never see *you*. And you see your character surrounded by trolls and warriors and devils and such, each of them possessing its collection of weapons and powers, and each controlled by someone you never see.

This is a great symbol for the world we live in, isn't it? Yet this stands in total contrast to our real home, where we dwell in perfect peace with God and with our brothers, and where no illusions can ever enter. We have the power to open the door to this home and usher in our brothers. How? By forgiving them, by realizing that the sinful characters they are playing in this MMORPG are not who they are.

> 11. How can the resting place of God turn on itself, and seek to overcome the One Who dwells there? And think what happens when the house of God perceives itself divided. The altar disappears, the light grows dim, the temple of the Holy One becomes a house of sin. And nothing is remembered <u>except</u> illusions. Illusions <u>can</u> conflict, because their forms <u>are</u> different. And they do battle <u>only</u> to establish which <u>form</u> is true.

What a harrowing image. The temple of the Holy One was established as the dwelling place of God and His holy Sons, where they exist in perfect harmony and love. The temple is filled with light, and shafts of brilliant light fall upon its most holy altar. But then the Sons begin to strive against each other. The harmony is shattered. "The altar disappears, the light grows dim, the temple of the Holy One becomes a house of sin." It turns into a darkened brothel, filled with sex and murder. However, the creatures that wait in the rooms and stalk the hallways are specters, shadows, who don't realize they are unreal. All are locked in endless combat, each seeking to establish that he or she is the truest illusion. Heaven has transformed into a macabre MMORPG.

> 12. Illusion meets illusion; truth, itself. The meeting of illusions leads to war. Peace, looking on itself, <u>extends</u> itself. War is the condition in which fear is born, and grows and seeks to dominate. Peace is the state where love abides, and seeks to share itself. Conflict and peace are opposites. Where one abides the other <u>cannot</u> be; where either goes the other disappears. So is the memory of God obscured in minds that have become illusions' battleground. Yet far beyond this senseless war it shines, ready to <u>be</u> remembered when you side with peace.

We now return to the section's beginning. There we were told, "The memory of God comes to the quiet mind. It cannot come where there is conflict." The entire section has expanded on this single idea. In the state of truth, there is only peace, for each truth is one with all other truth. Conflict is impossible. There is only perfect sharing and love. In the state of illusion, there is nothing but fragmentation, in which all the illusions splinter off from each other, each seeking to prove itself more real, even though they are all equally illusory. These two states—truth and illusion—never touch each other. Therefore, while our minds are caught up in the war of illusions, we cannot remember the truth, we cannot remember God. "So is the memory of God obscured in minds that have become illusions' battleground." Yet our war never touches God. His temple never really turns into a house of sin. And so the memory of Him is waiting for us, as soon as we choose to turn our computer off and walk away from our virtual battleground.

II. The Laws of Chaos
Commentary by Robert Perry

This long and important section continues from the previous section. To capture that section's vision of life on earth, I used the image of an MMORPG, a Massively-Multiplayer Online Role-Playing Game, in which computer gamers from all over the world can show up as characters in the same virtual world, a world that persists and evolves even as different players enter and exit. Each player appears as a fictional character in this world, where his character goes on quests and does battle with other characters.

If we see our world along these lines, what does it say about our world? It says that the characters we appear as in this world, and the characters we see others as, are illusions—fictional characters in an artificial environment. The characters that walk about in our world are not the actual people that are controlling the characters; those actual people are never seen in this virtual world. Being illusory, the characters are all the same—they are just different shapes and sizes of zero. Yet they *seem* different, and they do constant battle to establish this difference. Specifically, each one is battling with the others in the attempt to prove his illusion the most real. If he can defeat all the others, his illusory character will be shown to possess the most reality. This is the object of each character's quest. And this objective driving *each* of them produces endless warfare between *all* of them. It produces total chaos. Which brings us this next section.

> 1. The "laws" of chaos <u>can</u> be brought to light, though <u>never</u> understood. Chaotic laws are hardly meaningful, and therefore out of reason's sphere. Yet they <u>appear</u> to be an obstacle to reason and to truth. Let us, then, look upon them calmly, that we may look <u>beyond</u> them, understanding what they <u>are,</u> <u>not</u> what they would maintain. It <u>is</u> essential it be understood what they are <u>for,</u> because it is their <u>purpose</u> to make meaningless, and to <u>attack</u> the truth. Here are the laws that rule the world you made. And yet they govern nothing, and need <u>not</u> be broken; merely looked upon and gone beyond.

II. The Laws of Chaos

This first paragraph tells us that we are embarking on a process of looking calmly at "the laws that rule the world." This should make us sit up and take notice. After all, we've all been trying to figure out how this world works from day one. However, these laws don't deserve the name, since they are laws of *chaos*. They are the laws of lawlessness. They are the rules behind what has no rules. These laws, therefore, are really nonsense. And that is what we are trying to see. We are trying to look at the nonsense they really are, not the sage rules of order and justice they pass themselves off as.

Why is it so important to see their nonsense? Because then we can *stop obeying them*. We all love stories where the hero wakes up to the insanity of the system he is living in and then refuses to obey its laws. If we understand this section, we can be that hero. We can be like Neo in *The Matrix* who, once he understands how the Matrix works, doesn't even need to *dodge* the bullets.

> 2. The *first* chaotic law is that the truth is different for everyone. Like all these principles, this one maintains that each is separate and has a different set of thoughts that <u>set him off</u> [Ur: which *sets him off*] from others. This principle evolves from the belief there is a hierarchy of illusions; some are <u>more</u> valuable and <u>therefore</u> true. Each one establishes this <u>for himself,</u> and <u>makes</u> it true by his attack on what another values. And this is justified <u>because</u> the values differ, and those who hold them <u>seem</u> to be unlike, and <u>therefore</u> enemies.

What this brief paragraph says is extremely important. It adds to the picture that we have already been discussing, the picture of us being on illusions' battleground.

The first chaotic law, the one that leads to all the rest, is what these days passes for the height of spiritual wisdom and the epitome of tolerance: "The truth is different for everyone." Why is Jesus criticizing this sage bit of wisdom? Let me explain.

The fictional character that I show up as is to a large degree made up of the truths that I stand for. These truths can also be called values, since I believe that the things I value are *truly* valuable. For instance, I value the Course, and my family, and the Circle, and Mexican food, and hundreds of other things, and I think these values really are true. These truths of mine, arranged in a hierarchy from *most* valued to *least* valued, are the architecture of my personal identity—my *fictional* identity.

If, therefore, I can prove my hierarchy of values to be true, then I simultaneously prove my fictional identity to be true. But to do this, I have to wage war. I have to prove that your hierarchy of values is *not* true. I can do that in a million different ways, from holding up a placard that says, "God hates homosexuals" (followed by biblical citation), to silently but righteously replacing the top of the toothpaste tube that you left off.

Application: Ask yourself the following questions:

> You have obviously constructed your own value system that is different from that of others. Do you feel that if your value system is validated, then *you* are validated? Does your value system seem to make you better than others?
>
> How do you look on someone who holds a different set of values, especially a radically different one?
>
> If you think about someone with whom you have frequent conflict, do you think that a great deal of the conflict comes down to conflicting value systems?
>
> If you notice yourself attacking the value systems of others, could it be that you do this in order to make your value system true, so that your own identity becomes more validated?

> 3. Think how this <u>seems</u> to interfere with the first principle of miracles. For this establishes degrees of <u>truth</u> among illusions, making it seem that some of them are <u>harder</u> to overcome than others. If it were realized that they are all the same and <u>equally</u> untrue, it would be easy, then, to understand that miracles apply to <u>all</u> of them. Errors of <u>any</u> kind can be corrected *because* they are untrue. When brought to truth instead of <u>to each other</u> [to do battle], they merely disappear. No <u>part</u> of nothing <u>can</u> be more resistant to the truth than can another.

Are we willing to admit that, from the highest perspective, all of our values, all of our truths, are just illusion? In the end, does it really matter whether you leave the top of the toothpaste tube on or off, especially considering that there *is* no toothpaste tube? All of our values are so much straw before the eternal reality of our true Self.

Yet once we erect a hierarchy of illusions, we place outside of our reach the first principle of miracles—that there is no order of difficulty in miracles. For if some illusions are more true, more real, then some illusions are also harder to heal. If you've ever looked at the first principle of miracles and wondered why it wasn't active in your experience, this is why—because you have a hierarchy of values.

> 4. The *second* law of chaos, dear indeed to every worshipper of sin, is that each one *must* sin, and therefore <u>deserves</u> attack and death. This principle, closely related to the first, is the demand that errors call for punishment and <u>not</u> correction. For the <u>destruction</u> of the one who makes the error places him <u>beyond</u> correction and beyond forgiveness. What he has done is thus interpreted as an irrevocable sentence upon himself, which God Himself is powerless to overcome [Ur: overlook]. Sin cannot <u>be</u> remitted, being the belief the Son of God can make mistakes for which his own destruction becomes inevitable.

The first principle—that the truth is different for everyone—sends us all into battle to validate "our truth." It sends us on our own personal Crusade. In doing so, it seems to make us all into sinners. My sin is that I waged war on you to make you wrong, so that my identity could be validated over your dead body. *Your* sin was in possessing your stupid value system in the first place, and keeping it even after I pointed out how wrong it was.

Vampires are such great symbols for our behavior. To keep alive, they *have* to feed off others, for which they *deserve* that stake through the heart. To validate our identity, it seems that we *have* to invalidate that of others, we have to sin, for which we *deserve* attack and death. This is the second law of chaos, which, as you can see, follows directly from the first. To give our identity reality and substance, we have to rush into battle. We have no choice. But once we do, we have committed a sin that makes our own destruction inevitable.

Application: Again, ask yourself these questions:

Do you feel compelled to prove other people's value systems wrong? Because of your efforts in this direction, do you feel that you have blood on your hands?

5. Think what this <u>seems</u> to do to the relationship between the Father and the Son. Now it appears that they can <u>never</u> be one again. For one must <u>always</u> be condemned, <u>and by the other</u>. Now are they different, and <u>enemies</u>. And <u>their</u> relationship is one of opposition, just as the separate aspects of the Son meet <u>only</u> to conflict but <u>not</u> to join. One becomes weak, the other strong <u>by his defeat</u>. And fear of God and of each other now appears as sensible, made real by what the Son of God has done both to himself <u>and</u> his Creator.

If I have fed off of others, if I have validated myself by invalidating them, that makes me a sinner. And if I am a sinner, I am now at odds with my Father. For He is holy. An unbridgeable gulf has opened up between us. How can I ever go home to Him, given the things I have done?

Now one last character has joined the MMORPG—the God character. He is hidden from view most of the time, but occasionally He steps out from behind a cloud and rains death down on the other combatants. Now the battle is universal; everyone is involved. The peace of Heaven has degenerated into a deadly free-for-all. You can see why Jesus uses the term "chaos." Yet however extreme this sounds, is this so different from how our world seems to work, in which people are endlessly contending against each other, and God is up in the sky, sending thunderbolts down on the lot?

6. The arrogance on which the laws of chaos stand could not be more apparent than emerges here. Here is a principle that would define what the <u>Creator</u> of reality must be; what He <u>must</u> think and what <u>He</u> must believe; and how He must <u>respond</u>, believing it. It is not seen as even necessary that He be asked about the truth of what has been established for His belief. His Son can <u>tell</u> Him this, and He has but the choice whether to take his word for it or be mistaken. This leads directly to the *third* preposterous belief that seems to make chaos eternal. For if God cannot <u>be</u> mistaken, He must accept His Son's belief in what he is, and <u>hate</u> him for it.

Jesus has a point here. Isn't this all a bit arrogant? God says, "You are my beloved Son, created holy and forever so." Then we say, "I know that's how it looks to You, but I've got blood on my hands down here. I have done terrible things. I have changed myself into a monster." God replies, "But..." And we say, "Let me stop You right there. Look, You need to listen to what I'm telling You: I'm a sinner now. Since You're God and all, and can't be mistaken, You simply have to accept my status as sinner, and hate me for it."

This, of course, is the third law of chaos. It is obvious how it follows from the second, which followed from the first. And when put in the way I did above, it sounds ridiculous. Yet whenever we feel guilty, we are adopting the very stance I describe above.

Application: Think of something you feel terribly guilty about. Then realize that God claims that you have never sinned; you have never changed the holy state He gave you. According to Him, you have no basis for your guilt feelings. How does your guilt respond to that? Watch these two opposite beliefs respond to each other. Which side does most of the talking? Which side seems to win the debate?

7. See how the fear of God is <u>reinforced</u> by this third principle. Now it becomes <u>impossible</u> to turn to Him for help in misery. For now He has become the "enemy" Who caused it, to Whom appeal is useless. Nor can salvation lie within the Son, whose every aspect seems to be at war with Him, and <u>justified</u> in its attack. And now is conflict made inevitable, beyond the help of God. For now salvation <u>must</u> remain impossible, because the savior <u>has</u> become the enemy.

8. There can be <u>no</u> release and <u>no</u> escape. Atonement thus becomes a myth, and vengeance, <u>not</u> forgiveness, is the Will of God. From where all this begins, there <u>is</u> no sight of help that can succeed. <u>Only</u> destruction can <u>be</u> the outcome. And God Himself <u>seems</u> to be siding with it, to overcome His Son. Think not the ego will enable you to find <u>escape</u> from what it wants. <u>That</u> is the function of this course, which does <u>not</u> value what the ego cherishes.

At this point, why wouldn't we fear God? He has joined the game as a competitor, and He obviously has a few more powers than the rest of us. This brings to mind a *Far Side* cartoon, where God is on a TV game show, and of course He has racked up a bazillion points and is utterly trouncing the other contestants. This sounds funny, but it also captures how life can easily appear. God keeps sending us red lights and viruses and mechanical breakdowns and bills and treacherous friends. He is clearly winning this game. Now things seem truly hopeless. If God really cared about us, we could appeal to Him for help. But with Him as one of the combatants, there is literally nowhere to turn.

And that's the point. You see, the programmer that designed this particular MMORPG happens to be the ego, and the whole thing has been carefully designed to make sure that there is nowhere to turn and no way out.

But then one day, our character in the game gets lost and wanders into a room where no one ever goes. And there we find a book, even though this book was not part of the game's original programming. We open the book, and to our surprise, it tells us, plainly and in great detail, how to escape from the game.

> 9. The ego values only what it <u>takes</u>. This leads to the *fourth* law of chaos, which, if the others are accepted, <u>must</u> be true. This seeming law is the belief you <u>have</u> what you have taken. By this, another's loss becomes your gain, and thus it fails to recognize that you can never take away save from <u>yourself</u>. Yet all the other laws must lead to this. For enemies do <u>not</u> give willingly to one another, nor would they seek to <u>share</u> the things they value. And what your <u>enemies</u> would keep from you must <u>be</u> worth having, because [Ur: just *because*] they keep it hidden from your sight.

Without this fourth law of chaos—"you have what you have taken"— the universal melee wouldn't happen. There is obviously no point in battle unless you actually have what you take from the enemy. What he loses, you gain. And you have to *take* it; he is certainly not going to just give it to you.

This is a fundamental law (in our minds) of human relationship, yet one whose deeper dimensions we tend not to see. We realize that we can take another's money and possessions, but we probably don't realize that the most important things we take are intangible. In the Circle's first booklet, *Seeing the Face of Christ in All Our Brothers*, I drew a diagram meant to illustrate attack. The diagram pictures two balloons next to each other, both equally inflated. Then the one on the left punches the one on the right, puncturing it and causing it to deflate. And while it *deflates*, the attacker's balloon *inflates*. Surely, we are more than familiar with this scenario.

That booklet was published when my eldest son was very small, about two and a half years old. I showed him the drawings, hoping to acquaint him with spiritual principles at a young age. He grasped the lesson immediately. From then on, we would play this game where he punched me, causing me to deflate and him to inflate, so that he became all-powerful Power Man. He learned this spiritual teaching so well that we still play the game, years later, only now we call it *conversation*. As I think we all know, a great deal of normal conversation is actually subtle verbal fencing, in which, if you listen carefully, you can almost hear the air whooshing out of those punctured egos.

> 10. All of the mechanisms of madness are seen emerging here: The "enemy" made strong by keeping hidden the valuable inheritance that should be yours; your <u>justified</u> position [Ur: possession] and attack for what has been withheld; and the inevitable loss the enemy <u>must</u> suffer to save <u>yourself</u>. Thus do the guilty ones protest their "innocence." Were they not forced into this foul attack by the unscrupulous behavior of the enemy, they would respond with only kindness. But in a savage world the kind cannot survive, so they <u>must</u> take or else be taken <u>from</u>.

Who can't identify with this paragraph? Haven't you ever been in a situation where someone else seemed to possess the treasure that, if he would only give it to you, would solve everything? But he won't, and while he withholds it, he seems to hold your life in his hands, making him appear quite powerful. At that point, you have no choice but to attack him, and either take the treasure from him, force him to give it to you, or trick him into surrendering it. You hate being so barbaric, but there was really no other option. After all, you were clearly "forced into this foul attack by the unscrupulous behavior of the enemy." If that unnecessary guilt threatens to rise, you console yourself with that final line: "In a savage world the kind cannot survive, so they must take or else be taken from."

> 11. And now there is a vague unanswered question, not yet "explained." What <u>is</u> this precious thing, this priceless pearl, this hidden secret treasure, to be wrested in righteous wrath from this most treacherous and cunning enemy? It must be what you want but never found. And now you "understand" the reason <u>why</u> you found it not. For it was <u>taken</u> from you by this enemy, and hidden where you would not think to look. He hid it in his <u>body</u>, making it the cover for his guilt, the hiding place for what belongs to <u>you</u>. Now must his body be destroyed and

sacrificed, that you may have that which <u>belongs</u> to you. His treachery <u>demands</u> his death, that <u>you</u> may live. And you attack only in self-defense.

Again, you can surely relate to this paragraph. Inside that other person's body is "the hidden secret treasure" that would solve all your problems, that would make all your dreams come true. She holds within herself "what you want but never found." Why doesn't she let it out? Why don't her lips just say, "I love you"? Why won't her body just have sex with you? You don't know. For some reason, she keeps this treasure hidden inside, where you never see it. What you do know is that her withholding justifies whatever you do to her now. You have no choice but to take from her the treasure that is rightfully yours, either by cunning or by force.

But what is this thing you so desperately want? That is revealed in the fifth law of chaos, which we will see shortly.

Application: Again, ask yourself the following questions:

Have you ever felt like someone wasn't giving you the thing you deserved? And that if this person would just give you this thing, your life would be different?

Have you ever loved someone, but been driven crazy by the fact that he had the very thing you want but never found; that it was inside him to give, but he refused to give it to you?

Did this make you feel that you were justified in trying to take this thing from him? Wasn't your punishment of him (in whatever form that took) an attempt to wrest from him the treasure that was rightfully yours?

Before we go on, a brief recap: So far, we have seen a picture in which each of us carries our own truth, our own hierarchy of values (first law), which we are driven to validate by attacking other people's values. In this way, we confirm our personal identity; we prove this fictional identity to be true. To do this, however, we must sin (second law), which forces God to accept our status as sinner, and hate and punish us for it (third law). This section, then, pictures a universal melee, in which all the Sons and even the Father are engaged in endless battle. The battle is propelled by the belief that we genuinely possess what we take from each other (fourth law). But then the question arises: What are we trying to take from each other? This leads to the fifth and final law.

12. But what is it you want that <u>needs</u> his death? Can you be sure your murderous attack <u>is</u> justified unless you know what it is <u>for</u>? And here a *final* principle of chaos comes to the "rescue." It holds there is a <u>substitute</u> for love. This is the magic that will cure all of your pain; the missing factor in your madness <u>that makes it "sane."</u> <u>This</u> is the reason why you must attack. <u>Here</u> is what makes your vengeance justified. Behold, unveiled, the ego's secret gift, torn from your brother's body, hidden there in malice and in hatred for the one to whom the gift belongs [you]. <u>He</u> would deprive you of the secret ingredient that would give meaning to your life. The substitute for love, born of your enmity to your brother, <u>must</u> be salvation. <u>It</u> has no substitute, and there <u>is</u> only one. And <u>all</u> your relationships have but the purpose of seizing it and making it your own.

The final law is that "there is a substitute for love." This is the precious elixir that is hidden in our brother's body, "the secret ingredient that would give meaning to your life." If only his body would release to you this treasure, you would be saved. What is this substitute for love? A substitute, of course, takes the place of something else; looking like that something else while not *being* it. So a substitute for love takes the place of love, looking like love, but not being love.

This, along with everything else Jesus says here, leads me to think that the substitute for love is *special love*. This, of course, is what our brother's body could give to us, but generally does not. And since this "love" is rightfully ours, we seem justified in murdering him to take it from him. This sounds extreme, but it happens. O.J. Simpson comes to mind.

This final principle seems to clearly loop back to the first principle. In both, we are attacking others to get from them the validation of our personal identity. Is getting someone to say, "I should have put the top back on the toothpaste tube" really so different from getting him to say, "I should have loved you"? In both, you are forcing others to validate your illusory identity. In both, your fictional character in this Massively-Multiplayer Online Role-Playing Game has completed its quest. It has proven itself real, over the dead bodies of the others.

This quest to prove our illusory identity to be real, therefore, is the first and final principle. It is what sets this world's boundary-less battle into motion. It is the prize we seek from victory. It is the reason for the chaos. For chaos means that there is no overall order, no integration. And this is because none of the players in the game is truly integrated into the larger whole. Each character is out to validate his own identity. That is the cause of all the chaos we see around us, is it not?

> 13. Never is your possession made complete. And never will your brother cease his attack on <u>you</u> for what you stole. Nor will God end His vengeance upon both, for in His madness <u>He</u> must have this substitute for love, and kill you both. You who believe you walk in sanity with feet on solid ground, and through a world where meaning <u>can</u> be found, consider this: These *are* the laws on which your "sanity" appears to rest. These *are* the principles which make the ground beneath your feet seem solid. And it *is* here you look for meaning. These are the laws <u>you</u> made for your salvation. They hold in place the substitute for Heaven which you prefer. This is their <u>purpose</u>; they were <u>made</u> for this. There is no point in asking what they mean. That is apparent. The <u>means</u> of madness <u>must</u> be insane. Are you as certain that you realize the <u>goal</u> is madness?

The first sentences are a great summary of the result of the laws: total chaos. Everyone is vying to get that precious elixir of substitute love. Even God is involved. As we all know, the traditional God character is bent on wringing devotion and sacrifice from the bodies of His children. Isn't that what all the kneeling and almsgiving is about?

We can perhaps easily look out on the world and see that these "laws" rule it. We can see that, indeed, every character is on a quest to make his illusory identity the most real, the most valid. But can we see that we are on that same quest? That these are the laws by which *we* live? Can we see that we are trying to get our illusory character's identity validated by the other players, even if it means wringing their necks to get them to say the magic words?

Application: Have you ever felt like wringing someone's neck to get him or her to say the magic words? If so, can you accept this as a sign that you live by the laws of chaos?

> 14. <u>No one</u> wants madness, nor does anyone cling to his madness if he sees that this is what it <u>is</u>. What <u>protects</u> madness is the belief <u>that it</u>

is true. It is the <u>function</u> of insanity to <u>take the place</u> of truth. It must be seen <u>as</u> truth to be believed. And if it <u>is</u> the truth, then must its opposite, which was the truth before, be madness now. Such a reversal, <u>completely</u> turned around, with madness sanity, illusions true, attack a kindness, hatred love, and murder benediction, <u>is</u> the goal the laws of chaos serve. These are the means by which the laws of God <u>appear</u> to be reversed. Here do the laws of sin <u>appear</u> to hold love captive, and let sin go free.

If you saw that in order to prove your fictional character real, you were bent on the murder of your brothers, thus doing your small part to cause universal chaos, would you want this? No, this is madness, and madness must be passed off as sanity, as truth, before it can be embraced.

15. These do not <u>seem</u> to be the goals of chaos, for by the great reversal they appear to be the laws of <u>order</u>. How could it <u>not</u> be so? Chaos is lawlessness, and <u>has</u> no laws. To be believed, its <u>seeming</u> laws must be perceived as <u>real</u>. Their goal of madness <u>must</u> be seen as sanity. And fear, with ashen lips and sightless eyes, blinded and terrible to look upon, is lifted to the throne of love, its dying conqueror, its substitute, the savior from salvation. How lovely do the laws of fear make death appear. Give thanks unto the hero on love's throne, who saved the Son of God for fear and death!

These chaotic laws do pass as the laws of order in this world. Our laws, formal and informal, all assume that, yes, the validation of one's personal identity is the most sacred thing in this world, and that, yes, we must strive against each other to achieve this priceless treasure, and that, yes, the crimes we invariably commit in this striving must be harshly punished, because, yes, God Himself stands in hatred of those who commit them.

Somehow, we have turned all of this into the essence of justice. These are the unquestioned assumptions that drive human life. How did the laws of madness become the hallowed canons of order? Because we don't really look at them.

But we need to look. As we lift our validated identity onto the throne, we are really lifting *fear* onto the throne. And it gets worse. Look at the image Jesus uses. What has "ashen lips and sightless eyes"? A corpse, of course. Onto the throne that is supposed to be occupied by pure, sweet, perfect love, we have lifted a corpse, the symbol of fear. Do we realize that in following the laws of chaos, we have enthroned fear as what life is all about?

> 16. And yet, how can it be that laws like these can be believed? There is a strange device that makes it possible. Nor is it unfamiliar; we have seen how it appears to function many times before. In truth it does not function, yet in dreams, where only shadows play the major roles, it seems most powerful. No law of chaos could compel belief but for the emphasis on form and disregard of content. No one who thinks that one of these laws is true sees what it says. Some forms it takes seem to have meaning, and that is all.

How do we make the laws of chaos seem to be the laws of sanity and order? Simple—we dress their madness up in hallowed robes. You can make anything look sane and just if you just put it in the robes of a priest or a judge. How, though, do we accomplish this disguise? What does it mean in practical terms?

> 17. How can some forms of murder not mean death? Can an attack in any form be love? What form of condemnation is a blessing? Who makes his savior powerless and finds salvation? Let not the form of the attack on him deceive you. You cannot seek to harm him and be saved. Who can find safety from attack by turning on himself? How can it matter what the form this madness takes? It is a judgment that defeats itself, condemning what it says it wants to save. Be not deceived when madness takes a form you think is lovely. What is intent on your destruction is not your friend.

How do we dress up the laws of chaos in the robes of truth? By disguising attack as justified, even as love, and therefore not attack. This is the lie that dominates human life. It surrounds this earth like an extra atmosphere. All living things are engaged in disguising attack. You do it. I do it. We all do it. Even great spiritual masters do it. All attack in this world is justified by dressing it up as provoked, righteous, helpful, well intentioned, necessary, loving, concerned, benevolent, etc. This is how we make the laws of madness look like sanity. We know when our enemies are doing it, but we don't know when *we* are doing it.

18. You would maintain, and think it true, that you do <u>not</u> believe these senseless laws, nor act upon them. And when you look at what they <u>say</u>, they <u>cannot</u> be believed. Brother, you *do* believe them. For how else could you <u>perceive</u> the form they take, with content such as this? Can <u>any</u> form of this be tenable? Yet you believe them *for* the form [Ur: forms] they take, and <u>do not recognize</u> the content. <u>It</u> never changes. Can you paint rosy lips upon a skeleton, dress it in loveliness, pet it and pamper it, <u>and make it live</u>? And can you be content with an illusion that <u>you</u> are living?

The whole enterprise depends on staying fixated on the robes, on the form, and forgetting the content that lies beneath them—forgetting it while unconsciously relying on it. We are like a corporation that is making money off of activities that decimate villages in a far-off country. We don't talk about it. We try not to even think about it. But we depend on it.

The skeleton with rosy lips is one of the most arresting images in the Course. But what does the skeleton symbolize? Certainly it symbolizes the laws of chaos. But look more closely. Your illusion that *it* is living is your "illusion that *you* are living." The skeleton is your fictional identity in the MMORPG (Massively Multiplayer Online Role-Playing Game). It is what you think of as your *self.*

Application: Think of your identity in this world as an illusion that can never be real; specifically, as a skeleton that can never be made to live. Now think of yourself putting lipstick on your body, or in some way adorning it. Realize that you are trying to make real a fictional character that can never be real. Realize that you are painting rosy lips on a skeleton.

Now think of your attempts to make yourself look better—either with clothing, exercise, or by behaving intelligently, charmingly, or cleverly. Realize that you are trying to make real a fictional character that can never be real. Realize that you are dressing a skeleton in lovely clothes.

Now think of your attempts to make yourself more special, through achievements and victories, or through the love of a special someone. Realize that you are trying to make real a fictional character that can never be real. Realize that you are petting and pampering a skeleton. Then ask yourself:

Can I make a skeleton live?
*And can I be content with an illusion that **I** am living?*

19. There is no life outside of Heaven. Where God created life, there life must be. In any state apart from Heaven life is illusion. At best it seems like life; at worst, like death. Yet both are judgments on what is not life, equal in their inaccuracy and lack of meaning. Life not in Heaven is impossible, and what is not in Heaven is not anywhere. Outside of Heaven, only the conflict of illusion stands; senseless, impossible and beyond all reason, and yet perceived as an eternal barrier to Heaven. Illusions are but forms. Their content is never true.

Is our earthly identity truly real? Does it have real substance? Is it truly valid? As good Course students, you are thinking "no" as you read these questions. But every day you and I try to answer them with "yes," by getting dressed for battle and wading out into the fray to have our identity acknowledged as real. When we are not reading the Course, we think, "If I have the love of my family, the respect of my peers, and the approval of my community, then my earthly identity is real and valid."

Jesus, however, sees it differently. For him, there is only one measure that is relevant in deciding this question: Is your earthly identity outside of Heaven? If it is, it is not real. It is not valid. It is not even alive. "There is no life outside of Heaven." Outside of Heaven, there is only the Massively-Multiplayer Online Role-Playing Game that we call life. But it isn't life. Remember that old board game, "The Game of Life"? They should have called it "The Game of Death."

20. The laws of chaos govern all illusions. Their [illusions'] forms conflict, making it seem quite possible to value some [illusions] above the others. Yet each one [illusion] rests as surely on the belief the laws of chaos are the laws of order as do the others. Each one upholds these laws completely, offering a certain witness that these laws are true. The seeming gentler forms of the attack are no less certain in their witnessing, or their results. Certain it is illusions will bring fear because of the beliefs that they imply, not for their form. And lack of faith in love, in any form, attests to chaos as reality.

All illusions in this world have as their essence the laws of chaos. This includes our values. Notice the line "Their forms conflict, making it seem quite possible to value some above the others." Doesn't this remind you of the first law, which contained the idea that our *values conflict* with the values of others? Thus, our values, in the end, are made of the laws of chaos. Our values are like beautiful ice sculptures, whose frozen water is really the laws of chaos. Our values are attack wrapped up in noble disguises. Which means our very earthly "identity" is attack decked out in a lovely dress.

And here is the really unfortunate part: It doesn't matter how great the dress is. Even a beautiful, respectable, universally loved form cannot save the underlying content from being *fear* and *chaos*. No matter what the form, that is the content of the character we think we are.

> 21. From the belief in sin, the faith in chaos <u>must</u> follow. It is <u>because</u> it follows that it seems to be a logical conclusion; a valid step in ordered thought. The steps to chaos <u>do</u> follow neatly from their starting point. Each is a different form in the progression of truth's reversal, leading still deeper into terror and <u>away</u> from truth. Think not one step is smaller than another, nor that return from one is easier. The whole descent from Heaven lies in each one. And where your thinking starts, there must it end.

Notice how he says that the chaos follows from the starting point of *sin*. Yet all along we have been told that the starting point of chaos is the impulse to attack others to gain validation for our fictional identity. What is that but sin? As soon as we set foot on sin's ugly path, every other step seems totally logical and necessary, leading us inexorably to the final result of total chaos. What else could result? Imagine a world of vampires, in which there were no humans, just vampires craving *each other's* blood. How much order would such a world have? It would probably have about as much order as *our* world does.

> 22. Brother [Ur: Brothers], take not one step in the descent to hell. For <u>having</u> taken one, you will <u>not recognize</u> the rest for what they are. And they *will* follow. Attack in <u>any</u> form has placed your foot upon the twisted stairway that leads <u>from</u> Heaven. Yet any instant it is possible to have all this undone. How can you know whether you chose the stairs to Heaven or the way to hell? Quite easily. How do you feel? Is peace in your awareness? Are you <u>certain</u> which way you go? And are you sure the goal of Heaven <u>can</u> be reached? If not, you walk alone. Ask, then, your Friend to <u>join</u> with you, and <u>give</u> you certainty of where you go.

As soon as we attack another, for any reason, we are trying to make our warped wooden Pinocchio come to life by feeding it the blood of others. And then we are caught in the inexorable progression of the laws of chaos. We have set our foot, not on the stairway to Heaven, but on the twisted stairway *from* Heaven. Once we have set one foot on this stairway, every other step seems natural, necessary, and completely innocent. It seems like the only option available. And then, after a thousand steps, we find ourselves in a murky world of tortured, hollow, contending souls—something very like to hell—and we have no idea how we got there.

Even now, we don't realize that those "natural," "unavoidable" steps are taken in obedience to the laws of chaos. We don't even see that we are following their logic. We don't even realize that we are taking one step after another down their twisted stairway.

How, then, can we know? "Quite easily." The test is not our assessment of our beliefs. It is not our analysis of our behavior. It is our observation of our feelings. "Is peace in your awareness?" Do you walk right now with the serene confidence that everything is okay, knowing this will all end well—in Heaven? If not, then you are heading down that twisted stairway.

And when you recognize that you are heading down, rather than up, what do you do? "Ask...your Friend to join with you" (22:13). This is clearly the punch line to the whole section. This is the antidote to the laws of chaos. But what does it mean? Who is our "Friend"?

I have always assumed that our Friend is the Holy Spirit. The capital "F" makes that conclusion seem obvious. However, I now realize that this "Friend" is actually our brother. I am confident of this for a few reasons. First, you may not have noticed, but the Holy Spirit is nowhere to be seen in this section. In contrast, however, our brother is a major focus.

Second, this line, as I said, is the antidote to the laws of chaos. And to a significant degree, the laws of chaos are about treating our brother as our enemy. If that's the problem, then the solution is very likely joining with our brother as our friend.

Third, almost all references to "friend" for the last eight chapters have referred to our brother (almost all of which are capitalized in Helen's original notes), and not one has referred to the Holy Spirit. Here, for instance, is how 20.II.10:5-11:1 appeared in Helen's handwritten notes:

Walk with him now rejoicing, for the Saviour from illusion has come to greet you, and lead you home with *him*. Here is your Saviour and your Friend, *released* from crucifixion through *your* vision, and free to lead you now where *he* would be.

Doesn't this sound like the final sentences of our section? In both passages, we are meant to walk with this "Friend" and doing so helps us find our way home.

What, then, is the solution to the laws of chaos? We drop our ancient war upon our "enemy"; we stop trying to wrest from him the "hidden secret treasure" that we think he stole; we hold out our hand and say, "Will you walk home with me?"

III. Salvation without Compromise
Commentary by Robert Perry

1. Is it not true you do <u>not</u> recognize some of the forms attack can take? If it is true attack in <u>any</u> form will hurt you, and will do so just as much as in another form that you *do* recognize, then it <u>must</u> follow that you do not always <u>recognize</u> the source of pain. <u>Attack in any form is equally destructive.</u> Its <u>purpose</u> does not change. Its sole intent is murder, and what <u>form</u> of murder serves to cover the massive guilt and frantic fear of punishment the murderer <u>must</u> feel? He may deny he <u>is</u> a murderer and justify his savagery with smiles as he attacks. Yet he will suffer, and will look on his intent in nightmares where the smiles are gone, and where the purpose rises to meet his horrified awareness and pursue him still. For no one <u>thinks</u> of murder and escapes the guilt the thought entails. If the <u>intent</u> is death, what matter the form it takes?

This powerful paragraph continues the themes from "The Laws of Chaos," specifically the theme of disguised attack. The logic here is hard to deny. Let me break it down into three points.

First, attack is destructive to the attacker. Why? Because all attack carries murderous purpose, and expressing murderous purpose leads to "massive guilt and frantic fear of punishment."

Second, we try to disguise this murderous purpose. We try to make our attacks seem kind, and therefore innocent, by putting on a smiling face while we attack. It is uncomfortable hearing this, but let's face it— we all do it.

Third, these disguises blind us to the content of our attacks on a conscious level, but not on an *unconscious* level. Therefore, the attacks still cause us the exact same amount of pain as if they had been left undisguised, except that now we don't know where the pain is coming from.

These are some of the most sobering ideas you will ever encounter. They should hit you like a ton of bricks. Think about the last time you managed to cloak withering anger and judgment in polite words, said with a smile and a caring look on your face. Now think about this: That communication caused you the exact same amount of pain that it would have caused if you had expressed your feelings without *any* disguise. The only difference is that now, you will never track that pain back to its actual source. You will never know where it really came from.

This is the story of all the pain in your life.

> 2. Is death in <u>any</u> form, however lovely and charitable it may <u>seem</u> to be, a blessing and a sign the Voice for God speaks through you to your brother? The wrapping does not make the gift you give. An empty box, however beautiful and gently given, still contains nothing. And neither the receiver <u>nor the giver</u> is long deceived. <u>Withhold</u> forgiveness from your brother and you <u>attack</u> him. You <u>give</u> him nothing, and receive of him but what you gave.

We think there are many ways to let God's Voice speak through us, forgiveness being one of them. No, forgiveness is the only one. If you are not expressing forgiveness in some way to your brother, then you are giving him death. And is death "a sign the Voice for God speaks through you to your brother"? Your gift may be beautifully wrapped (referring to the smiles and caring looks), causing both of you to admire it. But once he opens it and you both see that the box is empty, neither of you will be deceived any longer. Moreover, what's in the box is what *you* receive.

> 3. Salvation is no compromise of any kind. To compromise is to accept but <u>part</u> of what you want; to take a little and <u>give up</u> the rest. Salvation gives up nothing. It is complete for everyone. Let the <u>idea</u> of compromise but enter, and the awareness of salvation's <u>purpose</u> is lost because it is not recognized. It is <u>denied</u> where compromise has been accepted, for compromise is the belief <u>salvation</u> is impossible. It [compromise] would maintain you can attack a little, love a little, <u>and know the difference</u>. Thus it would teach a little of the same can still be different, and yet the same remain intact, as one. Does this make sense? Can it <u>be</u> understood?

The key word here is "compromise." It is essential that we understand this word in context. Compromise here means to compromise between love and murder. This is what we do when we wrap *murderous* purpose in a *loving* form. We mix the two together, mixing in a little of each. We are attached to this kind of compromise, because we believe we have use for both, for both love *and* murder.

Yet if love contains everything you ever wanted, and yet you compromise between love and murder, then compromise takes on its usual meaning—accepting only *part* of what you want and giving up the rest. Is that a compromise you really want?

Further, if you have spent your life mixing love and murder, cloaking murder in loving forms, do you think you can really tell the difference between them? And if you can't tell love from murder, do you think you really know what love is?

> 4. This course is easy just <u>because</u> it makes no compromise. Yet it <u>seems</u> difficult to those who still believe that compromise is possible. They do <u>not</u> see that, if it is, <u>salvation is attack</u>. Yet it is certain the belief that salvation is impossible can<u>not</u> uphold a quiet, calm assurance it has come. Forgiveness cannot <u>be</u> withheld a little. Nor is it possible to attack for this and love for that and <u>understand</u> forgiveness. Would you not <u>want</u> to recognize assault upon your peace in <u>any</u> form, if only thus does it become impossible that <u>you</u> lose sight of it? It <u>can</u> be kept shining before your vision, forever clear and <u>never</u> out of sight, if <u>you</u> defend it not.

I have the perfect example for this paragraph's teaching. I recently saw a program on a woman named Audrey Kishline. She was a problem drinker who started a nationwide program called Moderation Management. The idea was that problem drinkers (but not alcoholics) didn't need total abstinence from alcohol. They could drink within carefully managed limitations and be fine. Audrey looked at a program of total abstinence like Alcoholics Anonymous and felt that it was too uncompromising, and therefore too difficult.

Years later, she admitted to everyone that she hadn't been following her own program. She had been going way over the limits. She quit the program and tried AA, but couldn't manage that either. She then left her family, so she could continue drinking. She drove away from the house on a drunken bender in a huge pickup, and ended up killing two people on the freeway. While serving jail time for this, she descended into profound guilt.

She is a great example of what this fourth paragraph is saying. She thought that uncompromising abstinence was too hard, but only because she was so attached to compromise. Yet wanting to play both sides caused her life to fall apart. It eventually convinced her that she was beyond redemption, that salvation was impossible for her. She finally realized that the easier road—indeed, the *only* road—for her was total lack of compromise.

Are we prepared to place ourselves in her shoes—not with alcohol, but with *attack*? Do we want to recognize all of our attempts at murder? We may feel an immediate "no," but this is the only way we can recognize what is assaulting our own peace. And once we recognize that, we will be able to keep our peace in clear sight at all times, and nothing, literally nothing, will be able to assault it.

> 5. Those who believe that peace can <u>be</u> defended, and that attack is <u>justified</u> on its behalf, can<u>not</u> perceive it lies within them. How <u>could</u> they know? Could they <u>accept</u> forgiveness side by side with the belief that murder takes some forms by which their peace is <u>saved</u>? Would they be <u>willing</u> to accept the fact their savage purpose is directed against themselves?

Of course, the reason we attack is to defend our peace. Our peace is threatened, and that makes murder justified (as we all know, if we have ever listened to any government). Yet if you attack to defend your peace, then you cannot know that your peace is in you, part of you, unassailable. Attack is therefore attack on *your own peace*. Can you consider the idea that on some level this is intentional—that you are actually *trying* to attack your own peace?

> No one unites with enemies, nor is at one with them in purpose. And no one <u>compromises</u> with an enemy but hates him still, for what he <u>kept</u> from him.
> 6. Mistake not truce for peace, nor compromise for the <u>escape</u> from conflict. To be <u>released</u> from conflict means that <u>it is over</u>. The door is open; you have <u>left</u> the battleground. You have <u>not</u> lingered there in cowering hope that it will not return because the guns are stilled an instant, and the fear that haunts the place of death is not apparent. There *is* no safety in a battleground. You can look down on it in safety from above and <u>not</u> be touched. But from within it you can find <u>no</u> safety. Not one tree left still standing will shelter you. Not one illusion of protection stands against the faith in murder. Here stands the body, torn between the natural desire to communicate [love] and the unnatural

intent to murder and to die. Think you the <u>form</u> that murder takes can offer safety? Can guilt be <u>absent</u> from a battlefield?

When we get too alarmed by our own attack, we turn to compromise. As we saw before, we compromise between murder and love, mixing the two together into the same behaviors. This is the same thing as compromising in the usual sense, between *our* needs and our *enemy's* needs. For our needs seem to summon us to murder, while acknowledging our enemy's needs compels us to mix in a little love. Hence, we throw in some of both, in proper proportions. This cajoles our enemy into doing the same, and we thereby restore the peace.

But have we? Isn't this really just a *truce*? A truce is where the motive for war remains, but is temporarily held back. Can we really call that peace? After all, the engine of war is still there, turning within us, right below the surface. We haven't, then, really left the battleground. We are still standing there, torn between the better angels of our nature and the devils within. The impulse to murder still boils in our blood, but outwardly we are forcing ourselves to be "loving." We are maintaining enough civility to preserve the fragile truce that keeps the guns quiet. Just for good measure, though, we are standing under the one scraggly, leafless tree that hasn't been blown to bits by the shelling, hoping that it will afford some protection should the truce collapse again, as it has so many times before.

Do you see yourself in this description? *This is our lives.* We are living on that battleground, under that one flimsy tree, hoping that the truce won't break down again. There is only one way out of this. We need to stop compromising. This doesn't mean going all the way over to murder (which is how our ego interprets this). It means going all the way over to *love*. Are we willing to admit that, when it comes to attack, moderation management will not work for us? Are we willing to commit to total abstinence? Are we willing to walk off the battleground once and for all?

IV. Above the Battleground
Commentary by Robert Perry

This section ends the battle discussion that was begun in Section I, "The Irreconcilable Beliefs." After pages of telling us about the battle, Jesus tells us how to get out.

> 1. Do not remain in conflict, for there *is* no war without attack. The fear of God is fear of life, and <u>not</u> of death. Yet He remains the only place of safety. In Him is no attack, and no illusion in any form stalks Heaven. Heaven is <u>wholly</u> true. No difference enters, and what is <u>all</u> the same cannot conflict. You are <u>not</u> asked to fight <u>against</u> your wish to murder. But you <u>are</u> asked to realize the <u>form</u> it takes conceals the <u>same</u> intent. And it is <u>this</u> you fear, and <u>not</u> the form. What is <u>not</u> love <u>is</u> murder. What is not loving <u>must</u> be an attack.

In our guilt (see the last line of the previous section), we fear that God is going to rain death on us, and so we fear Him. But in fearing Him and staying away from Heaven we are really fearing unlimited life. We fear the limitless safety of being off the battleground, in a place where there are no clashing forms. What a very odd fear!

"You are not asked to fight against your wish to murder." Thank goodness! All we are asked to do is realize that putting an innocent face on our attack doesn't rescue it from *being* an attack. The purpose is still murder. "What is *not* love *is* murder." We think there is this wide spectrum that goes from love to sort-of love, to neutral, to attacking, to murderous. Instead, there is no spectrum. There is only pure love and pure murder, combined together in uneasy mixtures. And that second purpose of ours scares the hell out of us. If we don't allow ourselves to hide it again, we will find it intolerable and get rid of it.

> <u>Every</u> illusion is an assault on truth, and every one [illusion] does violence to the <u>idea</u> of love because it [the illusion] <u>seems</u> to be of equal truth [to love].
> 2. What can be <u>equal</u> to the truth, yet different? Murder and love are incompatible. Yet if they <u>both</u> are true, then must they be the <u>same</u>, and

93

indistinguishable from one another. So <u>will</u> they be to those who see God's Son a body. For it is <u>not</u> the body that is like the Son's Creator. And what is lifeless cannot <u>be</u> the Son of Life. How can a body be extended to hold the universe? Can <u>it</u> create, and <u>be</u> what it creates? And can it offer its creations <u>all</u> that it is and <u>never</u> suffer loss?

If we think that both love and murder are true, then they become indistinguishable in our mind. The norm becomes murder-that-looks-loving. If we see our brother as a body, then this will be our normal way of operating. Jesus doesn't explain why this is, but he does explain very clearly why the body is not the Son of God. The Son of God can extend himself to hold the universe, can create something while still *being* what he creates, can give his creations all of himself without suffering any loss. Can a body do any of these things?

> 3. God does not share His function with a body. He <u>gave</u> the function to create unto His Son <u>because</u> it is His Own. It is <u>not</u> sinful to believe the function of the Son is murder, but it *is* insanity. What is the same can <u>have</u> no different function. Creation is the means for God's extension, and what is His <u>must</u> be His Son's as well. Either the Father <u>and</u> the Son are murderers, or neither is. Life makes not death, creating like itself.

While in the ego mode, we believe that our function is murder, that that is the most authentic expression of who we are. Yet God has ordained that our function is creation, to give life, rather than take it. He gave us that function because that is His Own function. Our function is of necessity the same as God's. If our function is murder, then God's must be that, too. Does that really make sense?

> 4. The lovely light of your relationship <u>is</u> like the Love of God. It cannot yet assume the holy function God gave His Son, for your forgiveness of your brother is not complete as yet, and so it cannot be extended to <u>all</u> creation. Each form of murder and attack that still attracts you and that you do not recognize for what it is, limits the healing and the miracles you <u>have</u> the power to extend to all. Yet does the Holy Spirit understand how to increase your little gifts and make them mighty. Also He understands how your relationship is raised <u>above</u> the battleground, <u>in</u> it no more. This is your part; to realize that murder in <u>any</u> form is <u>not</u> your will. The <u>overlooking</u> of the battleground is now your purpose.

94

Here we have one of the last references in the Text to the holy relationship. It says that the holy relationship is so like to God's Love that it will one day share His function of creating in Heaven. That is quite a statement. But the relationship cannot assume that function until its love is perfect, which will happen when its *forgiveness* is perfect. So that is its job now—to weed out all forms of murder and attack, to recognize them all for what they are, no matter how polite and loving they appear to be, and to realize that this is not what the two holy relationship partners really want. When they joined, the relationship itself was lifted above the battleground. Now they need to follow it there. They need to identify with the place above the battleground, rather than with the battle.

> 5. Be lifted up, and from a higher place look down upon it. From there will your perspective be quite different. Here in the midst of it, it <u>does</u> seem real. Here you have <u>chosen</u> to be part of it. Here murder <u>is</u> your choice. Yet from above, the choice is miracles <u>instead</u> of murder. And the perspective <u>coming from</u> this choice shows you the battle is <u>not</u> real, and easily escaped. Bodies may battle, but the clash of forms is meaningless. And it <u>is</u> over when you realize it never was begun. How can a battle be perceived as nothingness when you <u>engage</u> in it? How can the truth of miracles be <u>recognized</u> if murder is your choice?

This image of being lifted up and looking down on the battleground from a higher place is incredibly useful. Being above a battleground implies that you are "above it," in the sense of being incapable of the pettiness of war. It implies that the battle is small and insignificant, since that is how human dramas look from a great height. And it implies that you are safe from what is going on down there. So use this image. See yourself being above the battleground. From there you can see that the battle is just fictional forms clashing meaninglessly.

This is another way of saying: Back away from the computer screen and recognize that you are actually outside the MMORPG.

> 6. When the temptation to attack rises to make your mind darkened and murderous, remember you *can* see the battle from above. Even in forms you do <u>not</u> recognize, the signs you know. There is a stab of pain, a twinge of guilt, and above all, a <u>loss of peace</u>. This you know well. When they occur leave not your place on high, but quickly choose a miracle <u>instead</u> of murder. And God Himself and all the lights of

Heaven will gently lean to you, and hold you up. For you have chosen to remain where He would have you, and no illusion can attack the peace of God together with His Son.

Notice that Jesus says, "leave not your place on high." He wants us to *live* above the battleground. He wants us to see ourselves as constantly "above it all." Yet in this place on high, we need to be always on the lookout for the temptation to swoop down and do battle again. How do we know when this temptation comes over us? After all, this and the previous two sections have all stressed that we don't recognize our attacks because we have so successfully disguised them.

We know by watching our feelings. "There is a stab of pain, a twinge of guilt, and above all, a *loss of peace.*" While our exteriors lie, and while our assessment of our behavior lies as well, our feelings will not. They will tell us, "Hold on. Something is wrong here."

When they do that, we need to quickly say, "I choose a miracle instead of murder." And even as we start to lose altitude and sink toward the field of battle, "God Himself and all the lights of Heaven will gently lean to you, and hold you up." What a beautiful image.

> 7. See no one from the battleground, for there you look on him from nowhere. You have no reference point from where to look, where meaning can be given what you see. For only bodies could attack and murder, and if this is your purpose, then you must be one with them. Only a purpose unifies, and those who share a purpose have a mind as one. The body has no purpose of itself, and must be solitary. From below, it cannot be surmounted. From above, the limits it exerts on those in battle still are gone, and not perceived. The body stands between the Father and the Heaven He created for His Son *because* it has no purpose.

If you see someone from the battleground, what are you seeing? The battleground is all about form—forms taking forms from other forms. There is no meaning, only form. If you see your brother from this perspective, then he becomes a meaningless form, one that is withholding from you the forms you need. From this standpoint, the only option that exists is for you to take what he withholds.

That is why it is so crucial to see yourself above the battleground. There, you can join your brother in a genuinely common purpose. There, the body need not run the show. It may summon us to murder, but we can say, "No thanks. I'd rather join instead."

> 8. Think what is given those who share their Father's purpose, and who <u>know</u> that it is theirs. They want for nothing. Sorrow of any kind is inconceivable. Only the light they love is in awareness, and only love shines upon them forever. It is their past, their present and their future; always the same, eternally complete and wholly shared. They <u>know</u> it is impossible their happiness could <u>ever</u> suffer change of any kind. Perhaps you think the battleground <u>can</u> offer something you can win. <u>Can</u> it be anything that offers you a perfect calmness, and a sense of love so deep and quiet that no touch of doubt can <u>ever</u> mar your certainty? And that will last forever?

What a beautiful paragraph. The first sentences describe the condition of those who live above the battleground. They simply bask in the light of their Father's Love. It is their past, present, and future. They know its warm rays will never be obscured by a cloudy day. The sense of love they have is so deep and certain that they know it can never be shaken.

But we decide that we would rather chase after the prizes we win in battle. That *is* why we're on the battlefield, isn't it? There's something we are trying to win. It's as simple as that. But, whatever it is, could it *possibly* equal that deep, endless love that is enjoyed above the battleground?

> 9. Those with the strength of God in their awareness could never <u>think</u> of battle. What <u>could</u> they gain but <u>loss</u> of their perfection? For everything fought for on the battleground is of the body; something it seems to offer or to own. No one who knows that he has everything could seek for limitation, nor <u>could</u> he value the body's offerings. The senselessness of conquest is quite apparent from the quiet sphere above the battleground. What can conflict with everything? And what is there that offers <u>less</u>, yet could be wanted <u>more</u>? Who with the Love of God upholding him could find the choice of miracles or murder hard to make?

Imagine floating on a cloud above the battleground, basking in your Father's Love. You are perfect. You have everything. You don't even have a solid outline. Being one with everything, you can conflict with nothing. Having all of your Father's strength, you cannot imagine being threatened by anything.

Then, a helicopter comes up to your level and hovers. A recruiter from the military lifts a megaphone to his mouth and says, "Boy do we have a great opportunity for you! We would like you to come down from your cloud and murder for us. You can be a little pile of meat and join thousands of other piles of meat that will do battle with still other piles of meat, all to gain the priceless treasure of meaningless forms. You will feel weak and vulnerable. You will lose your feeling of being perfect. There will be blood on your hands that will never wash off. You will believe that your Father can never love you again. Great benefits package. Join today!"

This recruiter makes his pitch to us every day. Why, oh why, do we answer yes?

Application: Think of a situation in your life in which you feel as if you are on a battlefield.

Watch your behavior in this situation. See how you've justified it to yourself. You had good reasons for everything you did, no matter what it was. You really had no choice.

See how appropriate you are on the outside, how measured your words are, how you've tried to be considerate of others, how you've refrained from striking back so many times, how you've held your tongue, how you've tried so hard to be good.

Realize that these are the "loving" forms with which you have covered over your attack. The attack was there, in your mind, in your unloving perceptions of others, and in your desire to see them suffer for what they've done. It was there all along behind your smiling facade.

Hear these words from the Course:

"You are not asked to fight against your wish to murder.
[You don't need to wrestle with your inner demon, to forcibly keep it at bay, safely repressed inside of you.]
But you are asked to realize the form it takes conceals the same intent [murder].
[Be willing to consider that your intent in this situation has been murder.]

98

And it is this [intent of murder] you fear, and not the form.
What is not love is murder.
What is not loving must be an attack."

Realize that the smiling, patient masks you've placed over your attack
    have fooled even you,
so that you yourself can't see your attack for what it is.
But now you want to see attack for what it is.
And there is a way to tell.

See yourself operate in the situation.
See yourself, for instance, talking to someone in the situation, trying
    to be as nice and as restrained as you can.
Or see some bit of difficult news reach your ears.
Or see yourself make some cold decision that you'll later regret.
While seeing these things, watch for the following signs in your mind:
"a stab of pain, a twinge of guilt, and above all, a loss of peace. This
    you know well."
These signs are your cue, your cue to rise above the battleground.

"Be lifted up, and from a higher place look down upon it."
Imagine yourself rising up--physically, but also mentally and
    emotionally.
"From there will your perspective be quite different."
From this higher perspective, you see the battle as inconsequential,
as trivial, as a meaningless clash of forms.
Its forms are small, its sounds remote.
"The senselessness of conquest is quite apparent from the quiet sphere
    above the battleground."
In this quiet sphere you realize that this battle cannot touch you.
You are above it, in every way.
In this quiet sphere you realize that the battle is not real, and easily
    escaped.
And in this place you say to yourself: "I choose a miracle instead of
    murder."
"I choose a miracle instead of murder."

This quiet sphere is more than just an absence of battle, it is a place of peace.

Repeat these words to yourself:

"In this place I want for nothing.
Sorrow of any kind is inconceivable.
Only the light I love is in awareness,
and only love shines upon me forever.
It is my past, my present, and my future;
always the same, eternally complete, and wholly shared.
I know it is impossible my happiness could ever suffer change of any kind."

Hear these words:

"Perhaps you think the battleground can offer you something you can win.

[What have you been trying to win from this battleground?]

Can it be anything that offers you a perfect calmness, and a sense of love so deep and quiet that no touch of doubt can ever mar your certainty?

And that will last forever?"

And so repeat, *"I choose to remain above the battleground.*
And God Himself and all the lights of Heaven will gently lean to me, and hold me up.
I choose a miracle instead of murder."

Commentaries on Chapter 24

THE GOAL OF
SPECIALNESS

Introduction
Commentary by Robert Perry

This important chapter is about our need to be special, something that the world celebrates, yet which Jesus says is the source of all the trouble. This chapter's importance is reflected in the fact that when Helen Schucman originally finished dictating it, she felt Jesus' gratitude for her taking it down. Note that this is not about special relationships, but specialness itself, the private, internal prize we hope to gain from those relationships.

> 1. Forget not that the motivation for this course is the attainment and the <u>keeping</u> of the state of peace. Given this state the mind is quiet, and the condition in which God is remembered is attained. It is not necessary to tell Him what to do. He will not fail. Where He can enter, there He is already. And can it be He can<u>not</u> enter where He wills to be? Peace will be yours *because* it is His Will. Can you believe a shadow can hold back the Will that holds the universe secure? God does not wait upon illusions to let Him be Himself. No more His Son. They *are*. And what illusion that idly seems to drift between Them has the power to defeat what <u>is</u> Their Will?

Jesus has already told us (see T-8.I.1:1-2) that the goal of the Course is peace, for peace is the gateway to heavenly knowledge. After the last chapter, though, this takes on a deeper meaning. Now peace is not just inner peace, it is *interpersonal* peace. It is the absence of battle. Jesus is telling us that all we need do is stop the guns, and God will enter. And we *will* stop the guns, because He wills to enter. After all, the general that ordered the guns to fire is only an illusion, a shadow. And how can a shadow "hold back the Will that holds the universe secure?"

> 2. To learn this course requires willingness to question <u>every</u> value that you hold. Not one can be kept hidden and obscure but it will jeopardize your learning. <u>No</u> belief is neutral. Every one has the power to dictate each decision you make. For a decision is a <u>conclusion</u> based on <u>everything</u> that you believe. It is the <u>outcome</u> of belief, and follows it

[belief] as surely as does suffering follow guilt and freedom sinlessness. There is no substitute for peace. What God creates has no alternative. The truth arises from what He knows. And your decisions come from your beliefs as certainly as all creation rose in His Mind *because* of what He knows.

To find the peace that the Course is leading us to, we need to question every value that we hold. With each one, we have to say, "I value this, but is this *really* valuable?" The reason for this is that we have values that don't lead to peace, that lead to *war*.

Before we can question these values, however, we have to find them. Many of them are hidden, obscure, unrecognized. Yet concealing them doesn't neutralize them. They still cause sweeping effects. For these values are also beliefs, and we make decisions *based* on our beliefs. When we decide anything, we first take a survey of all that we believe. Thus, until we identify our hidden beliefs in war, they will continue to inspire the decision to rush into battle. And the door to knowledge will remain closed.

I. Specialness as a Substitute for Love
Commentary by Robert Perry

1. Love <u>is</u> extension. To withhold the smallest gift is not to know love's purpose. Love offers everything forever. Hold back but <u>one</u> belief, <u>one</u> offering, and love is gone, because you asked a substitute to take its place. And now must war, the <u>substitute</u> for peace, come with the one alternative that you <u>can</u> choose for love. Your <u>choosing</u> it has given it <u>all</u> the reality it seems to have.

"Love is extension." Love gives. Therefore, to withhold even a little bit of love means you don't understand love. This also applies to those hidden beliefs. If you withhold just one such belief, keeping it apart from love, then love is gone. And now that it is gone, it is replaced by its opposite: murder. And peace is replaced by its opposite: war.

2. Beliefs will never <u>openly</u> attack each other because conflicting outcomes <u>are</u> impossible. But an <u>unrecognized</u> belief is a decision to war in secret, where the results of conflict are kept unknown and <u>never</u> brought to reason, to be considered sensible or not. And many senseless outcomes <u>have</u> been reached, and meaningless decisions have been made and kept hidden, to become beliefs now <u>given</u> power to direct all subsequent decisions. Mistake you not the power of these hidden warriors to disrupt your peace. For it <u>is</u> at their mercy while you decide to leave it there. The secret enemies of peace, your least decision to choose attack instead of love, unrecognized and swift to challenge <u>you</u> to combat and to violence far more inclusive than you think, are there by your election. Do not deny their presence nor their terrible results. All that can <u>be</u> denied is their <u>reality</u>, but <u>not</u> their outcome.

This is an important paragraph. We have a chain of three things: *beliefs*, which lead to *decisions*, which lead to *outcomes*. Problems arise in this chain when we have conflicting beliefs. When this happens, one side of the conflict will always submerge itself. This is what happens with our beliefs in war (the same as our *valuing* of war). These conflict with our beliefs in peace, and so they dive down beneath the surface.

There, beneath the surface, they inspire decisions to go to war, which naturally result in loss of peace.

If we really looked at this chain of cause and effect, we would let it go, but unfortunately, we keep the whole chain hidden. We deny the beliefs. Then we deny the decisions that come out of the beliefs. Then we deny the results of those decisions. It's a whole criminal underground. The godfather is hidden away, his hit men work in secret, and the bodies are buried and never found.

Meanwhile, the whole thing grows. Small decisions to go to war "challenge you to combat and to violence far more inclusive than you think." Then these decisions become enthroned as new beliefs, with power to direct future decisions. The final outcome is that we have completely lost our peace, and we have no idea why.

> 3. All that is ever cherished as a hidden belief, to be defended though unrecognized, is <u>faith in specialness</u>. This takes many forms, but <u>always</u> clashes with the reality of God's creation and with the grandeur that He gave His Son. What else <u>could</u> justify attack? For who could hate someone whose Self is his, and Whom he <u>knows</u>? Only the special <u>could</u> have enemies, for they are different and <u>not</u> the same.

Here we have the main theme of this key chapter: specialness. Being special means that you are *set apart* (specific) and *set above* (superior). It's that last one—set above—that we are all seeking. Spiritual people will tell you "I feel special in a negative way—I feel especially unworthy." I never feel these statements are fully sincere. Rather, I think they are testament to what Jesus is saying here: the warriors are *hidden*. In fact, such statements are the warriors in action. For hidden within them is another statement: "I'm better than all those people who think they are so superior."

Specialness is the common essence of all those hidden beliefs that call us to war. It is the reason behind all our attacks. It is the root cause of seeing anyone as an enemy. If we knew our brother was not different, not separate, but shared the same Self, how could we attack him? But specialness sees our brothers as strangers, separate and different, and therefore dangerous.

> And difference of <u>any</u> kind imposes orders of reality, and a need to judge that cannot <u>be</u> escaped.

4. What God created <u>cannot</u> be attacked, for there is nothing in the universe unlike itself. But what is different <u>calls</u> for judgment, and this <u>must</u> come from someone "better," someone incapable of being like what he condemns, "above" it, sinless <u>by comparison</u> with it. And thus does specialness become a means and end at once. For specialness not only sets apart, but serves as grounds from which attack on those who seem "beneath" the special one is "natural" and "just." The special ones feel weak and frail <u>because</u> of differences, for what would make them special *is* their enemy. Yet they <u>protect</u> its enmity and call it "friend." On its behalf they fight against the universe, for nothing in the world they value more.

As soon as your brother is different from you, you have to figure out what he is. You have to evaluate him, judge him. And since you are now in the position of being his judge, you must be better than him. As we all know, a judge has to be above what he judges.

Specialness, then, serves as both means and end. How so? The fact that you are special makes it only natural and just that, from your great height, you judge and attack your brother (specialness as means). And, of course, you judge and attack your brother *in order* to feel more special (specialness as end). It is a very, very vicious cycle.

There is nothing in the world we value more than our specialness. We think that it is self-esteem, that it means we have value. Therefore, it is the core of our value system. We fight against the universe in order to obtain it. And yet, specialness is *not* self-esteem. Being based on differences, it makes us feel weak and frail, and thus eclipses our grandeur.

5. Specialness is the great dictator of the wrong decisions. Here is the grand illusion of what you are and what your brother is. And here is what <u>must</u> make the body dear and <u>worth</u> preserving. <u>Specialness must be defended.</u> Illusions <u>can</u> attack it, and they <u>do</u>. For what your brother <u>must</u> become to <u>keep</u> your specialness *is* an illusion. He who is "worse" than you <u>must</u> be attacked, so that your specialness can live on his defeat. For specialness is triumph, and its victory <u>is</u> his defeat and shame. How can he live, with all your sins upon him? And who <u>must</u> be his conqueror but you?

Specialness is victory. It means that my illusion of me (centered on my body) has gone to battle with your illusion of you, and has emerged on top—set above. This contest can be about all sorts of things, including innocence. By projecting my sins onto you and making you seem like the sinner, I can claim the title of being the most innocent. Yet once I have gained this specialness, I have to defend it—constantly. It's an exceedingly fragile thing, because it's an illusion.

Application: Think of someone you feel more special than. Say to yourself,

> *I have to attack him to establish him as worse than me,*
> *so that my specialness can live on his defeat.*

6. Would it be <u>possible</u> for you to hate your brother if you were like him? <u>Could</u> you attack him if you realized you journey <u>with</u> him, to a goal that is the <u>same</u>? Would you not help him reach it in every way you could, if his attainment of it were perceived as <u>yours</u>? You <u>are</u> his enemy in specialness; his friend in a <u>shared</u> purpose. Specialness can <u>never</u> share, for it depends on goals that you <u>alone</u> can reach. And he must <u>never</u> reach them, or <u>your</u> goal is jeopardized. Can love <u>have</u> meaning where the goal is triumph? And what decision <u>can</u> be made for this that will <u>not</u> hurt you?

Specialness is a goal which, by definition, has to be reached alone. It is a mountain whose summit you have to reach by yourself. Even if you and your brother are walking side by side up this mountain, you need to be secretly plotting some accident that will keep him from getting there. Now imagine going up that same mountain and thinking not "If he gets there, I don't get there," but "*Unless* he gets there, I don't get there."

Application: Think again of someone you feel more special than, and ask yourself these questions:

> *Could I hate him if I realized that I am like him?*
> *Could I attack him if I realized I journey with him, to a goal that*
> *is the same?*
> *Would I not help him reach it in every way I could, if his attainment*
> *of it were perceived as mine?*

7. Your brother is your friend <u>because</u> his Father created him like you. There <u>is</u> no difference. You have been <u>given</u> to your brother that love might be extended, <u>not</u> cut off from him. What you <u>keep</u> is lost to you. God gave you and your brother Himself, and to remember this is now the <u>only</u> purpose that you share. And so it is the only one you <u>have</u>. Could you attack your brother if you chose to see <u>no</u> specialness of any kind between you and him? Look fairly at whatever makes you give your brother only partial welcome, or would let you think that you are better off apart. Is it not <u>always</u> your belief your specialness is <u>limited</u> by your relationship? And is not <u>this</u> the "enemy" that makes you and your brother illusions to each other?

The real situation is this. God created us like each other, with no differences of any kind. This made us friends for eternity. Further, He gave Himself to both of us. This means that our only purpose now is to remember that eternal Fact together. That is the mountain we need to climb, side by side.

But then specialness comes in like a destructive addiction and says, "I am your only friend. Put me above all others. That guy over there, the one you thought was your brother—he's your enemy." Before our eyes, our eternal friend turns into our enemy. Now he stands next to us at the starting line, about to race against us for the grand prize of specialness, in a race where anything goes.

However, Jesus has twice now said the real truth. It is so radical that perhaps you didn't catch it. Here it is: *Specialness is our enemy.*

Application: Think about two ways in which you consider yourself better than others. With each one, say this to yourself,

> *This thought is my enemy.*
> *It shuts out my grandeur and makes me feel weak and frail.*
> *On its behalf I fight against the universe, for nothing in the world*
>   *do I value more.*
> *It turns my dear, eternal friends into my competitors, my enemies.*
> *Yet it is my **real** enemy.*

8. The fear of God and of your brother [Ur: each other] comes from each unrecognized belief in specialness. For you demand your brother

109

[Ur: For each demands the other] bow to it <u>against his will</u>. And God Himself must honor it or suffer vengeance. Every twinge of malice, or stab of hate or wish to separate arises here. For here the purpose that you and your brother [in this case, your holy relationship partner] share becomes obscured from <u>both</u> of you. You would oppose this course because it teaches you you and your brother are alike [Ur: *you are alike*]. You have <u>no</u> purpose that is not the same, and none your Father does not share with you. For your relationship has been made clean of special goals. And would you now <u>defeat</u> the goal of holiness that Heaven gave it? What perspective can the special have that does <u>not</u> change with every seeming blow, each slight, or fancied judgment on itself?

Specialness requires that we bend everyone's resistant will, even God's Will, into acknowledging how rare and amazing we are. And we fear that all this will-bending and arm-twisting will one day catch up with us. Specialness, therefore, leads to fear of God and of our brothers.

Notice that line: "Every twinge of malice, or stab of hate or wish to separate arises here." This clearly sounds like a line from the previous section: "There is a stab of pain, a twinge of guilt, and above all, a loss of peace" (T-23.IV.6:3). Specialness, in other words, is what gives rise to the stabs of *hate* that make us feel the stabs of *pain*. It is what gives rise to the twinges of *malice* that cause our twinges of *guilt*.

Specialness is also what blocks the goal of the holy relationship. While we are outwardly saying, "How beautiful it is to be walking to God together," inwardly we are thinking, "What am I doing with this bozo? He is so obviously beneath me." In the previous paragraph, Jesus asked us to look fairly on why we give our brother only partial welcome, or think we are better off apart. Isn't it because we think this person somehow hurts our chances for being special?

9. Those who are special <u>must</u> defend illusions against the truth. For what <u>is</u> specialness but an attack upon the Will of God? You love your brother not while it is this you would defend <u>against</u> him. This is what <u>he</u> attacks, and <u>you</u> protect. Here is the ground of battle which you wage against him. Here <u>must</u> he be your enemy and <u>not</u> your friend. Never can there be peace among the different. He is your friend *because* you are the same.

I. Specialness as a Substitute for Love

This paragraph confirms what various clues have already made us suspect, that this discussion is a continuation of the battle discussion from the previous chapter. There, the language I used was that what started the battle was our need to have our illusory identity validated. Yet what is that but our need to have our specialness confirmed? The craving to be special, then, is the single impulse that starts all the madness. This is the dark underbelly of life on earth, the thing we all covet and seek and celebrate, yet the thing that sets in motion all the wars, all the chaos.

This is everyone's dirty little secret. This is the thing that drives us, yet which we dare not voice, even to ourselves. Do not underestimate your own investment in specialness, nor in keeping that investment hidden. Jesus has taken twenty-four chapters to get to this place for a reason. This is the ugly core of the ego's ugly system.

I am watching a documentary on the genocide in Rwanda. They interviewed a man who, with his own hands, hacked his neighbors apart with a machete, because they were Tutsis and he was a Hutu. He said, "It was as if we were taken over by Satan. When Satan is using you, you lose your mind. We were not ourselves. You couldn't be normal when you started butchering people for no reason. We'd been attacked by the devil." This section tells us what the devil is, and reveals that he lives within each one of us, and that he isn't sleeping.

II. The Treachery of Specialness
Commentary by Robert Perry

1. Comparison <u>must</u> be an ego device, for love makes none. Specialness <u>always</u> makes comparisons. It is <u>established</u> by a lack seen in another, and maintained by searching for, and keeping clear in sight, all lacks it can perceive. This does it seek, and this it looks upon. And <u>always</u> whom it thus diminishes would be your savior, had you not chosen to make of him a tiny measure of your specialness instead. Against the littleness you see in him you stand as tall and stately, clean and honest, pure and unsullied, by comparison with what you see. Nor do you understand it is <u>yourself</u> that you diminish thus.

Jesus has captured so well what we do—too well. We look at another person, and search for his lacks, his faults, his shortcomings. Once we find them, we keep them clearly in sight. The result is that this person looks *maximally small*. Then, he becomes the yardstick for our stature. We measure ourselves against his smallness and think, "Well, maybe I'm only five two, but look at him. He's two and a half feet tall!" Compared to him, we "stand as tall and stately, clean and honest, pure and unsullied, by comparison." This process should be very, very familiar to all of us.

Perhaps we don't plan to stop this anytime soon, but this should give us pause: By belittling the one whose holiness and grandeur could save us, it is *ourselves* that we diminish.

2. Pursuit of specialness is always at the cost of peace. Who can attack his savior and cut him down, yet recognize his strong support? Who can detract from his omnipotence, yet <u>share</u> his power? And who can use him as the gauge of littleness, and be <u>released</u> from limits? You have a function in salvation. <u>Its</u> pursuit will bring you joy. But the pursuit of specialness <u>must</u> bring you pain. Here is a goal that would <u>defeat</u> salvation, and thus run <u>counter</u> to the Will of God. To value specialness is to esteem an alien will to which illusions of yourself <u>are</u> dearer than the truth.

Specialness brings us pain? It defeats salvation? It runs counter to God's Will? These thoughts turn our world upside down. Doesn't Jesus

112

know that the happy ones in this world are the winners? Hasn't he ever heard of the elect—the special ones who are predestined by God to be saved while everyone else goes to hell? Hasn't he ever heard of God's Chosen People?

No matter how different Jesus' ideas are, though, his logic remains airtight. If our stature is gauged against our brother's littleness, how can we be limitless? If our brother's omnipotence is what saves us, how can we cut him down and still receive salvation? This logic leads to a radical conclusion: We will be saved only as we build our brother up and up and up, until he becomes heavenly in our sight.

> 3. Specialness is the idea of sin <u>made real</u>. Sin is impossible even to imagine without this base. For sin arose from it, out of nothingness; an evil flower with no roots at all. Here is the self-made "savior," the "creator" who creates <u>unlike</u> the Father, and which made His Son like to itself and <u>not</u> like unto Him. His "<u>special</u>" sons are many, <u>never</u> one, each one in exile from himself, and Him of Whom they are a part. Nor do they love the Oneness Which created them as one with Him. They chose their specialness <u>instead</u> of Heaven and <u>instead</u> of peace, and wrapped it carefully in sin, to keep it "safe" from truth.

In the Course's philosophy, sin (attack viewed as real) is the starting point for all that goes wrong. Out of it comes guilt and then fear and then death. Yet here Jesus says that specialness is actually the *root* of sin. This gives specialness the preeminent place in the entire system of separation. And this makes sense. The Course says the separation flowed from two things: the desire to be above our brothers (the desire for God to love us more), and the desire to be above God Himself (the desire to create Him, rather than be created by Him). Notice what they both have in common: *the desire to be above.* This is specialness—being set above, being better than. This is what started it all. This is what we chose instead of Heaven. Thus, when we belittle our brother and then compare ourselves to him, and then celebrate how special we are, we are repeating the ancient act that started the separation. We may think we enjoy it, but is it really better than Heaven?

> 4. You are <u>not</u> special. If you think you are, and would defend your specialness against the truth of what you <u>really</u> are, how can you know the truth? What answer that the Holy Spirit gives can reach you,

when it is your specialness to which you listen, and which asks <u>and answers</u>? Its tiny answer, soundless in the melody that pours from God to you eternally in loving praise of what you are, is all you listen to. And that vast song of honor and of love for what you are seems silent and unheard before <u>its</u> "mightiness." You strain your ears to hear <u>its</u> soundless voice, and yet the Call of God Himself is soundless to you.

This paragraph plays off of our ability to tune into small sounds even when surrounded by loud noise. In doing so, it completely reverses the traditional notion of "the still, small voice."

Imagine that you are attending an opera, and you are the guest of honor. In fact, the entire opera is about you. The lead singer plays the role of God, and he sings in the most beautiful voice a song of loving praise of what you are. It is a vast song of honor and of love for your eternal grandeur. The music pours to you, rising and falling with almost painful beauty. It reveals to you a truth about yourself that, though surprising, should fill you with sweet, endless happiness.

Yet you are not paying attention. You have a little hand-held tape recorder in your hand. On it is a recording made by you. Its small, tinny sound is so quiet that you can barely hear it. Yet all of your attention is trained on it, as if you were tuning into a conversation at a party while tuning out the din of the party. What does your tape player say? It is your voice repeating a long list: "I'm better than Jim because his taste in clothing is clearly inferior. I'm better than Jane because she can't spell. I'm better than Joe because he doesn't keep his lawn well manicured."

This is a colorful depiction of our literal situation. *Right now* this vast song is pouring to us, and yet we have tuned it out, so focused are we on the tinny squeaks that tell of our specialness. Could this be why, when we ask the Holy Spirit for guidance, we don't hear anything? Could this be why the Voice for God Himself seems still and small?

5. You <u>can</u> defend your specialness, but never will you hear the Voice for God beside it. They speak a different language and they fall on different ears. To every special one a <u>different</u> message, and one with <u>different</u> meaning, is the truth. Yet how <u>can</u> truth be different to each one? The special messages the special hear convince them <u>they</u> are different and apart; each in his special sins and "safe" from love, which does not see his specialness at all. Christ's vision <u>is</u> their "enemy," for

it sees not what <u>they</u> would look upon, and it <u>would</u> show them that the specialness they think they see <u>is</u> an illusion.

Notice how we've looped back to the first law of chaos. The truth that is different for everyone (first law) is each person's specialness. Whenever I say, "This is my truth," the real, underlying essence of "my truth" is "I'm special." If we were listening to the Voice for God, we would all hear the same truth and be united in the same truth. But instead, we each have headphones on and are listening to recordings of our own voice talking about how special we are. That is why there is such a gap between us and others. And that is why we are afraid of Christ's vision, for it would show us that every single person out there is exactly the same as us.

> 6. What would they see instead? The shining radiance of the Son of God, so like his Father that the memory of Him springs instantly to mind. And with this memory, the Son remembers his own creations, as like to him as he is to his Father. And all the world he made, and all his specialness, and all the sins he held in its defense <u>against</u> himself, will vanish as his mind accepts the truth about himself, as it returns to take their place. This is the only "cost" of truth: You will no longer see what never was, nor hear what makes no sound. Is it a sacrifice to give up nothing, and to receive the Love of God forever?

If we saw with Christ's vision, we would see nothing but the shining radiance of God's Son, wherever we look, whoever we look at. Everyone would be the same. And in that sameness, we would awaken to full awareness of God. True, our world would vanish, along with our specialness, and all the sins we wrapped it in to keep it intact. But so what? We would have *Heaven*. As Jesus says, "Is it a sacrifice to give up nothing, and to receive the Love of God forever?"

> 7. You who have chained your savior to your specialness, and given it <u>his</u> place, remember this: He has <u>not</u> lost the power to forgive you all the sins you think you placed between him and the function of salvation <u>given</u> him for you. Nor will you <u>change</u> his function, any more than you can change the truth in him and in yourself. But be you certain that the truth is just the same in both [unlike what the first law of chaos says]. It gives no different messages, and has <u>one</u> meaning. And

it is one you and your brother <u>both</u> can understand, and one that brings release to <u>both</u> of you. Here stands your brother with the key to Heaven in his hand, held out to you. Let not the dream of specialness remain between you. What is one <u>is</u> joined in truth.

Application: A visualization:

Begin by visualizing your specialness as a person.
How does this person look? What does he wear?
Now picture an actual person in your life, ideally a spouse or partner.
This makes three figures in the scene: you, the actual person (spouse or partner), and your specialness.
See the other person literally chained to your specialness.
See your specialness occupying the place in your life that this other person is meant to occupy.
If the other person is a spouse, see your specialness, rather than your spouse, sleeping next to you.
If a business partner, see your specialness, rather than your partner, conferring with you in meetings.
And all the while the other person remains chained to your specialness.
She is on a leash of iron links.
Now realize that this person is in your life to be your savior.
She came to save you from your sins, by giving you the blessing of her holiness.
She still has that function; it will never change.
Look at her there, in shackles.
Notice that despite her chains, she still holds the key to Heaven's gate in her hand.
See her eyes meet yours.
They are strong and clear, empty of blame.
Then see her hold out the key to you.
To accept the key, all you have to do is unchain her and order your specialness to leave, to disappear.
Then together, the two of you can place the key in Heaven's gate and turn it.
Finish the scene in your mind however you like.

8. Think of the loveliness that you will see within yourself, when you have looked on him as on a friend. He *is* the enemy of specialness, but only friend to what is real in you. Not one attack you thought you made on him has taken from him the gift that God would have him give to you. His need to give it is as great as yours to have it. Let him forgive you all your specialness, and make you whole in mind and one with him. He waits for your forgiveness only that he may return it unto you. It is not God Who has condemned His Son [you], but [Ur: *only*] you, to save his [your] specialness and kill his [your] Self.

Please read this paragraph slowly as a continuation of the visualization I asked you to do before.

I want to draw out the fourth through sixth sentences. They make it clear that this gift, the key to Heaven, is something our brother *actively* gives us. The process goes like this. First, we forgive him for all his delusions of specialness, all his proud ideas of how superior he is. This is what he has been waiting for. Now he is free to return to us this forgiveness. Now he forgives us for all our arrogance and conceit, all our delusions of grandiosity. Giving this gift to us is what saves him. That is why "His need to give it is as great as yours to have it."

This is another example of what Greg and I have said many times: Our job is to release our saviors, so that they can perform their function of saving *us*.

9. You have come far along the way of truth; too far to falter now. Just one step more, and every vestige of the fear of God will melt away in love. Your brother's specialness and yours *are* enemies, and bound in hate to kill each other and deny they are the same. Yet it is not illusions that have reached this final obstacle which seems to make God and His Heaven so remote that They cannot be reached. Here in this holy place does truth stand waiting to receive you and your brother in silent blessing, and in peace so real and so encompassing that nothing stands outside. Leave all illusions of yourself outside this place, to which you come in hope and honesty.

I remember when they were recording "We Are the World" back in the eighties. They had all these superstar recording artists in one room, people typically known for having huge egos. Imagine the chaos that could ensue in a room full of fragile, celebrity-size egos. However, I heard things went off very well because the motto of the producers was "Check your ego at the door."

That is what we need to do when we and our brother come before the final obstacle to peace: the fear of God. Our illusory identities—made of the stuff of specialness—have been battling it out for eons (as we saw in "The Laws of Chaos"). They have sworn to kill each other. Yet now the two of us have finally reached the holy place where the journey ends. We have reached the holy ground before the veil across the face of Christ. All we have to do is lift the veil together and we will disappear into God. But unless we want a brawl in the sanctuary, we will need to check our feuding egos at the door.

> 10. Here is your savior *from* your specialness. He is in need of your acceptance of himself as part of you, as you for his. You [two] are alike to God as God is to Himself. He is not special, for He would not keep one part of what He is unto Himself, <u>not</u> given to His Son but kept for Him alone. And it is this you fear, for if He is not special, then He willed His Son to be like Him, and your brother *is* like you. Not special, but possessed of everything, <u>including</u> you. Give him but what he has [everything], remembering God gave Himself to you and your brother [Ur: to *both* of you] in equal love, that both might share the universe with Him Who chose that love could never be divided, and kept separate from what it <u>is</u> and must forever be.

Here we have the underlying reason why specialness is false: God is not special. What does that mean? It means that God does not see His value lying in possessing something that no one else has, something He keeps to Himself. Instead, He shares everything He has, with everyone. God, then, is the polar opposite of special. Yet if God is the Author of all things real, where, then, does that leave our specialness? This is what we are afraid of. We are afraid that what God is leaves our specialness without any foundation in reality.

But we aren't looking at the benefits here. If we can admit that we are not special, if we can admit that our brother is like us and part of us, then we can accept that both of us have everything that God has, and *are* everything that God *is*.

> 11. You *are* your brother's; part of love was not <u>denied</u> to him. But can it be that <u>you</u> have lost because <u>he</u> is complete? What has been given

him makes you complete, as it does him. God's Love gave you to him and him to you because He gave Himself. What is the same as God is one with Him. And only specialness could make the truth of God and you as one seem anything but Heaven, with [Ur: And] the hope of peace at last in sight.

God gave everything to your brother. Nothing was denied to him. God even gave your brother *you*. Can you feel the envy arise in you? Why should *he* get everything? Yet God did the exact same thing with you. He gave you everything, including your brother. For God's Nature is to give Himself, to everyone, thus making everyone one with Him. How can this not be an unparalleled blessing? How can being special ever equal the wonder of being at one with God?

12. Specialness is the seal of treachery upon the gift of love. Whatever serves its purpose must be given to kill. No gift that bears its seal but offers treachery to giver and receiver. Not one glance from eyes it veils but looks on sight of death. Not one believer in its potency but seeks for bargains and for compromise that would establish sin love's substitute, and serve it faithfully. And no relationship that holds its purpose dear but clings to murder as safety's weapon, and the great defender of all illusions from the "threat" of love.

The language here is colorful. When specialness is given as a gift, the gift will betray both giver and receiver. Specialness is like some foul being that veils its eyes, so you cannot see where it looks and thus cannot tell what it's really after. But it always looks on sight of death. It attracts devotees that believe in its power and thus become faithful servants of sin. And everything and everyone that serves its purpose ends up murdering on its behalf.

What is this colorful language talking about? It seems to be talking about special love. To give a *special* love, a love that says, "I love only you," is to give a treacherous love, a love that will turn out to be love's opposite. You are giving a Trojan horse, and when night falls, out of its stomach will pour murderers, who kill both the receiver *and* the giver of this gift. The image may seem stark, but haven't we all received Trojan horses? And haven't we all given them?

13. The hope of specialness makes it seem possible God made the

body as the prison house that keeps His Son from Him. For it <u>demands</u> a special place God cannot enter, and a hiding place where none is welcome but your tiny self. Nothing is sacred here but unto you, and you alone, apart and separate from all your brothers; safe from <u>all</u> intrusions of sanity upon illusions; safe from God and safe for conflict everlasting. Here [referring to the body] are the gates of hell you closed upon yourself, to rule in madness and in loneliness your special kingdom, <u>apart</u> from God, <u>away</u> from truth and from salvation.

The hope of specialness made the body necessary. What? At first, the connection between the two is not obvious, but then it becomes clear. The whole idea of specialness is "I have something you don't have." I have this unique value, this special magic, this extraordinary something that you sadly lack.

In order to have this, though, I need a special hiding place for it, a special vault that is my private space, where no one but me can enter. That special hiding place, where I keep my precious diamonds of specialness, is my body. (This is why, in the final law of chaos, you keep trying to crack the safe of my body so you can get those diamonds and put them in your own safe.)

Application: Think of your body as a safe that contains your specialness, making sure that specialness remains yours and yours alone. Then say,

> *Here are the gates of hell I closed upon myself to rule in madness and in loneliness my special kingdom, apart from God, away from truth and from salvation.*

14. The key you threw away God gave your brother, whose holy hands would offer it to you when you were ready to accept His plan for your salvation in the place of yours. How could this readiness be reached save through the sight of all your misery, and the awareness that your plan has failed, and will forever fail to bring you peace and joy of <u>any</u> kind? Through this despair you travel now, yet it is but <u>illusion</u> of despair. The death of specialness is <u>not</u> your death, but your awaking into life eternal. You but emerge from an illusion of what you are to the acceptance of yourself as God created you.

Application: Ask yourself,

> *Has my specialness made me happy?*
> *Has it made me truly and wholeheartedly value and esteem myself?*
> *Based on how well it has done so far, will specialness **ever** make me happy?*

Be aware that for some time you have been gradually realizing that the answer is "no."

As a result, you have been despairing of ever finding happiness.

But this is just an *illusion* of despair.

You actually have cause for rejoicing.

For the death of specialness is not your death, but your awaking into life eternal.

Picture your body as a vault, within which you enclosed your "priceless" special self.

Picture you locking yourself in and throwing away the key.

After all these years inside this vault, you finally realize that the door you closed on yourself was the gate of hell, and you have no key.

Now see that on the outside of the vault, there is a brother (choose someone) and he holds the key. God gave it specifically to him.

All you need to do is see him as holy, not sinful, as being powerful, not little and insignificant, and as being the same as you, and he will turn the key, and let you out of hell.

Picture this happening.

III. The Forgiveness of Specialness
Commentary by Robert Perry

1. Forgiveness is the end of specialness. Only illusions can <u>be</u> forgiven, and then they disappear. Forgiveness is release from <u>all</u> illusions, and that is why it is impossible but <u>partly</u> to forgive. No one who clings to <u>one</u> illusion can see himself as sinless, for he holds one error to himself as lovely still. And so he calls it "unforgivable," and makes it sin. How can he then give <u>his</u> forgiveness wholly, when he would not receive it for himself? For it is sure he <u>would</u> receive it wholly the instant that he gave it so. And thus <u>his</u> secret guilt would disappear, forgiven by himself.

All our beliefs in being special are illusions. After all, how can we be special if God created us all the same? That is why we need to let our beliefs in specialness go—all of them. If we hold onto even one such belief, then there is one error that we still cling to. And holding it dear, we will view that error as a sin, a sin we want because we believe that it elevates us above others. Then we won't want to give forgiveness to others—truly, wholly. Why? Because if we gave it, then we would receive it, and then our specialness, terrifying yet regal, would be revealed as nothing more than a quaint and groundless mistake.

2. Whatever form of specialness you cherish, you have made sin. Inviolate it stands, strongly defended with all your puny might against the Will of God. And thus it stands against <u>yourself</u>; *your* enemy, <u>not</u> God's [the third time specialness has been called our enemy]. So does it seem to split you off from God, and make you separate from Him as its defender. <u>You</u> would protect what God created not. And yet, this idol that seems to <u>give</u> you power has taken it away. For you have given your brother's birthright to it [another reference to the story of Jacob and Esau], leaving <u>him</u> alone and unforgiven, and yourself in sin beside him, both in misery, before the idol that can save you not.

This paragraph reminds me of an experience from a number of years ago. There was a man who was the leader of a small spiritual group. He lived in his trailer on a piece of land the group believed it was meant to have. Their attempt to buy the land, however, fell through, and this devastated the group. Shortly after this occurred, the man, who was still on the land, found there what he called "the gift." In excited letters, he described "the gift" as deposited on this special piece of land perhaps millions of years ago by some extraterrestrial intelligence. This artifact was able to do absolutely amazing things, which, he said, made the special effects in movies look like cheap dime store tricks. This thing would change world history, and he was the one who found it.

Unfortunately, the others in the group who were privileged to see "the gift" saw only an ordinary rock. They were mystified. You can imagine the mental gymnastics this man must have gone through to convince himself that this rock was something earth-shattering. The group disintegrated as this man spiraled into increasingly fantastic delusions of grandeur.

We each have our own version of "the gift." What others see as a mindless piece of stone, we see as our god, who will save us. We defend it against all reason and truth. And for its sake we sacrifice our brothers, the only ones who could really save us.

> 3. It is not *you* who are so vulnerable and open to attack that just a word, a little whisper that you do not like, a circumstance that suits you not, or an event that you did not anticipate upsets your world, and hurls it into chaos. Truth is not frail. Illusions leave it perfectly unmoved and undisturbed. But specialness is <u>not</u> the truth in you. *It* can be thrown off balance by <u>anything</u>. What rests on nothing <u>never</u> can be stable. However large and overblown it <u>seems</u> to be, it still must rock and turn and whirl about with every breeze.

Why is our self-esteem so incredibly fragile? Have you ever wondered? Sometimes, all it takes is just one word, just a whisper you thought you overheard, and our world is hurled into chaos. Jesus here explains why. It is not *you* who are this vulnerable. It is your specialness. It is vulnerable because it has no real foundation, because it is not true.

Application: A visualization:

Picture your specialness as a massive block of granite, perhaps eight
    feet high.
It looks ageless, noble, and enduringly strong.

You might even imagine that it is carved with shapes or letters designed to depict how special you are.

See yourself admiring it.

Now notice that a breeze kicks up and it actually moves, just a little.

Then the breeze gets stronger, and then it rocks and turns and whirls about.

You realize that this is not a real rock.

It must be made of papier-mâché or some ultra-light material, so that what should weigh ten tons weighs just ten *pounds*.

Then you realize that the rock of your specialness can so easily be thrown off balance because it is artificial; it is not real.

Is this what you want to identify with?

4. Without foundation nothing is secure. Would God have left His Son in such a state, where safety <u>has</u> no meaning? No, His Son is safe, resting on Him. It is your specialness that is attacked by everything that walks and breathes, or creeps or crawls, or even lives at all. Nothing is safe from its attack, and it is safe from nothing. It will forevermore <u>be</u> unforgiving, for that is what it <u>is</u>; a secret vow that what God wants for you will never be, and that you will oppose His Will forever. Nor is it possible the two can ever be the same, while specialness stands like a flaming sword of death between them [a reference to the flaming sword that barred Adam's return to Eden], and makes them enemies.

Isn't it true that our self-esteem seems to be "attacked by everything that walks and breathes, or creeps or crawls, or even lives at all"? Does it make sense that God would create us this unstable, this insecure? He wouldn't and He didn't. He created us eternally secure, resting in Him. Our *specialness* is what is so insecure, for the simple reason that it is not true.

Application: Say to yourself,

I am not insecure.
My specialness is insecure,
because it is not true.

Now realize that your specialness is really a secret vow that you will never be one with God again. Imagine yourself as Adam, standing outside the Garden of Eden, yearning to go back in. But there at the entrance to the Garden stands a flaming sword, barring your return. Now realize that this flaming sword is not of God; it is your own specialness.

> 5. God asks for your forgiveness. He would have no separation, like an alien will, rise between what He wills for you and what <u>you</u> will. They [God's Will and our will] *are* [Ur: *They* are] the same, for neither one wills specialness. How could they will the death of love itself? Yet they are powerless to make attack upon illusions. They are <u>not bodies</u>; as one Mind they wait for all illusions to be <u>brought</u> to them, and left behind. Salvation challenges not even death. And God Himself, Who knows that death is <u>not</u> your will, must say, "Thy will be done" because <u>you</u> think it is.

Our will and God's Will want exactly the same thing. Both wills simply want to be together; that's all. Neither one wants specialness, for specialness is the death of love, and love is the thing that is most valued by both wills. Outside of time, standing together as one Mind, our will and God's wait for our illusions of specialness to be brought to them, and disappear. They merely wait; they will not attack our illusions of specialness. Therefore, "God Himself, Who knows that death is not your will, must say, 'Thy will be done' because you think it is."

Notice the irony. In our attachment to specialness, we refuse to say, "Thy Will be done," even though God's Will is only for our happiness and our eternal life. Yet even while we refuse, God says to us, "Thy will be done," refusing to block our desire for death in the firm knowledge that we will eventually return to our true will, which is exactly the same as His.

> 6. Forgive the great Creator of the universe, the Source of life, of love and holiness, the perfect Father of a perfect Son, for your illusions of your specialness. Here is the hell you chose to be your home. He chose not this for you. Ask not He enter this. The way is barred to love and to salvation. Yet if you would release your brother from the depths of hell, you have forgiven Him Whose Will it is you rest forever in the arms of peace, in perfect safety, and without the heat and malice of one thought

of specialness to mar your rest. Forgive the Holy One the specialness He could not give, and that you made instead.

This paragraph hearkens back to "The Fear of Redemption" (T-13. III), which tells us that the separation started when we asked God to make us more special than the rest of our brothers. He refused, knowing this could only make us lonely. So we separated and made a world where we *could* be special.

Our experiment in specialness, however, turned out to be a nightmare. Yet rather than accepting that we were wrong, we still blame God. If only He had made our specialness fully real, so real that it could never be challenged by anything, we would be happy in this dream. Somewhere inside, then, we blame it all on God. He could have made us the philosopher-king of the world, for all time, but He didn't.

We need to forgive God, just as a child needs to forgive its parents for not giving it something desired but dangerous. How do we forgive God? By releasing our "brother from the depths of hell."

> 7. The special ones are all asleep, surrounded by a world of loveliness they do not see. Freedom and peace and joy stand there, beside the bier on which they sleep, and call them to come forth and waken from their dream of death. Yet they hear nothing. They are lost in dreams of specialness. They hate the call that would awaken them, and they curse God because He did not make their dream reality. Curse God and die, but not by Him Who made not death; but only in the dream. Open your eyes a little; see the savior God gave to you that you might look on him, and give him back his birthright. It is <u>yours</u>.

What a powerful image. We, the special ones, are asleep, each one of us on our own bier. A bier, of course, is a stand for a corpse. We, however, are not dead; we are lost in *dreams* of death—dreams of specialness. We are deeply attached to our dream of death, despite the fact that we are surrounded by a paradise of loveliness. Freedom and peace and joy stand by our side and call to us to awaken. You'd think we would want to bolt out of a dream of death in answer to such a call. Yet we will not respond. We hate the call and curse God because He would not make our dream real. What an ironic image! Can we accept that this image applies to us, that the world we see before us is a dream of death, while we sleep, surrounded by loveliness and called to by freedom and joy?

How do we awaken? We open our eyes ever so slightly on our bier, and see our savior sleeping beside us, and then give him back the birthright we gave our specialness.

> 8. The slaves of specialness will yet be free. Such is the Will of God and of His Son. Would God condemn Himself to hell and to damnation? And do you will that this be done unto your savior? God calls to you from him to join His Will to save you both from hell. Look on the print of nails upon his hands that he holds out for your forgiveness. God asks your mercy on His Son and on Himself. Deny Them not. They ask of you but that your will be done. They seek your love that you may love yourself. Love not your specialness instead of Them. The print of nails is on your hands as well. Forgive your Father it was not His Will that you be crucified.

Application:

Choose someone in your life who has been hurt by your devotion to your specialness.

Visualize this person before you.

See her hold her hands to you, asking for your forgiveness.

Look at her hands, and see the print of nails on them.

Your specialness has crucified her in order to elevate yourself.

As she silently asks for forgiveness, realize that God is asking this through her.

He asks for your mercy not only on her, but on Himself, and on *you.*

He asks only that your true will be done.

Now you have a choice: You can continue loving your specialness.

Or you can love her, your savior, instead.

While you ponder this choice, look down at your own hands, and see the print of nails on them as well.

No one has been left unharmed by your specialness.

Forgive this person for all her crimes against your specialness, and heal *both* of you.

IV. Specialness versus Sinlessness
Commentary by Robert Perry

1. Specialness is a lack of trust in anyone except yourself. Faith is invested in yourself alone. Everything else becomes your enemy; feared and attacked, deadly and dangerous, hated and worthy only of destruction. Whatever gentleness it offers is but deception, but its hate is real. In danger of destruction it <u>must</u> kill, and <u>you</u> are drawn to it to kill it first. And such is guilt's attraction. Here is death enthroned as savior; crucifixion is now redemption, and salvation can <u>only</u> mean destruction of the world, <u>except yourself</u>.

The Ring of Power in *The Lord of the Rings* is a great metaphor for specialness. While you possess it, it essentially possesses you, warping your perception of everyone, making everyone seem to be secretly plotting to take the ring. If someone offers to help, you are suspicious, assuming that this must be a trick. If someone overtly attacks, though, you know that he is showing his true colors. As long as the ring is in your possession, everyone is seen through its warped and jealous eyes.

So it is with specialness. We think we serve it out of attraction to a sense of self-worth. Can we entertain the idea that we serve it out of an attraction to *guilt*?

2. What could the purpose of the body be <u>but</u> specialness? And it is this that makes it frail and helpless in its own defense. It was <u>conceived</u> to make *you* frail and helpless. The goal of separation is its curse. Yet <u>bodies</u> have no goal. Purpose is of the mind. And minds can change as they desire. What they <u>are</u>, and all their attributes, they <u>cannot</u> change. But what they hold as purpose <u>can</u> be changed, and body states must shift accordingly. Of itself the body can do nothing. See it as means to hurt, and it is hurt. See it as means to heal, and it is healed.

It is no secret that we use our body to enhance our specialness. We make it look better than other bodies. We try to make it more strong and able than other bodies. And we use its abilities to prove to the world that we really are superior to others. We use it for specialness because we made it for that very purpose.

Yet specialness makes us separate and different. It makes us a tiny particle split off from everyone and everything. And therefore it makes us frail and helpless. Dedication to specialness is thus dedication to frailty and helplessness.

A consistent Course teaching is that when we dedicate the body to a purpose, the body's condition will then reflect that purpose. Thus, if you dedicate your body to the purpose of specialness, which is really the purpose of frailty and helplessness, the body will become frail and helpless. This, then, is where our search to have a superior body leads us—to having a frail and helpless body.

> 3. <u>You can but hurt yourself.</u> This has been oft repeated, but is difficult to grasp as yet. To minds intent on specialness it is impossible. Yet to those who wish to heal and <u>not</u> attack, it is quite obvious. The purpose of attack is in the <u>mind</u>, and its effects are felt but where it <u>is</u>. Nor is the mind limited; so must it be that harmful purpose hurts the mind <u>as one</u>. Nothing could make <u>less</u> sense to specialness. Nothing could make <u>more</u> sense to miracles. For miracles are merely change of purpose from hurt to healing. This shift in purpose <u>does</u> "endanger" specialness, but only in the sense that all illusions are "threatened" by the truth. They will <u>not</u> stand before it. Yet what comfort has ever been in them, that you would keep the gift your Father asks from Him, and give it there instead? Given to <u>Him</u>, the universe is yours. Offered to <u>them</u>, no gifts can be returned. What you have given specialness has left you bankrupt and your treasure house barren and empty, with an open door inviting everything that would disturb your peace to enter and destroy.

Specialness is counting on the fact that when you defeat someone else, you win. You have hurt only him, and helped yourself. The truth, however, is that you can only hurt yourself. When he loses, you lose. Yet your brother is part of you, and so your loss is also his. "Harmful purpose hurts the mind [of the Sonship] as one."

This makes no sense to specialness, but it makes perfect sense to miracles. For miracles are just a case of changing our purpose from hurt to healing, from winning the race to helping along our lagging brother. Yes, this does threaten our victory, but has victory ever given us what we wanted? Has it ever brought real peace? Or has it just brought worry about the next contest, and secret guilt over all those we trampled on along the way to glory?

The paragraph ends on a stark image. We have spent years doting on our specialness. We have opened the door of our treasure house and gradually taken every bit of treasure out of there, and laid it respectfully before the stone idol of our specialness. What did we get from all these acts of devotion? Bankruptcy. Our specialness is like a crooked preacher who is intent on eliciting lavish gifts from rich widows, until they have nothing left to show for all their pious generosity.

> 4. Earlier I [Ur: Long ago we] said consider not the means by which salvation is attained, nor how to reach it. But <u>do</u> consider, and consider well, whether it is your <u>wish</u> that you might see your brother sinless. To specialness the answer <u>must</u> be "no." A sinless brother *is* its enemy, while sin, if it were possible, <u>would</u> be its friend. Your brother's sin would justify itself, and <u>give</u> it meaning that the truth denies.

In Chapter 20, Jesus stressed repeatedly that we shouldn't worry about how to acquire vision. All we need do is want it—just want to see our brother sinless—and vision will be given us. His point now is that we can't want to see our brother sinless *and* want to be special. Perhaps the chief way of being better than is being more sinless, more pure, more righteous. At the heart of specialness, therefore, is the attitude of "holier than thou." If we want vision, we have to give up specialness.

> All that is real proclaims his sinlessness. All that is false proclaims his sins as real. If <u>he</u> is sinful, then is <u>your</u> reality not real, but just a dream of specialness that lasts an instant, crumbling into dust.
> 5. Do not defend this senseless dream, in which God is bereft of what He loves, and you remain beyond salvation. Only this is certain in this shifting world that has <u>no</u> meaning in reality: When peace is not with you <u>entirely</u>, and when you suffer pain of <u>any</u> kind, you have beheld some sin within your brother, <u>and have rejoiced</u> at what you thought was there. Your specialness seemed safe <u>because</u> of it. And thus you saved what <u>you</u> appointed to be your savior, and crucified the one whom God has given you instead. So are you bound with him, for you <u>are</u> one. And so is specialness <u>his</u> "enemy," and <u>yours</u> as well [the fourth time Jesus has called our specialness our enemy].

Is peace with you entirely? Is peace with any of us entirely? No, it's not. Why not? Because we have seen sin in our brother *and rejoiced.* We rejoiced because his sin meant, "I am better than he." His sin was such great news because it made our specialness seem safe. Thus we saved what we thought of as our savior, and crucified the one God sent us to be our savior. It's like one of those scenes in movie where to save your protector you shoot the intruder, only to discover that the "protector" was really out to get you, and the "intruder" knew this and was really trying to save you. In this case, though, the "protector" is really just a senseless dream, a fantasy that is incredibly insecure *because* it's a fantasy. The intruder, on the other hand, is real and is one with us. By shooting him, then, we shoot ourselves.

V. The Christ in You
Commentary by Robert Perry

The Text is sliding into iambic pentameter now. It began doing so in the sections before this, but this section is more consistently in iambic pentameter. Iambic pentameter is composed of lines of ten syllables each, with the accent on every *second* syllable. I've laid the first paragraph out in this form of verse:

> The Christ in you is very still. He looks
> on what He loves, and knows it as Himself.
> And thus does He rejoice at what He sees,
> because He knows that it is one with Him
> and with His Father. Specialness, too, takes joy [one extra syllable]
> in what it sees, although it is not true.
> Yet what you seek for is a source of joy
> as you conceive it. What you wish is true for you. [two extra syllables]
> Nor is it possible that you can wish
> for something and lack faith that it is so.
> Wishing makes real, as surely as does will create. [two extra syllables]
> The power of a wish upholds illusions [one extra syllable]
> as strongly as does love extend itself.
> Except that one deludes; the other heals.

As you can see, the iambic pentameter is a bit rough. Four of the lines don't fit the pattern. But the other lines fit it perfectly. From here, the Text will slowly slide into ever more perfect iambic pentameter. The reason Jesus uses this is surely the same reason that any poet uses it: to enhance the beauty of the language. If you listen to the words as you read them, you will notice a kind of heartbeat that runs through the lines.

> 1. The Christ in you is very still. He looks on what He loves, and knows it as Himself. And thus does He rejoice at what He sees, because He knows that it is one with Him and with His Father. Specialness, too, takes joy in what it sees, although it is not true. Yet what you seek for <u>is</u>

132

a source of joy as you conceive it. What you wish <u>is</u> true for you. Nor is it possible that you can wish for something and <u>lack</u> faith that it is so. <u>Wishing makes real</u>, as surely as does will create. The power of a wish upholds illusions as strongly as does love extend itself. Except that one deludes; the other heals.

Christ is the single Self that everyone shares, and though the Sons of God (plural) may have fallen asleep, their one Self, the Christ, never did. His presence in us "is very still," rather than frantic and striving. From this stillness, He looks on a world of holy brothers who are exactly the same as He. He sees no specialness, no unique identities locked up in special containers. He sees only Himself, and rejoices.

Specialness also rejoices at what it sees. And as the previous section told us, it sees sin. It sees a world of dangerous idiots who are so clearly beneath it.

This reflects a principle of perception. Once we want to see something we will see it, and we will take joy in it and have faith that it is true. Therefore, if sin seems like an undeniable reality in the world, that is because we *want* to see it. Our specialness needs to see bad people so that it can feel better than them.

> 2. There is no dream of specialness, however hidden or disguised the form, however lovely it may seem to be, however much it delicately offers the hope of peace and the escape from pain, in which you suffer not your condemnation. In dreams effect and cause are interchanged, for here the maker of the dream believes that what he made is happening <u>to</u> him. He does <u>not</u> realize he picked a thread from here, a scrap from there, and wove a picture out of nothing. For the parts do <u>not</u> belong together, and the whole contributes nothing to the parts to <u>give</u> them meaning.

Have you ever wondered at how warped some people's stories can get? It's as if they "picked a thread from here, a scrap from there, and wove a picture out of nothing," isn't it? What is harder to accept is that we are doing the same thing. The picture we are weaving is a picture of our specialness and our brother's sinfulness. Isn't that the main theme of most of our stories? And isn't that why our stories differ from those of others? Somewhere inside, we know that we are the weaver, and we condemn ourselves for it. This is why every dream of specialness, however glorious it may seem, ends up being a dream of self-condemnation.

> 3. Where could your peace arise *but* from forgiveness? The Christ in you looks only on the truth, and sees no condemnation that could need forgiveness. He is at peace *because* He sees no sin. Identify with Him, and what has He that you have not? He is your eyes, your ears, your hands, your feet. How gentle are the sights He sees, the sounds He hears. How beautiful His hand that holds His brother's, and how lovingly He walks beside him, showing him what can be seen and heard, and where he will see nothing and there is no sound to hear.
>
> 4. Yet let your specialness direct his [your brother's] way, and you will follow. And both will walk in danger, each intent, in the dark forest of the sightless, unlit but by the shifting tiny gleams that spark an instant from the fireflies of sin and then go out, to lead the other to a nameless precipice and hurl him over it. For what can specialness delight in but to kill? What does it seek for but the sight of death? Where does it lead but to destruction? Yet think not that it looked upon your brother first, nor hated him before it hated you. The sin its eyes behold in him and love to look upon it saw in you, and looks on still with joy. Yet is it joy to look upon decay and madness, and believe this crumbling thing, with flesh already loosened from the bone and sightless holes for eyes, is like yourself?

These paragraphs give us a choice. We can identify with the Christ in us or with our specialness. If we identify with the Christ, we will look out on the world and see no sin. Can you imagine what peace would arise from the sight of a world cleansed of all sin? Through this world we can walk, letting Christ be our eyes that look on holiness, letting Him be our ears that listen to the song of Heaven, letting Him be our feet to guide us where we need to go, and letting Him be our hands which hold our brother's hand in theirs, so that Christ guides him as safely as He guides us.

Or we can identify with our specialness and let it guide us. This picture is rather different, isn't it? Rather than walking on a clear road through a world of divine radiance, we walk through "the dark forest of the sightless." The only light comes from the "fireflies of sin." And rather than the two of us banding together in this dire situation, we are each intent on leading the other to a nameless cliff and pushing him off of it. That way, our specialness can live off of his defeat. Though the language is extreme, the fact remains that we are in that dark forest right now. Indeed, there may be someone now that we would like to see hurled over a nameless precipice.

What we don't realize is that our specialness doesn't just rejoice at the sin it sees in others. It rejoices at the sin it sees in *us*. It rejoices to see in us what is best described as a rotting corpse, "with flesh already loosened from the bone and sightless holes for eyes." This is perhaps the single most stomach-turning image in the Course, but it's there for a purpose. While holding it in mind, we need to ask ourselves these questions:

> *Is this what I want to see in myself?*
> *Is this what I want to rejoice at in myself?*
> *Is this what I want to believe is myself?*

5. Rejoice you <u>have</u> no eyes with which to see; no ears to listen, and no hands to hold nor feet to guide. Be glad that <u>only</u> Christ can lend you His, while you have need of them. They are illusions, too, as much as yours. And yet because they serve a different purpose, the strength their <u>purpose</u> holds is given <u>them</u>. And what <u>they</u> see and hear and hold and lead is given light, that <u>you</u> may lead as you were led.

Application: Say to yourself,

I will rejoice that I have no eyes with which to see—my body's eyes are blind.
I will rejoice that I have no ears to listen—my body's ears are deaf.
I will rejoice that I have no hands to hold—my body's hands cannot bring about real joining.
I will rejoice that I have no feet to guide—my body's feet cannot really guide anyone.
I will only be glad that Christ can lend me His.
I am glad that His eyes can see for me.
I am glad that His ears can hear for me.
I am glad that His hands can bring about true joining.
I am glad that His feet can lead me, so that I can lead my brothers.

6. The Christ in you is very still. He knows where you are going, and He leads you there in gentleness and blessing all the way. His Love for God replaces <u>all</u> the fear you thought you saw within yourself. His holiness shows you Himself in him [the brother] whose hand you hold, and whom you lead to Him. And what you see <u>is</u> like yourself. For what but Christ <u>is</u> there to see and hear and love and follow home? He looked upon you <u>first,</u> but recognized that you were not complete. And so He sought for your completion in each living thing that He beholds and loves. And seeks it still, that each might offer <u>you</u> the Love of God.

How could we read these paragraphs and not want Christ to be our guide? He is still; we are often frantic. He knows where we are going; the Course reminds us many times that we don't. He leads us in gentleness and blessing; we lead ourselves in fear and trembling. He fills us with love for God; this replaces the fear with which we filled ourselves. He shows us our brother's holiness; we look for our brother's sinfulness. He shows us a world in which everything is like us; we see a world of strangers, different from us. He sees each living thing as completing us; we look for completion in certain special ones, and never find it. He sees a world in which everything offers us the Love of God; we see a world in which everything is wounding our self-esteem.

7. Yet is He quiet, for He knows that love is in you now, and safely held in you by that same hand that holds your brother's in your own. Christ's hand holds all His brothers in Himself. He gives them vision for their sightless eyes, and sings to them of Heaven, that their ears may hear no more the sound of battle and of death. He reaches through them, holding out His hand, that everyone may bless all living things, and see their holiness. And He rejoices that these sights are <u>yours,</u> to look upon with Him and share His joy. His perfect <u>lack</u> of specialness He offers you, that you may save all living things from death, receiving from each one the gift of life that your forgiveness offers to your Self. The sight of Christ is all there is to see. The song of Christ is all there is to hear. The hand of Christ is all there is to hold. There is no journey but to walk with Him.

Again, after hearing these paragraphs, who wouldn't want to walk the world with Christ as their guide? Just imagine what this paragraph says being true for you. Imagine Christ giving you vision, so that what you see is not meaningless forms but holiness. Imagine Christ singing to you of Heaven, so that your ears will hear no more the sound of battle. Imagine Christ reaching through you, holding up His hand to bless all living things. Imagine Christ walking through you, that everyone may see a higher example to follow.

And there is one last gift we should imagine Christ giving us: "His perfect lack of specialness He offers you." In light of everything we have read, can we see this as a gift?

Notice that each of the final four lines is a discrete line of iambic pentameter. I'll italicize the stressed syllables so you can see clearly how this kind of meter works. Notice the beat as you read these lines:

> *The sight of Christ is all there is to see.*
> *The song of Christ is all there is to hear.*
> *The hand of Christ is all there is to hold.*
> *There is no journey but to walk with Him.*

Now please read the lines again, and this time focus on really believing what they say.

> 8. You who would be content with specialness, and seek salvation in a war with love, consider this: The holy Lord of Heaven has Himself come down to you, to offer you your own completion. What is His is yours because in your completion is His Own. He Who willed not to be without His Son could never will that you be brotherless. And would He give a brother unto you except he be as perfect as yourself, and just as like to Him in holiness as you must be?

The opening sentence is one of those "you who" lines that we often find in the Course. Their usual form goes like this: "You who...think about..." They are Jesus' way of addressing us very directly and then getting us to reflect on something. So in that spirit, let's read this paragraph again, with the help of some parenthetical remarks, and adding our own name in at the suggested places:

> You who would be content with specialness [realize this means you], and seek salvation in a war with love [which specialness is], consider this: The holy Lord of Heaven has Himself come down to you [name],

to offer you your own completion. [Really consider this.] What is His is yours [name] because in your completion is His Own. [Could this really be?] He Who willed not to be without His Son could never will that you [name] be brotherless. And would He give a brother unto you [name] except he be as perfect as yourself, and just as like to Him in holiness as you must be? [Would He?]

9. There must be doubt <u>before</u> there can be conflict. And <u>every</u> doubt must be about yourself. Christ <u>has</u> no doubt, and from His certainty His quiet comes. He will exchange His certainty for <u>all</u> your doubts, if you agree that He is one with you, and that this oneness is endless, timeless, and within your grasp <u>because</u> your hands are His. He is within you, yet He walks beside you and before, leading the way that He must go to find Himself complete. His quietness becomes <u>your</u> certainty. And where is doubt when certainty has come?

The stillness and quietness of Christ has been a refrain for this section. Now that notion is contrasted with both doubt and conflict. How are we to understand these ideas? We really have to see them in light of the earlier discussions of quietness, conflict, and God's memory (T-23.I), and the battleground (T-23.I-IV).

Our self-doubt sends us into battle, in the hopes that victory will shore up our illusory identity and calm our doubts. Yet the memory of God will never come into minds that are full of conflict. We are so used to living lives undermined by self-doubt that we can hardy imagine the alternative. Yet the alternative is wonderful. The Christ in us has no doubt about Himself, and His utter Self-certainty can be ours, if we will simply agree that He is one with us, has always been one with us, and that this oneness is within our grasp. If we will only do this one thing, we will share His certainty, and in that certainty we will be quiet, and will have no need to enter battle anymore.

VI. Salvation from Fear
Commentary by Robert Perry

This section is virtually a hymn to our brother's holiness. I am going to comment on it only minimally, because I'd like us to use it as an extended exercise. Please try to set aside about a half hour for the exercise I have included at the end. It is something that we have used in the past at forgiveness retreats and have consistently heard that it is one of the most powerful elements of the retreat.

> 1. Before your brother's holiness the world is still, and peace descends on it in gentleness and blessing so complete that not one trace of conflict still remains to haunt you in the darkness of the night. He is your savior from the dreams of fear. He is the healing of your sense of sacrifice and fear that what you have will scatter with the wind and turn to dust. In him is your assurance God is here, and with you now. While he is what he is, you can be sure that God is knowable and <u>will</u> be known to you. For He could never leave His Own creation. And the sign that this is so lies in your brother, offered you that all your doubts about yourself may disappear before his holiness. See in him God's creation. For in him his Father waits for your acknowledgment that He created <u>you</u> as part of Him.

The world is locked in conflict.

> And we are here as on a darkling plain,
> Swept with confused alarms of struggle and flight
> Where ignorant armies clash by night. (from Matthew Arnold's "Dover Beach")

Yet in the midst of this conflict appears the radiant light of your brother's holiness, and everything stops. Weapons drop from hands as everyone gazes transfixed on this wonder. Peace descends over what, only a moment before, had been a battleground. And you, as one of the former combatants, are transformed. Your fear has vanished. Your brother's holiness is the sign you have been waiting for, the sign God is here, the sign that He could never leave you. As you gaze on this sign, all the doubts you had about your substance and reality, all the insecurities that sent you into battle, disappear. At last you know that you are part of God Himself.

I have long felt that this is one of the sweetest, most beautiful images in the Course.

> 2. Without you there would be a lack in God, a Heaven incomplete, a son without a Father. There could be no universe and no reality. For what God wills is whole, and part of Him <u>because</u> His Will is one. Nothing alive that is not part of Him, and nothing is but <u>is</u> alive in Him. Your brother's holiness shows you that God is one with him <u>and</u> you; that what he has is yours <u>because</u> you are not separate from him nor [Ur: *or*] from his Father.

The Course teaches us that we are infinitely precious in God's eyes. Yet we are blind to this. How can we see it? It is our brother's holiness that shows it to us.

> 3. Nothing is lost to you in all the universe. Nothing that God created has He failed to lay before you lovingly, as yours forever. And no Thought within His Mind is absent from your own. It is His Will you <u>share</u> His Love for you, and look upon yourself as lovingly as He conceived of you before the world began, and as He knows you still. God changes not His Mind about His Son with passing circumstance which has no meaning in eternity where He abides, and you with Him. Your brother *is* as He created him. And it is this that saves <u>you</u> from a world that He created not.

God treats us truly like a king treats his son. Everything in His Kingdom is ours. Everything He created He lays before us lovingly. All He wants is for us to look upon ourselves as lovingly as He did when He created us and as lovingly as He looks on us now. He will never change His Mind about us. And the way that we know this is to see that He has never changed His Mind about our brother.

> 4. Forget not that the healing of God's Son is all the world is for. That is the <u>only</u> purpose the Holy Spirit sees in it, and thus the only one it <u>has</u>. Until you see the healing of the Son as all you wish to be accomplished by the world, by time and <u>all</u> appearances, you will <u>not</u> know the Father

140

nor [Ur: *or*] yourself. For you will use the world for what is <u>not</u> its purpose, and will <u>not</u> escape its laws of violence and death. Yet it is <u>given</u> you to be <u>beyond</u> its laws in <u>all</u> respects, in <u>every</u> way and <u>every</u> circumstance, in <u>all</u> temptation to perceive what is <u>not</u> there, and <u>all</u> belief God's Son can suffer pain because he sees himself as he is not.

What is my computer for? The healing of God's Son. What is the cracker I am eating for? The healing of God's Son. What are the streets for? The healing of God's Son. What is government for? The healing of God's Son.

When we don't use the world for the healing of God's Son, we bind ourselves to its laws, and its laws are laws of violence and death. We think of physical laws in more neutral terms, but that is where they end up, in violence and death. Yet we can be free of these laws, by using the world not as an end in itself, but as a means to the healing of God's Son.

> 5. Look on your brother, and behold in him the whole reversal of the laws that <u>seem</u> to rule this world. See in his freedom <u>yours</u>, for such it <u>is</u>. Let not his specialness obscure the truth in him, for not one law of death you bind him to will <u>you</u> escape. And not one sin you see in him but keeps you <u>both</u> in hell. Yet will his perfect sinlessness <u>release</u> you both, for holiness is quite impartial, with <u>one</u> judgment made for all it looks upon. And that is made, <u>not</u> of itself, but through the Voice that speaks for God in everything that lives and shares His Being.

If we can only look on our brother, and instead of seeing a special, sinning body, we can see a holiness that transcends earthly laws, we will be released. We will find ourselves free of the laws of this world. Why? When we look on holiness we see that its essence is impartiality, we see that its very nature is to not be doled out selectively, but given equally to all. If, therefore, our brother has it, then we must have it.

> 6. It is <u>His</u> [God's] sinlessness that eyes that see can look upon. It is <u>His</u> loveliness they see in everything. And it is <u>He</u> they look for everywhere, and find no sight nor place nor time where He is <u>not</u>. Within your brother's holiness, the perfect frame for <u>your</u> salvation and the world's, is set the shining memory of Him in Whom your brother lives, and you along with him. Let not your eyes be blinded by the veil of specialness that hides the face of Christ from him, and you as well.

And let the fear of God no longer hold the vision you were <u>meant</u> to see from you. Your brother's <u>body</u> shows not Christ to you. He *is* set forth within his holiness.

Our goal on earth is to look on God's sinlessness, His loveliness, and see them everywhere. How? They are set forth in our brother's holiness. It is depicted as a glowing frame, within which is the face of Christ and memory of God. Wouldn't it be amazing if we could walk into a museum and see such a picture? And yet, such pictures are walking by us everywhere we go. We cannot see the pictures, however, because we are too fixated on the veil that hangs in front of each one, the veil of specialness. On this veil is painted a body.

> 7. Choose, then, his body <u>or</u> his holiness as what you <u>want</u> to see, and which you choose is yours to look upon. Yet will you choose in countless situations, and through time that seems to have no end, until the truth be your decision. For eternity is <u>not</u> regained by still one more denial of Christ in him. And where is <u>your</u> salvation, if he is but a body? Where is <u>your</u> peace but in his holiness? And where is God Himself but in that part of Him He set forever in your brother's holiness, that <u>you</u> might see the truth about yourself, set forth at last in terms you recognized and understood?

This choice of seeing our brother's body or his holiness is so low on our priority list. It gets pushed out by so many other, "more important" things. And yet on the true list of our priorities, it is not only high; it is the only thing on the list. And we will keep choosing for thousands, even millions, even billions of years, "until the truth be your decision." A saying comes to mind: "That which you deny becomes the focus of your life."

> 8. Your brother's holiness is sacrament and benediction unto <u>you</u>. His errors can<u>not</u> withhold God's blessing from himself, nor you who see him truly. His mistakes can cause delay, which it is given <u>you</u> to take from him, that both may end a journey that has never begun, and <u>needs</u> no end. What never was is <u>not</u> a part of you. Yet you will think it is, until you realize that it is not a part of him who stands beside you. He is the mirror of yourself, wherein you see the judgment you have laid on <u>both</u> of you. The Christ in you beholds his holiness. Your specialness looks on his body and beholds him not.

142

The principle here is that whatever you see in your brother is what you have chosen to see in both of you. "He is the mirror of yourself, wherein you see the judgment you have laid on both of you." If you see in your brother a special person, struggling along on an endless journey, then that is how you will see yourself. If you see his holiness, then you will see God's blessing shining from him to you.

Yes, he has made mistakes. And yes, those mistakes do delay his journey, yet you have the ability to save him from that delay, by realizing his reality never set foot on that torturous journey. Are we willing to see the people in our lives in this way, as never having left God in the first place?

> 9. See him as what he is, that your deliverance may not be long. A senseless wandering, without a purpose and without accomplishment of any kind, is all the other choice can offer you. Futility of function not fulfilled will haunt you while your brother lies asleep, till what has been assigned to you is done and he is risen from the past. He who condemned himself, and you as well, is given you to save from condemnation, along with you. And both shall see God's glory in His Son, whom you mistook as flesh, and bound to laws that have no power over him at all.

Have you ever felt that you were just wandering, not sure where you were going? Have you ever been haunted by a sense that there was some function you were supposed to perform but weren't doing it? Both of these feelings are about the same thing: letting your brother remain asleep in dreams of self-condemnation. Until you raise him from this tomb, both feelings will persist. When you read this, is there a particular person that comes to mind?

> 10. Would you not gladly realize these laws are not for you? Then see him not as prisoner to them. It cannot be what governs part of God holds not for all the rest. You place yourself under the laws you see as ruling him. Think, then, how great the Love of God for you must be, that He has given you a part of Him to save from pain and give you happiness. And never doubt but that your specialness will disappear before the Will of God, Who loves each part of Him with equal love and care. The Christ in you can see your brother truly. Would you decide against the holiness He sees?

What laws do we see our brothers as prisoners to? There's the law of entropy, that everything has to run down. There's the laws of disease. There's the law of lack which says that we are inherently lacking and must fill our lack by acquiring from the outside. If we choose to see our brother through the Christ in us, we will see him as free of all such laws. What do *we* get out of this? "You place *yourself* under the laws you see as ruling *him*" (Urtext version). By seeing him as free of these laws, we will set him free from pain, and then he will turn around and set us free from all the laws of limitation.

We can see this as proof of God's Love for us. His Love for us must be great indeed for Him to grant us the privilege of saving an actual part of Him—our brother.

> 11. Specialness is the function that you gave yourself. It stands for you alone, as self-created, self-maintained, in need of nothing, and unjoined with anything beyond the body. In its eyes you are a separate universe, with all the power to hold itself complete within itself, with every entry shut against intrusion, and every window barred against the light. Always attacked and always furious, with anger always fully justified, you have pursued this goal with vigilance you never thought to yield, and effort that you never thought to cease. And all this grim determination was for this; you wanted specialness to be the truth.

Can we accept this picture as applying to us? Can we admit that, at least in little ways, we see ourselves as "always attacked and always furious, with anger always fully justified"? Can we confess that we have pursued the goal of specialness "with vigilance you never thought to yield, and effort that you never thought to cease"? Whenever we have worked with that kind of unrelenting focus, isn't a great deal of the prize we were pursuing the trophy of specialness? And doesn't this make us (at least in our eyes) "a separate universe…with every entry shut against intrusion, and every window barred against the light"?

> 12. Now you are merely asked that you pursue another goal with far less vigilance; with little effort and with little time, and with the power of God maintaining it, and promising success. Yet of the two, it is this one you find more difficult. The "sacrifice" of self you understand, nor do you deem this cost too heavy. But a tiny willingness, a nod to God, a greeting to the Christ in you, you find a burden wearisome and

tedious, too heavy to be borne. Yet to the dedication to the truth as <u>God</u> established it <u>no</u> sacrifice is asked, <u>no</u> strain called forth, and all the power of Heaven and the might of truth itself is given to provide the means, and <u>guarantee</u> the goal's accomplishment.

This paragraph puts the lie to all of our complaints about the Course asking too much of us. The following dialogue is my attempt to capture what is really going on:

Jesus: Can I have just five minutes of your time?
Us: You know, I'm booked solid till Friday. Just today I have chants to my specialness from 10-12. Then from 12-5 I go to the hairstylist, followed by a manicure, a pedicure, and a facial. And from 5-10 I am writing my specialness memoirs. Every day is like that.
Jesus: So you can't spare five minutes before Friday?
Us: You ask so much of me. You load burden after burden onto my shoulders.
Jesus: You don't find spending all day throwing your Self away a burden? All I'm asking is a tiny willingness, a nod to God, a greeting to the Christ in you.
Us: But how do I know that your program will succeed?
Jesus: All the power of Heaven and the might of truth itself will provide the means, and guarantee the goal's accomplishment.
Us: Sorry, off to my pedicure. We'll do this again some time. Ta-ta.

13. You who believe it easier to see your brother's body than his holiness, be sure you understand what made this judgment. Here is the voice of specialness heard clearly, judging <u>against</u> the Christ and setting forth for <u>you</u> the purpose that you <u>can</u> attain, and what you can<u>not</u> do. Forget not that this judgment <u>must</u> apply to what you do with <u>it</u> [your specialness] as your ally. For what you do through Christ it does not know. To Him this judgment makes no sense at all, for <u>only</u> what His Father wills is possible, and there <u>is</u> no alternative for Him to see. Out of His <u>lack</u> of conflict comes your peace. And from His purpose comes the means for effortless accomplishment and rest.

It is not, as we have believed, objectively easier and more obtainable to pursue the goal of being special. It is objectively harder and totally unobtainable. Yet we are listening to the voice of our specialness, and it tells us an entirely false story. It tells us that it is far easier to see our brother's illusory body than his true holiness. It tells us that *its* purpose is within our reach, while our true purpose is completely beyond us.

We accept these parameters, and then within them, we struggle along on the Course's path, pushing timidly forward, taking rests, giving up, getting back to it. We could, however, question this whole story. Maybe our true Self knows better what is possible for us. Maybe the Christ in us knows the goal that we can reach, and provides the means for effortless accomplishment. Could it be that we have been seeing the Course's journey through the eyes of the very thing that wants to *thwart* that journey?

Exercise: As I said, give yourself about a half hour for this. Choose a person you need to forgive, especially someone you see as inferior to you in important ways. Then read the following selections from "Salvation from Fear." Read them slowly, drinking in every word. Take your time. This is for you. Visualize the images, think about the ideas, imagine the statements as literally true. Above all, *apply everything specifically to the person you have chosen.*

Before your brother's holiness the world is still [picture this],
and peace descends on it [because it looks upon your brother's
    holiness]
in gentleness and blessing so complete
that not one trace of conflict still remains
to haunt you in the darkness of the night.
[You might imagine your brother's holiness appearing before a battle
    of which you are part, causing peace to descend on everyone,
    causing the night to be replaced by the dawn.]
He [name] is your savior from the dreams of fear.
He is the healing of your sense of sacrifice
and fear that what you have will scatter with the wind and turn to dust.
[Feel the sight of his holiness healing this fear of yours.]
In him is your assurance God is here, and with you now.
While he is what he is,
you can be sure that God is knowable and will be known to you.
For He could never leave His Own creation.

And the sign that this is so lies in your brother [name],
offered you that all your doubts about yourself
may disappear before his holiness.
[Imagine your doubts about yourself disappearing as you gaze on his
  holiness.]

Your brother's holiness shows you that God is one with him and you;
that what he has [everything, including all of God] is yours
because you are not separate from him nor from his Father.

God changes not His Mind about His Son with passing circumstance
which has no meaning in eternity where He abides, and you with Him.
Your brother *is* as He created him.
And it is this that saves you from a world that He created not.

Look on your brother [name],
and behold in him the whole reversal of the laws that seem to rule
  this world [the laws of sin, death, attack, selfishness—all these are
  reversed in who he really is].
See in his freedom [from these imprisoning laws] yours, for such it is.
Let not his specialness [the appearance that he is a unique and special
  person] obscure the truth in him, for not one law of death you bind
  him to will you escape [and binding him to specialness *is* binding
  him to laws of death].
And not one sin you see in him [think of a "sin" you see in him] but
  keeps you both in hell.
Yet will his perfect sinlessness release you both, for holiness is quite
  impartial, with one judgment made for all it looks upon.
[Feel his holiness looking upon you and releasing you from all your
  chains.]
And that is made, not of itself, but through the Voice that speaks for
  God in everything that lives and shares His Being.

Within your brother's holiness, the perfect frame for your salvation
  and the world's, is set the shining memory of Him in Whom your
  brother lives [God], and you along with him.
[Imagine your brother's holiness as a frame, within which is the light

of your salvation and the blazing memory of God.]

Let not your eyes be blinded by the veil of specialness [the appearance that he is a unique person, with a unique body and personality] that hides the face of Christ from him, and you as well....

[You might picture this veil hanging over both picture and frame.]

Your brother's body [picture it] shows not Christ to you.

He [Christ] *is* set forth within his holiness [within the frame of your brother's holiness].

Choose, then, his body or his holiness as what you want to see [try to make this choice], and which you choose is yours to look upon.

Yet will you choose in countless situations, and through time that seems to have no end [take this literally], until the truth be your decision.

For eternity is not regained by still one more denial of Christ in [name].

And where is your salvation, if he is but a body? [Indeed, *where*?]

Where is your peace but in his holiness?

And where is God Himself but in that part of Him He set forever in your brother's holiness [set in the frame of your brother's holiness], that you might see the truth about yourself [within this frame], set forth at last in terms you recognized and understood?

Your brother's holiness is sacrament and benediction unto you.

His errors [think of specific ones] cannot withhold God's blessing from himself, nor you who see him truly.

His mistakes can cause delay, which it is given you to take from him [appreciate this fact], that both may end a journey that has never begun, and needs no end.

What never was [the mistake-filled journey] is not a part of you.

Yet you will think it is, until you realize that it is not a part of him who stands beside you.

He is the mirror of yourself, wherein you see the judgment you have laid on both of you.

[Picture your view of him as a mirror in which you see your judgment of yourself].

The Christ in you beholds his holiness [this is happening right now].

Your specialness looks on his body and beholds him not.

See him as what he is, that your deliverance [from the journey] may
not be long.

A senseless wandering, without a purpose and without accomplishment
of any kind, is all the other choice can offer you [and this is what
you have already had].

Futility of function not fulfilled will haunt you while your brother
[name] lies asleep, till what has been assigned to you is done
and he is risen from the past. [Raising him from the past *is* your
assignment.]

He who condemned himself, and you as well, is given you to save
from condemnation, along with you.

And both shall see God's glory in His Son [picture this happening],
whom you mistook as flesh, and bound to laws that have no power
over him at all.

VII. The Meeting Place
Commentary by Robert Perry

1. How bitterly does everyone tied to this world defend the specialness he <u>wants</u> to be the truth! His wish is law to him, and he obeys. Nothing his specialness demands does he withhold. Nothing it needs does he deny to what he loves. And while it calls to him he hears no other Voice. No effort is too great, no cost too much, no price too dear to save his specialness from the least slight, the tiniest attack, the whispered doubt, the hint of threat, or anything but deepest reverence. This is your son, beloved of you as you are to your Father. Yet it stands in place of your creations, who *are* son to you, that you might <u>share</u> the Fatherhood of God, not snatch it <u>from</u> Him. What <u>is</u> this son that you have made to be your strength? What is this child of earth on whom such love is lavished? What is this parody of God's creation that takes the place of <u>yours</u>? And where are <u>they</u> [your creations], now that the host of God has found another son whom he prefers to them?

Can you see that you treat your specialness like a doting father treats a spoiled son? Nothing this kid demands do you hold back. Nothing the kid needs do you deny to the apple of your eye. And when the boy calls out, you drop everything, hearing nothing else, even if God Himself should call you (say I, having just returned from dealing with my crying baby daughter). "No effort is too great, no cost too much, no price too dear" to save this pampered prince from the neighbors' slightest disrespectful remark, for only deepest reverence will do.

The problem, though, is that this is an imaginary son. He exists only as an image in your mind. Worse yet, you have a real son, who is so neglected that you have forgotten that he even exists. This real son is your creations in Heaven.

If this situation happened in earthly terms—if someone forgot about their actual child because they had become consumed with doting over an imaginary child—we would consider this the depths of madness. Yet in larger terms, this is the exact situation we are in.

2. The memory of God shines not alone. What is within your brother still contains <u>all</u> of creation, everything created and creating, born

150

and unborn as yet, still in the future or apparently gone by. What is in him is changeless, and your changelessness is recognized in its acknowledgment. The holiness in you belongs to him. And by your seeing it in him, returns to you. All of the tribute you have given specialness belongs to him, and thus returns to you. All of the love and care, the strong protection, the thought by day and night, the deep concern, the powerful conviction this is you, belong to him. Nothing you gave to specialness but is his due. And nothing due him is not due to you.

The memory of God shines in your brother, but not by itself. Along with it shines all of heavenly creation, everything that has been created and everything that will be created. All you need do is look on him, on his everlasting holiness, and you will see all this in yourself.

Application: In the final sentences, the idea of giving to our specialness what belongs to our creations changes to giving to our specialness what belongs to our brother. Choose someone in your life and repeat to yourself—*slowly*—the following lines:

> *All of the tribute I have given my specialness belongs to [name].*
> *All of the love and care I have given my specialness belongs to [name].*
> *All of the strong protection I have given my specialness belongs to [name].*
> *All of the thought by day and night that I have given my specialness belongs to [name].*
> *All of the deep concern that I have given my specialness belongs to [name].*
> *All of the powerful conviction that this is me that I have given my specialness belongs to [name].*
> *There is nothing I have given to specialness that is not [name's] due.*
> *And everything that I give to [name] returns to me.*

3. How can [Ur: will] you know your worth while specialness claims you instead? How can you fail to know it in his holiness? Seek not to make your specialness the truth, for if it were you would be lost indeed.

Be thankful, rather, it is given you to see his holiness *because* it is the truth. And what is true in him <u>must</u> be as true in you.

We are trying so hard to make our specialness the truth, in the firm conviction that this is how we find a sense of worth. Yet our brother's holiness is the truth, and seeing that is how we will really find a sense of worth.

> 4. Ask yourself this: <u>Can</u> *you* <u>protect the mind</u>? The body, yes, a little; not from time, but temporarily. And much you think you save, you hurt. What would you save it *for*? For in that choice lie both its health <u>and</u> harm. Save it for show, as bait to catch another fish, to house your specialness in better style, or weave a frame of loveliness around your hate, and you condemn it to decay and death. And if you see this purpose in your brother's, such is your condemnation of your own. Weave, rather, then, a frame of holiness around him, that the truth may shine on him, and give *you* safety from decay.

In trying to protect our specialness, we are trying to protect a very fragile and subjective image. But we are not this image. We are a mind. And how exactly do you protect a mind? It either *is* or it *isn't*. And if it *is*, what can anything do about that?

In trying to protect the image of our specialness, we generally try to protect another image: our body.

Application: Ask yourself the following questions and repeat the statements to yourself:

> *Am I trying to preserve my body for show?*
> *Am I trying to preserve my body as bait to catch another fish?*
> *Am I trying to preserve my body to house my specialness in better style?*
> *Am I trying to preserve my body as a lovely frame for my hateful specialness?*
> *If so, then I condemn it to decay.*
>
> *Do I see these purposes in the bodies of others?*
> *Do I take pleasure in the bodies that put themselves on show?*

Am I the fish that takes the bait?

Do I admire the beautiful house that houses someone's specialness?

Do I gaze on the lovely frame for someone's hateful specialness?

If so, then I condemn my own body to decay.

5. The Father keeps what He created [your mind] safe. You cannot touch it with the false ideas you made, because it was created not by you. Let not your foolish fancies frighten you. What is immortal cannot be attacked; what is but temporal has no effect. Only the purpose that you see in it has meaning, and if that is true, its safety rests secure. If not, it has no purpose, and is means for nothing. Whatever is perceived as means for truth shares in its holiness, and rests in light as safely as [truth] itself. Nor will that light go out when it [the temporal thing] is gone. Its holy purpose gave it immortality, setting another light in Heaven, where your creations recognize a gift from you, a sign that you have not forgotten them.

Our mind was created by God. Nothing that we do and nothing that is done to us can touch it. We try to convince ourselves it is special, which also implies that it is sinful. Yet none of our ideas about it have any effect on it whatsoever.

We try to convince ourselves that our body, too, is special (probably without success, for most of us). But unlike the mind, the body is totally meaningless. Only the purpose we see in it has any meaning. If we dedicate it to serve the purpose of specialness, then it becomes a reflection of its corrupt purpose and turns into a thing of corruption and decay. It ages and dies.

Yet there is another road we can take. We can dedicate our body to the purpose of truth. It can become a messenger of truth, not a piece of lovely bait on a hidden hook. Dedicated to the purpose of truth, it shares in the holiness of truth. "Now is the body holy" (W-pII.5.4:4), says the Workbook. Now, once it passes away, its light will not go out. It will be like one of those heroes of old who, once he dies, becomes one of the stars in the heavens. So will our body's light become one of the lights in Heaven. And as this new star takes its place in the heavenly firmament, our creations will exclaim in relief, "Thank God! We knew our father hadn't completely forgotten us."

6. The test of <u>everything</u> on earth is simply this; "What is it *for?*" The answer makes it what it <u>is</u> for you. It has <u>no</u> meaning of itself, yet you can <u>give</u> reality to it, according to the purpose that <u>you</u> serve. Here <u>you</u> are but means, along with it. God is a Means as well as End. In Heaven, means and end are one, and one with Him. This is the state of true creation, found not within time, but in eternity. To no one here is this describable. Nor is there any way to learn what this condition means. Not till you go <u>past</u> learning to the Given; not till you make again a holy home for <u>your</u> creations is it understood.

The meaning that we experience in all the objects and bodies around us is not in them, for they are completely devoid of meaning. Rather, it is in the purpose we assign to them.

Everything on earth, including our own activities, is a means to a greater purpose, a greater end. Yet in Heaven, means and end are not related in the same way as here. Indeed, they are not related at all. They are one. Thus, when God creates something, there is not the activity of creation and then the thing created. Those two things are exactly the same thing. If you are struggling to understand this, you can go ahead and give up. It can only be understood in Heaven. No one on earth has ever understood it or ever will.

Application: Look around the place you are in, and ask these two questions of several things that your eyes alight on:

> *What is this for in my eyes?*
> *Is it for enhancing my specialness or for serving God's plan of forgiveness?*

7. A co-creator with the Father must have a Son. Yet must this Son [of the co-creator] have been created like Himself [the co-creator].[:] A perfect being, all-encompassing and all-encompassed, nothing to add and nothing taken <u>from</u>; not born of size nor place nor time, nor held to limits or uncertainties of <u>any</u> kind. Here do the means and end unite as one, nor does this one have any end at all. All this is true, and yet it has no meaning to anyone who still retains one unlearned lesson in his memory, one thought with purpose still uncertain, or one wish with a divided aim.

Here is the only overt description of our creations in the Course. This is easily missed, both because the language is convoluted and because the creations are described in the singular as a "Son." Let me try to rephrase this paragraph to draw out its meaning:

If you are the Father's Son, and if you also create with Him, then you yourself must have a Son (created by you and God together). And this Son must have been created to be just like you: "a perfect being, all-encompassing and all-encompassed, nothing to add and nothing taken from, not born of size nor place nor time, nor held to limits or uncertainties of any kind." You were the means for this perfect being, yet the means (you) and the end (your Son) are one, and this one has no end at all. Though this is all perfectly true, it has no meaning to anyone who has one lesson left to learn, one thought with an uncertain purpose, "or one wish with a divided aim."

> 8. This course makes no attempt to teach what cannot easily be learned. Its scope does not exceed your own, except to say that what is yours will come to you when you are ready. Here are the means and the purpose separate because they were so made and so perceived. And therefore do we deal with them as if they were. It is essential it be kept in mind that <u>all</u> perception still is upside down until its <u>purpose</u> has been understood. Perception does not <u>seem</u> to be a means. And it is this that makes it hard to grasp the whole extent to which it <u>must</u> depend on what you see it <u>for</u>. Perception seems to <u>teach</u> you what you see. Yet it but witnesses to what <u>you</u> taught. It is the outward picture of a wish; an image that you <u>wanted</u> to be true.

At this point, we may be sorely tempted to make sense of the means and end being actually one. I can imagine long discussions about that. But we need to just let it go. The Course is not trying to teach us what is beyond us now, but rather what is easily within our reach. And so it talks about means and end as being separate, not because that is so, but because that is what makes sense to us.

One means that the Course returns to again and again is perception. Perception does not seem to be a means. It does not seem to be an instrument we use to reach a chosen end. It seems like a fact. It "seems to *teach* you what you see." But the truth is that our perception will change entirely if we see it as serving a different purpose.

9. Look at yourself, and you will see a body. Look at this body in a different light and it looks different. And without a light it seems that it is gone. Yet you are reassured that it is there because you still can feel it with your hands and hear it move. Here is an image that you <u>want</u> to be yourself [see the previous paragraph: "an image that you <u>wanted</u> to be true"]. It is the means to make your wish come true. It <u>gives </u>the eyes with which you look on it, the hands that feel it, and the ears with which you listen to the sounds it makes. <u>It proves its own reality to you.</u>

Now Jesus gives us an experiment to do:

Look at yourself, and you will see a body.
Look at this body in a different light and it looks different.
And without a light it seems that it is gone.
Yet you are reassured that it is there because you still can feel it with
  your hands and hear it move.

Okay, we can't dispute this, but what is his point here? His point is that we wanted to believe that this image, the body, is us. That was our goal. And so we invented the means to that goal. We invented the physical instruments that look on it and tell us it's real. How do we know it is real? Its eyes tell us it is. Its hands tell us it's there. Its ears listen to the sounds it makes. It's all rather circular, isn't it? Where exactly is the evidence for the body beyond the body's own word? It's as if we are saying, "I know that that hallucination I'm seeing is real because it just told me it is."

Now we can better understand his point that perception is a means we use to reach an end. We use the body's senses to reach our desired end of believing that the body is us.

10. Thus is the body made a <u>theory</u> of yourself, with <u>no</u> provisions made for evidence <u>beyond</u> itself, and <u>no</u> escape within its sight. Its course is sure, when seen through its own eyes. It grows and withers, flourishes and dies. And you cannot conceive of you <u>apart</u> from it. You brand it sinful and you hate its acts, judging it evil. Yet your specialness whispers, "Here is my own beloved son, in whom I am well pleased." Thus does the "son" become the <u>means</u> to serve his "father's" purpose. <u>Not</u> identical, not even like, but still a means to offer to the "father" <u>what he wants</u>. Such is the travesty on God's creation. For as His Son's creation gave <u>Him</u> joy and witness to <u>His</u> Love and shared <u>His</u> purpose,

so does the body testify to the idea that made it, and speak for its reality and truth.

The body is really a myth about ourselves. It is one of those sacred myths that no one dares question. It's like the Bible in some circles. "How do we know this happened?" "Because the Bible says it did." "How do we know the Bible is telling us the truth?" "Because the Bible says it is." We have a deeply ambivalent relationship with this body. We don't like it growing old. We believe that its instincts and desires make us do sinful things. Yet we also can't conceive of ourselves apart from it.

Yet while we look on it with ambivalence, a bat (rather than a dove) flutters down to it and a voice in the air says, "Here is my own beloved son, in whom I am well pleased." This is not the Voice of God announcing that Jesus is His Son, His chosen instrument in the world. This is the voice of our specialness, announcing that our body is its beloved son, its chosen instrument.

And now we understand why we are so attached to our physical senses. It is because they "prove" our body to be real, which in turn proves our *specialness* to be real. That is the goal for which physical perception is the means.

> 11. And thus are two sons [God's Son and your body] made, and both appear to walk this earth without a meeting place and no encounter. One [the body] do you perceive outside yourself, your own beloved son. The other [the real Son] rests within, his Father's Son, within your brother as he is in you. Their difference does not lie in how they look, nor where they go, nor even what they do. They have a different purpose [Ur: *They share a different purpose*]. It is this that joins them to their like, and separates each from all aspects with a different purpose. The Son of God retains his Father's Will. The son of man perceives an alien will [specialness] and wishes it were so. And thus does his perception [his body's senses] serve his wish by giving it appearances of truth. Yet can perception serve another goal. It is not bound to specialness but by your choice. And it is given you to make a different choice, and use perception for a different purpose. And what you see will serve that purpose well, and prove its own reality to you.

Now there are two sons. There is God's Son, which is who you really are. He walks this earth as the means to his Father's purpose. And there is

157

your body, the son of your specialness. It walks the earth as the means to your specialness. These two sons have nothing in common. They never really meet each other. Yet both of them present themselves as you. The essential way in which they differ is that they have a different purpose. One has the purpose of holiness, the other the purpose of specialness. One serves God's Will, the other serves the alien will of specialness.

While we serve the will of specialness, we will use perception on its behalf, and that means seeing the body as real, seeing our body as *us*. "Yet can perception serve *another* goal." If we choose a different purpose, "what you see will serve that purpose well, and prove its own reality to you." It will prove the reality of holiness to you.

Commentaries on Chapter 25

THE JUSTICE OF GOD

Introduction
Commentary by Robert Perry

1. The Christ in you inhabits <u>not</u> a body. Yet He <u>is</u> in you. And thus it <u>must</u> be that <u>you</u> are not within a body. What is within you <u>cannot</u> be outside. And it is certain that <u>you</u> cannot be <u>apart</u> from what is at the very <u>center</u> of your life. What gives you life cannot be housed in death. <u>No more can you.</u> Christ is within a frame of holiness whose <u>only</u> purpose is that He may be made manifest to those who know Him not, that He may call to them to come to Him and see Him where they <u>thought</u> their bodies were. Then will their bodies melt away, that they may frame His holiness in them.

Imagine if you said, "I have a memory of the pivotal event of my life. This memory is inside me. Indeed, it is at the very heart of me. It is inseparable from me. And yet this memory is *not* inside a body—any body." You immediately understand the implication: "*I* am not inside a body."

This memory, of course, corresponds to what this paragraph says about Christ. Christ is in you. He is the very center of your life. But He is not inside a body. How can life be housed in death? How can eternal divinity be framed in the corruptible? No, Christ is framed in holiness.

The image of a frame figures prominently in the next few sections, so let's talk about it a bit. A frame, of course, is a presentation device. It sets something off and thereby showcases it, making it more visible and hopefully more attractive. Our brother's holiness is the frame for Christ. It is what makes Christ "visible" to us. Seeing our brother's holiness will allow us to see Christ; we will see Him within the frame of our brother's holiness. And then He will call to us to come to Him, and see Him in us, instead of seeing us in our body. And then our body will melt away, as we ourselves become frames for Christ's holiness.

2. No one who carries Christ in him can fail to recognize Him everywhere. *Except* in <u>bodies</u>. And as long as he believes he is in a body [Ur: As long as they believe *they* are in bodies], where he thinks he is He cannot be [Ur: where they think they are He *cannot* be]. And

so he carries [Ur: they carry] Him unknowingly, and does [Ur: do] not make Him manifest. And thus he does [Ur: they do] not recognize Him where He <u>is</u>. The son of man is <u>not</u> the risen Christ. Yet does the Son of God abide <u>exactly</u> where he is, and walks with him within his holiness, as plain to see as is his specialness set forth within his body.

Right now, as we walk the world, we have two separate frames and two separate pictures. Our body is the frame for our specialness. The body is there to showcase our specialness. Our holiness is the frame for the Christ in us. If someone looks on our holiness, then he *will* see Christ, the Self that we all share. If, instead, someone looks on our body, then he will see our specialness—and that, of course, is usually our plan.

The same goes for us. If we see ourselves as residing in the frame of our body, then we will see ourselves as our specialness. We will see ourselves as that special person who is strutting around in that special body. Because we are looking at the wrong frame, we will not see the Christ, for He is not *in* that frame. You don't see Leonardo's *Mona Lisa* by looking at the frame for Van Gogh's *Starry Night*.

> 3. The body needs <u>no</u> healing. But the mind that thinks it <u>is</u> a body is sick indeed! And it is here that Christ sets forth the remedy. His <u>purpose</u> folds the body in His light, and fills it with the holiness that shines from <u>Him</u>. And nothing that the body says or does but makes <u>Him</u> manifest. To those who know Him not it carries Him in gentleness and love, to heal their minds. Such is the mission that your brother has for <u>you</u>. And such it <u>must</u> be that <u>your</u> mission is for <u>him</u>.

Just thinking that we live in a body means we are psychologically ill, and this illness will get projected onto the body in the form of physical illness. But we can mentally step outside the body and identify with Christ. Then our body will be dedicated to His purpose. As a result, it will become folded into His light. "Folded" here has the meaning it would have in a recipe book: "to incorporate (a food ingredient) into a mixture by repeated gentle overturnings without stirring or beating." Think about that in this context. Imagine your body being folded into His light. At that point, everything it did would shine with His light and so make Him manifest to others, even to those who look only upon the body.

162

I. The Link to Truth
Commentary by Robert Perry

1. It <u>cannot</u> be that it is hard to do the task that Christ appointed you to do, since it is <u>He</u> Who does it. And in the <u>doing</u> of it will you learn the body merely <u>seems</u> to be the means to do it. For the Mind is <u>His</u>. And so it <u>must</u> be yours. <u>His</u> holiness directs the body <u>through</u> the mind at one with Him. And <u>you</u> are manifest unto your holy brother, as he to you. Here is the meeting of the holy Christ unto Himself; nor <u>any</u> differences perceived to stand between the aspects of His holiness, which meet and join and raise Him to His Father, whole and pure and worthy of His everlasting Love.

Christ does give us tasks that must be carried out bodily in order to further His purpose in this world. A common response of ours to these tasks is, "This is too hard. This is too big. I am not up to this." But can it really be hard when you are not the one doing it? If your mind is at one with His, then His holiness will flow through your mind and direct your body—reminiscent of the early discussion of Jesus actually controlling our behavior (see T-2.VI.2:9). Can these tasks be that hard if He is actually moving our limbs for us?

When this happens, one aspect of the Christ—you—becomes manifest to another aspect of the Christ—your brother. Thus, two aspects of Christ "meet and join and raise [Christ, now restored to wholeness] to His Father, whole and pure and worthy of His everlasting Love."

2. How can you manifest the Christ in you <u>except</u> to look on holiness and see Him there? Perception tells you <u>you</u> are manifest in what you see. Behold the body, and you <u>will</u> believe that you are there. And every body that you look upon reminds you of yourself; <u>your</u> sinfulness, <u>your</u> evil and, above all, your <u>death</u>. And would you not despise the one who tells you this, and seek <u>his</u> death instead? The message and the messenger <u>are</u> one. And you <u>must</u> see your brother as yourself. Framed in his body you will see <u>your</u> sinfulness, wherein <u>you</u> stand condemned. Set in his holiness, the Christ in him proclaims <u>Himself</u> as you.

Jesus is telling us over and over that our whole mission on this earth is to manifest Christ. This sounds wonderful, even if quite lofty. But then the question arises: How do we make Christ manifest? The answer is, you have to see Christ framed in your brother's holiness. "Perception tells you *you* are manifest in what you see." If you look on the frame of your brother's holiness, you will see the Christ in him and recognize that you are looking on your Self. If you look on the frame of his body, you will see his sinful specialness, and be reminded of your own sinfulness, your evil, and your death. And then you'll shoot the messenger. You'll despise the one who reminded you of this. This hardly adds up to manifesting the Christ.

> 3. Perception is a choice of what you want <u>yourself</u> to be; the world you <u>want</u> to live in, and the state in which you think your mind will be content and satisfied. It chooses where you think your safety lies, <u>at your decision</u>. It reveals yourself to you as <u>you</u> would have you be. And <u>always</u> is it faithful to your purpose, from which it never separates, nor gives the slightest witness unto anything the purpose <u>in your mind</u> upholdeth not. Perception is a <u>part</u> of what it is your purpose to behold, for means and end are <u>never</u> separate. And thus you learn what <u>seems</u> to have a life <u>apart</u> has none.

Perception, as we were recently told, is a means. In other words, the world we see around us is a means. But what is the end? The end is a belief about ourselves. It is what we want to believe that we are. If we want to believe that we are special (end), we will see a world of bodies (means). If we want to believe that we are Christ (end), we will see a world of holiness (means). Since we all see bodies and are struggling to see even a glimmer of holiness, we would like to squirm out of this. Surely there must be a loophole, so that even though my purpose is to believe that I am Christ, I still see a world of bodies. Maybe it's because of painful life experiences that have scarred me. But Jesus says that there is no way around this. "Means and end are never separate." As means, your perception does not float eerily disconnected from your purpose. The two are in absolute lockstep.

> 4. *You* are the means for God; <u>not</u> separate, nor with a life apart from His. <u>His</u> Life is manifest in you who are His Son. Each aspect

of Himself [an aspect being a Son] is framed in holiness and perfect purity, [is framed in] in love celestial and [love] so complete [that] it [the aspect] wishes <u>only</u> that it may release <u>all</u> that it looks upon unto itself [so that all it looks upon can behold it—its true nature, the Christ]. Its radiance shines through each body that it looks upon, and brushes <u>all</u> its darkness into light merely by looking <u>past</u> it *to* the light. The veil is lifted through its gentleness, and <u>nothing</u> hides the face of Christ from its beholders. You and your brother stand [Ur: And *both* of you stand there,] before Him now, to let <u>Him</u> draw aside the veil that <u>seems</u> to keep you separate and apart.

This paragraph is not an easy one to follow. Let me paraphrase it. You are a means for God, an aspect of God, whose calling here is to make God manifest. As an aspect of Him, your true nature (as Christ) is framed in holiness and in celestial love. This love in you is so complete that all you really want is to release everyone from blindness, to open their eyes so that they can look on the Christ in you. The radiance of your true nature shines through each body that you look on, brushing all that body's darkness into light merely by looking past it *to* the light. This lifts the veil that had blocked that person's sight, so that now he can gaze in wonder on the face of Christ in you.

> 5. Since you believe that <u>you</u> are separate, Heaven presents itself to you as separate, too. <u>Not</u> that it is in truth, but that the link that has been given you to <u>join</u> the truth may reach to you through what you understand. Father and Son and Holy Spirit are as One, as all your brothers join as one in truth. Christ and His Father <u>never</u> have been separate, and Christ abides within your understanding, in the part of you that <u>shares</u> His Father's Will. The Holy Spirit links the other part—the tiny, mad desire to be separate, different and special—<u>to</u> the Christ, to make the oneness clear to what is <u>really</u> one. In this world this is not understood, but <u>can</u> be taught.

The previous section told us that we simply cannot understand how means and end are completely one in reality, and so the Course must talk to us as if means and end are separate. Now this section tells us that we are a means for God—He is the End. As His means, we cannot be separate from Him. But we cannot understand that in this world. And so Heaven presents itself to us as if it were separate. It needs to do this in order to reach us through what we understand.

Imagine that the one hundred most spiritually advanced people currently on the planet come up to you, and they all say, "We used to believe in a Holy Spirit that was somehow distinct from us and could guide us and make plans for us and all that. But then we came to understand that we are not separate from the Holy Spirit, or from God, or all our brothers and sisters. So we no longer relate to the Holy Spirit as a 'Him.' Now we realize that 'He' is us."

Question: How many of them do you estimate are telling you the truth?

Answer: None of them are. As long as they are in this world, it is impossible to understand the oneness of Heaven. As long as they are in this world, they need a Holy Spirit Who presents Himself as separate (at least to some degree) and Who leads them to the point at which they transcend this world altogether. *Then* they will understand oneness.

> 6. The Holy Spirit serves Christ's purpose in your mind, so that the aim of specialness <u>can</u> be corrected where the error lies. Because His purpose still is one with both the Father <u>and</u> the Son, He <u>knows</u> the Will of God and what you <u>really</u> will. But this is understood by mind <u>perceived</u> as one, <u>aware</u> that it is one, <u>and so experienced</u>. It is the Holy Spirit's function to teach you <u>how</u> this oneness is experienced, <u>what</u> you must do that it can <u>be</u> experienced, and <u>where</u> you should go to do it.

The Holy Spirit knows what we can't know right now. He knows the oneness of Heaven. He knows God's Will and our own true will. His job is to come from that place of oneness into the mind that believes in specialness. He doesn't try to teach that mind oneness, because that mind simply can't understand that. What He does is lead that mind towards the memory of oneness. He tells the mind what it must do and where it must go to journey to the final experience of perfect oneness.

> 7. All this takes note of time and place <u>as if</u> they were discrete, for while <u>you</u> think that part of <u>you</u> is separate, the concept of a oneness <u>joined</u> as one is meaningless. It is apparent that a mind so split could <u>never</u> be the teacher of a Oneness Which unites <u>all</u> things within Itself. And so What <u>is</u> within this mind, and <u>does</u> unite all things together,

<u>must</u> be its Teacher. Yet must It use the language that this mind can understand, in the condition in which it <u>thinks</u> it is. And It must use all learning to transfer illusions <u>to</u> the truth, taking all <u>false</u> ideas of what you are, and leading you <u>beyond</u> them to the truth that *is* beyond them. All this can very simply be reduced to this:

What is the same can not be different, and what is one can not have separate parts.

We can't be our own teacher of oneness. That role is reserved for the Holy Spirit in our mind. He tells us what to do and where to go, speaking as if there really were such things as different places and different times. He speaks our language, even though it is not His Own. He addresses the condition we think we are in, even though He knows our true condition is something else altogether. In doing all these things, He leads us down a long road in which we walk past a succession of different false images of ourselves, until finally at the end, we have passed them all and take one last step into the truth that lies beyond them. And at last we *know* that we are what God is, what the Holy Spirit is, what Christ is, what all our brothers are. We realize that this oneness does not allow for us being a separate part, that we are the same as everything else in Heaven.

II. The Savior from the Dark
Commentary by Robert Perry

1. Is it not evident that what the body's eyes perceive <u>fills you with fear</u>? Perhaps you think you find a hope of satisfaction there. Perhaps you fancy to attain some peace and satisfaction in the world as <u>you</u> perceive it. Yet it <u>must</u> be evident the outcome <u>does not change</u>. Despite your hopes and fancies, <u>always</u> does despair result. And there is <u>no</u> exception, nor will there ever be. The <u>only</u> value that the past can hold is that you learn it gave you <u>no</u> rewards which you would <u>want</u> to keep. For only thus will you be <u>willing</u> to relinquish it, and have it gone forever.

Application: The first three paragraphs of this section require no explanation. But they do require careful, personal reading. So please go ahead and do that. Read each line separately as I have laid it out below. Read it slowly as if it is written directly to you. And read it with the help of the comments and questions I have put in brackets. I have left in the emphasis from the Urtext.

Is it not evident that what the body's eyes perceive *fills you with fear*? [Look around the room, take note of the fear associated with each object.]

Perhaps you think you find a hope of satisfaction there. [Isn't this true?]

Perhaps you fancy to attain some peace and satisfaction in the world as *you* perceive it. [Do you?]

Yet it *must* be evident the outcome *does not change*. Despite your hopes and fancies, *always* does despair result. [Isn't it true that countless disappointments have meant that you are not able to raise your hopes as high as you used to?]

And there is *no* exception, nor will there ever be. [Can you accept this?]

The *only* value that the past [your past search for happiness] can hold

168

is that you learn it gave you *no* rewards which you would *want* to keep. [Does this seem true?]

For only thus will you be *willing* to relinquish it, and have it gone forever. [Wouldn't it be wonderful to be free of the past?]

> 2. Is it not strange that you should cherish still some hope of satisfaction from the world you see? In <u>no</u> respect, at <u>any</u> time or place, has <u>anything</u> but fear and guilt been your reward. How long is needed for you to realize the chance of <u>change</u> in this respect is hardly worth delaying change that might result in better outcome? For one thing is sure; the way <u>you</u> see, and long <u>have</u> seen, gives <u>no</u> support to base your future hopes, and <u>no</u> suggestions of success at all. To place your hopes where no hope lies <u>must</u> make you hopeless. Yet is this hopelessness your choice, while you would seek for hope where none is <u>ever</u> found.

Is it not strange that you should cherish still some hope of satisfaction from the world you see? [Hear Jesus asking you this.]

In *no* respect, at *any* time or place, has *anything* but fear and guilt been your reward [though sometimes disguised as pleasure].

How long is needed for you to realize the chance of *change* in this respect is hardly worth delaying change that might result in better outcome? [How will it take you to give up on this losing horse and try something more promising?]

For one thing is sure; the way *you* see, and long *have* seen, gives *no* support to base your future hopes, and *no* suggestions of success at all. [You have been hoping for luck, haven't you?]

To place your hopes where no hope lies *must* make you hopeless. [Can you see the logic of this? Has this happened in your own life?]

Yet is this hopelessness your choice, while you would seek for hope where none is *ever* found. [If you are hopeless, haven't you chosen it by placing your hopes where no hope lies?]

> 3. Is it not <u>also</u> true that you have found some hope <u>apart</u> from this; some glimmering,—inconstant, wavering, yet dimly seen,—that hopefulness <u>is</u> warranted on grounds that are <u>not</u> in this world? And yet your hope that they may <u>still</u> be here prevents you still from giving up the hopeless and unrewarding task you set <u>yourself</u>. Can it make sense to hold the fixed belief that there <u>is</u> reason to uphold pursuit of what has

<u>always</u> failed, on grounds that it will suddenly succeed and bring what it has <u>never</u> brought before?

Is it not *also* true that you have found some hope *apart* from this; some glimmering— inconstant, wavering, yet dimly seen—that hopefulness *is* warranted on grounds that are *not* in this world? [Isn't this true? Isn't this exactly what the Course has brought you?]
And yet your hope that they [the grounds for hopefulness] may *still* be here [in the happenings of this world] prevents you still from giving up the hopeless and unrewarding task you set *yourself* [and fully devoting yourself to the Course's way].
Can it make sense to hold the fixed belief that there *is* reason to uphold pursuit of what has *always* failed, on grounds that it will suddenly succeed and bring what it has *never* brought before? [Ask yourself this.]

4. Its [your pursuit of happiness's] past *has* failed. Be glad that it is gone within your mind, to darken what <u>is</u> there. Take not the form for content, for the form is but a <u>means</u> for content. And the frame is but a means to hold the picture up, so that it can be seen. A frame that <u>hides</u> the picture <u>has</u> no purpose. It cannot <u>be</u> a frame if <u>it</u> is what you see. <u>Without</u> the picture is the frame without its meaning. Its <u>purpose</u> is to set the <u>picture</u> off, and <u>not</u> itself.

The message I see in this paragraph is this: Do not mistake the hopeful forms of this world (specifically, the body) for the hopeless content they actually deliver. The forms are only the frame for the content. Yet unlike these forms, a frame is supposed to *present* its picture, not hide it.

This talk of frame and picture sounds very much like "The Two Pictures" in Chapter 17, where we seek for love by going after bodies, not realizing that they are just the frame for the picture of death.

This search has gotten us into trouble time and again, yet we can be glad, for what really drives this search was uprooted when we joined with our brother. Now, only the *habit* of looking for love in bodies remains. This habit is like a fan that is still spinning even after it has been unplugged. Its momentum is keeping it going, but only for so long. And that is why we can genuinely, as Jesus says, "be glad."

5. Who hangs an empty frame upon a wall and stands before it, deep in reverence, as if a masterpiece were there to see? Yet if you see your brother as a body, it is but this you do. The masterpiece that God has set within this frame is all there is to see. The body holds it for a while, without obscuring it in any way. Yet what God has created needs no frame, for what He has created He supports and frames within Himself. His masterpiece He offers you to see. And would you rather see the frame instead of this? And see the picture not at all?

Imagine someone standing before an empty frame on a wall, "deep in reverence, as if a masterpiece were there to see." It's a ludicrous image. Yet that is what we are doing when we see our brother as a body. The body is just a frame, nothing more. The only thing really worth seeing is the masterpiece that God set in this frame. Yet the body is not this masterpiece's *real* frame. *God* is its real frame. How exactly would you put a nonphysical masterpiece into a physical frame? How can you have a 36 X 44 rectangular infinite spirit?

Application: Picture yourself looking on someone's beautiful body. Now realize that you are gazing on an empty frame, as if a masterpiece were there to see. Now say to yourself,

> *The only thing worth seeing here is this person's reality.*
> *For this person's reality is God's masterpiece,*
> *the work that reveals all of His limitless creativity.*

6. The Holy Spirit is the frame God set around the part of Him that you would see as separate. Yet its frame is joined to its Creator, one with Him and with His masterpiece. This is its purpose, and you do not make the frame into the picture when you choose to see it in its [proper] place. The frame that God has given it but serves His purpose, not yours apart from His. It is your separate purpose that obscures the picture, and cherishes the frame [of the body] instead of it. Yet God has set His masterpiece within a frame [the Holy Spirit] that will endure forever, when yours has crumbled into dust. But think you not the picture is destroyed in any way. What God creates is safe from all corruption, unchanged and perfect in eternity.

Who would ever think of saying that the frame we are within is the Holy Spirit? And yet, what frame we see ourselves in makes a huge difference. You can test this out for yourself. First, think of someone close to you and say,

> *You are a picture set in the frame of your body.*

Now think of that same person and say,

> *You are a picture set in the frame of the Holy Spirit Himself,*
> *a frame that is joined to its Creator.*

Notice how, without saying anything about the picture, the person seems different depending on which frame he or she is seen in.

7. Accept God's [Ur: *His*] frame instead of yours, and you <u>will</u> see the masterpiece. Look at its loveliness, and understand the Mind that thought it, <u>not</u> in flesh and bones, but in a frame as lovely as Itself. Its holiness lights up the sinlessness the frame of darkness hides, and casts a veil of light across the picture's face which but reflects the light that shines from it to its Creator. Think not this face was ever darkened because <u>you</u> saw it in a frame of death. God kept it safe that <u>you</u> might look on it, and <u>see</u> the holiness that He has given it.

Application: Choose a person, and see before you two frames for this person. One is the body, a frame of flesh and bones, a frame of death (you might want to visualize it as a jumbled mass of rotting flesh and bones). This frame is so dark you cannot see any picture within it. The other is the Holy Spirit, a frame of pure and radiant light. It contains God's masterpiece. This masterpiece is a face like none you have ever seen, a face that is beauty and sinlessness itself, the majestic face of Christ. With this image in mind, go through the paragraph and try to experience each sentence.

Accept God's frame [the Holy Spirit] instead of yours [this person's body], and you will see the masterpiece [this person's reality,

172

which will make you want to kneel at his or her feet.]
Look at its loveliness, and understand the Mind that thought it, not in
flesh and bones, but in a frame [the Holy Spirit] as lovely as Itself.
[Do your best to carry out this instruction.]
Its [the frame's] holiness lights up the sinlessness the frame of darkness
[the body] hides, and casts a veil of light across the picture's face
[the face of Christ, the symbol of this person's true Identity] which
but reflects the light that shines from it to its Creator.
Think not this face [the face of Christ, the face of who this person
really is] was ever darkened because you saw it in [the body] a
frame of death.
God kept it safe that you might look on it, and see the holiness that
He has given it.

8. Within the darkness see the savior *from* the dark, and understand your
brother as his Father's Mind shows him to you. He will step forth from
darkness as you look on him, and you will see the dark no more. The
darkness touched him not, nor you who brought him forth for you to
look upon. His sinlessness but pictures yours. His gentleness becomes
your strength, and both will gladly look within, and see the holiness
that must be there because of what you looked upon in him. He is the
frame in which your holiness is set, and what God gave him must be
given you. However much he overlooks the masterpiece in him and
sees only a frame of darkness, it is still your only function to behold in
him what he sees not. And in this seeing is the vision shared that looks
on Christ instead of seeing death.

Application: Choose someone, perhaps the same person as in the
previous exercise, and make him the focus of the following visualization:

Within the darkness of the world of bodies, see your brother as he
really is, as God's radiant masterpiece.
See him step forth, stepping through the frame of the body, shining
with blazing light.
The light is so bright that it is now all you can see.
The dark world of bodies behind it is no longer visible.

173

Your brother has become your savior from the dark.

Realize that the masterpiece of light you see before you is a picture of your own sinlessness.

The beautiful face of Christ you see in this light is your own true face.

For everything that God gave this brother, He must also have given you.

You, too, are God's masterpiece.

And since you and your brother are the same, what could the two of you do but unite, and look within upon the holiness that God gave both of you, discovering that both of you are the Christ?

9. How could the Lord of Heaven <u>not</u> be glad if you appreciate His masterpiece? What <u>could</u> He do but offer thanks to you who love His Son as He does? Would He not make <u>known</u> to you His Love, if you but <u>share</u> His praise of what He loves? God cherishes creation as the perfect Father that He is. And so His joy is made complete when any part of Him <u>joins</u> in His praise, to <u>share</u> His joy. This brother is His perfect gift to you. And He is glad and thankful when you thank His perfect Son for being what he <u>is</u>. And <u>all</u> His thanks and gladness shine on you who would <u>complete</u> His joy, along with Him. And thus is <u>yours</u> completed. Not one ray of darkness can be seen by those who will to make their Father's happiness complete, and theirs along with His. The gratitude of God Himself is freely offered to everyone who shares His purpose. It is not His Will to be alone. And neither is it <u>yours</u>.

This whole paragraph turns on the familiar image of an artist who has completed his masterpiece and loves it, and who wants others to appreciate and praise it, too. And when they do, his joy is complete, and so he thanks them and overflows with love for them.

It is amazing when you realize how Jesus is applying this image. God is the artist, our brother is His masterpiece, and we are the viewers. Try to take this seriously. Imagine that your brother really is God's masterpiece, into which He poured all of His infinite creativity. This masterpiece is so perfect that God loves it with all His Heart. Like any artist, He yearns for others to see its perfection, too, and appreciate and praise it along with Him. And when they do, His joy is made complete, and then "all His thanks and gladness shine on you who would complete His joy."

10. Forgive your brother, and you <u>cannot</u> separate yourself from him nor from his Father. <u>You</u> need <u>no</u> forgiveness, for the wholly pure have never sinned. Give [to your brother], then, what He has given you [the recognition of sinlessness], that <u>you</u> may see His Son as one, and thank his [the Son's] Father as He [the Father] thanks <u>you</u>. Nor [And do not] believe that all His praise is given not to you. For what you give [the recognition of sinlessness] is <u>His</u>, and giving it, you learn to understand His gift to you. And give the Holy Spirit what He offers unto the Father <u>and</u> the Son alike. Nothing has power over you <u>except</u> His Will <u>and</u> yours, which but extends [Ur: who but *extend*] His Will. It was for this <u>you</u> were created, and your brother <u>with</u> you and at <u>one</u> with you.

This paragraph is a plea to give your brother the gift of forgiveness, the recognition that he is wholly pure because he never sinned. Only then will you believe that this is true of you, that you are wholly pure and have never sinned, and that you are one with both your brother and your Father. Then will you rediscover the reason you and your brother were created: to limitlessly extend the Will of God, which is one with yours.

11. You and your brother [Ur: *You*] are the same as God Himself is One, and <u>not</u> divided in His Will. And <u>you</u> must have one purpose, since He gave the same to <u>both</u> of you. His Will is brought together as you join in will, that <u>you</u> be made complete by offering completion to your brother. See not in him the sinfulness <u>he</u> sees, but give him honor that you may esteem yourself <u>and</u> him. To you and your brother [Ur: To each of you] is given the power of salvation, that escape from darkness into light be yours to share; that you may see as one what never <u>has</u> been separate, nor apart from <u>all</u> God's Love as given equally.

The two of us are each a part of God's Will. We therefore are one, and were each given the exact same purpose. That is why "His Will is brought together as you join in will." It is as if when we join, the scattered parts of God's Will come back together. Now His Will, reassembled, has real power on earth. Yet before the two of us can truly exercise this power, we need to save each other. I need to look past the sinfulness you see in yourself and give you the honor that is due God's masterpiece. And you need to do the same for me. God has commissioned us to be each other's savior. That is our calling. And when we at last answer this calling, we will "see as one what never has been separate."

III. Perception and Choice
Commentary by Greg Mackie

1. To the extent to which you value guilt, to that extent will you perceive a world in which attack is justified. To the extent to which you recognize that guilt is meaningless, to that extent you will perceive attack cannot *be* justified. This is in accord with perception's [Ur: vision's] <u>fundamental</u> law: You see what you believe is there, and you believe it there because you <u>want</u> it there. Perception <u>has</u> no other law than this. The rest but stems from this, to hold it up and offer it support. This is perception's form, adapted to this world, of God's more basic law; that love creates itself, and nothing <u>but</u> itself.

In Heaven, God's law is the law of extension: Love wants to extend, so it *does* extend outward in creation. When we seemed to separate, though, that law was adapted to become "perception's fundamental law," which is essentially a law of projection: What we want to see we project outward and see it in the world.

If we want guilt, we will see a world in which our attack on it is justified, because "guilt is the result of attack" (T-13.I.11:1). We see a world that gives us a rationale for attack—"Look at what she did to me! How can I let her get away with that?"—and we attack, thus accumulating the guilt we want. But if we realize that guilt is meaningless and totally undesirable, we'll see that nothing the world "does" to us is a justification for attack at all.

2. God's laws do not obtain directly to a world perception rules, for such a world could not have been created by the Mind to which perception has no meaning. Yet are His laws reflected everywhere. <u>Not</u> that the world where this reflection is, is real at all. <u>Only</u> because His Son <u>believes</u> it is, and from His Son's belief He <u>could</u> not let Himself be separate entirely. He could not enter His Son's insanity with him, but He could be sure His sanity went there <u>with</u> him, so he could not be lost forever in the madness of his wish.

God's laws in their pure form do not apply to this illusory world at all. But when we made the world, He didn't just blithely ignore what

176

happened or say, "My laws are just too pure to be sullied by that mess you made." He *responded*, because He loves His Son so much that He couldn't let him separate completely. His response was to *adapt* His laws to this world, so that even in his madness the Son had a way out of madness, a way to return to sanity. We'll see how this works as the section proceeds.

> 3. Perception rests on choosing; knowledge does not. Knowledge has but one law <u>because</u> it has but one Creator. But this world has two who made it, and they do <u>not</u> see it as the same. To each it has a <u>different</u> purpose, and to each it is a perfect means to serve the goal for which it is perceived. For specialness, it is the perfect frame to set it off; the perfect battleground to wage its wars, the perfect shelter for [Ur: the] illusions which it would make real. Not one [illusion] but it upholds in its perception; not one but can be fully justified.

Knowledge does not involve choice at all; it is completely one. But perception does involve choice: the choice is between two options, two "makers" of the world. This choice is crucial because the two makers see the world very differently and have very different goals for it.

The first maker is "specialness." When we value specialness, we see a world in which our attack is justified in the name of defending our specialness. This world *is* soaked in the quest for specialness, is it not? From the dating game to the corporate rat race to wars between nations to spiritual teachers showing off their great attainments, everybody's trying to be the top dog at something. This world of differences is the perfect place for endless competition to decide which differences are *better*. And thus it seems to be a world where God's loving laws are forever banished.

> 4. There is another Maker of the world, the simultaneous Corrector of the mad belief that <u>anything</u> could be established and maintained without some link that kept it still within the laws of God; <u>not</u> as the law itself upholds the universe as God created it, but in some form adapted to the need the Son of God believes he has. Corrected error <u>is</u> the error's end. And thus has God protected still His Son, even in error.

The second Maker is the Holy Spirit, Who corrects our mad belief that God's loving laws have been banished. He does this by showing us that even in this world, God's laws apply in adapted form. Thus our erroneous belief that this world is a battleground for specialness is corrected by God's loving Voice. And "corrected error is the error's end."

I think the "world" made by the Holy Spirit here is primarily the real world, the nonphysical world of forgiveness and love revealed by the eyes of Christ. Yet based on the early Urtext material which suggested that God created the world as a teaching device to free us from separation, I think this section may also be referring to the Holy Spirit's remaking of the physical world. We made this world as an "attack on God" (W-pII.3.2:1), a hell from which we could never escape. But the Holy Spirit simultaneously remade it into a place where we could learn the means of escape. "Thus has God protected still His Son, even in error." He gave us a doorway *out* of error.

> 5. There is another purpose in the world that error made, because it has another Maker Who can reconcile its goal with His Creator's purpose. In His perception of the world, nothing is seen but justifies forgiveness and the sight of perfect sinlessness. Nothing arises but is met with instant and complete forgiveness. Nothing remains an instant, to obscure the sinlessness that shines unchanged, beyond the pitiful attempts of specialness to put it out of mind, where it must be, and light the body up instead of it. The lamps of Heaven are not for mind [Ur: it] to choose to see them where it will. If it elects to see them elsewhere from their home, as if they lit a place where they could never be, [Ur: and you agree,] then must the Maker of the world correct your error, lest you remain in darkness where the lamps are not.

The other Maker, the Holy Spirit, "makes" another world by giving the world that error made another purpose. Remember, our specialness made the world to be a place where attack is justified in the name of defending our specialness. This serves the ego's purpose of compounding sin and accumulating guilt. The star attraction in this quest for specialness is the body, which the ego spotlights like a swiveling rock star. "Look at me! Look at me!"

The Holy Spirit's purpose for the world is the exact opposite. His purpose is to restore our awareness of sinlessness, so in His eyes, the world is a place where only *forgiveness* is justified. He shows us that real light comes not from our pitiful attempts to spotlight the body but from the sinlessness of the "lamps of Heaven."

6. Everyone here has entered darkness, yet no one has entered it alone. Nor need he stay more than an instant. For he has come with Heaven's Help within him, ready to lead him <u>out</u> of darkness into light at <u>any</u> time. The time he chooses can be <u>any</u> time, for help is there, awaiting but his choice. And when he chooses to <u>avail</u> himself of what is given him, then will he see each situation that he thought before was means to justify his anger turned to an event which justifies his love. He will hear plainly that the calls to war he heard before are really calls to peace. He will perceive that where he gave attack is but another altar where he can, with equal ease and <u>far</u> more happiness, bestow forgiveness. And he will reinterpret <u>all</u> temptation as just another chance to bring him joy.

The "light" of this world is really darkness, but the other Maker of the world is here to lead us from the darkness to real light at any time. We don't have to wait; He's ready whenever we choose to let Him in. And when we make this choice, every situation in our lives will be transformed. Having abandoned the quest for specialness and accepted the Holy Spirit's purpose for the world instead, we will see every situation that seemed to justify attack become a situation that justifies complete forgiveness.

Application: Think of a situation in your life in which you are tempted to attack another person, a situation where you are harboring unforgiveness. Then, apply these words:

I have seen this situation as a justification for attack.
But when I choose to avail myself of the Holy Spirit's help, I will see this situation transformed
from one that justifies anger to one that justifies love, from a call to war to a call to peace, from a battleground where I attack to an altar where I bestow forgiveness, from a temptation to accumulate sin and guilt to a chance to bring myself joy.
Holy Spirit, I choose to avail myself of your help right now.

7. How <u>can</u> a misperception be a sin? Let <u>all</u> your brother's errors be to you nothing except a chance for <u>you</u> to see the workings of the Helper given <u>you</u> to see the world <u>He</u> made instead of yours. What, then, *is*

justified? <u>What do you want?</u> For these two questions <u>are</u> the same. And when you see them <u>as</u> the same, your choice is made. For it is <u>seeing</u> them as one that brings release from the belief there are two ways to see. This world has much to offer to your peace, and many chances to extend your own forgiveness. Such its <u>purpose</u> is, to those who <u>want</u> to see peace and forgiveness descend on <u>them</u>, and offer <u>them</u> the light.

When we see the world's purpose as being to inflate our specialness, another person's loss becomes our gain. The more sin and guilt we see in our brother, the more "innocent" (and therefore special) we feel. When we look at the world this way, it seems that the answers to the two questions in the third and fourth sentences are different: I want innocence for myself, so attack on others for their "sins" is justified.

But this violates perception's fundamental law. That law says that I see in the world what I want to see—not just in the world, but in *myself.* So, if I want innocence in myself, I must see innocence in the other person as well. I must give the same answer to both of those questions. What do I want? Forgiveness for myself. What, then, *is* justified? Only forgiveness of my brother.

Seeing the answers to these two questions as the same enables us to recognize that we cannot see our brother in one way and ourselves in another—both of us must be seen in one way, the Holy Spirit's way. This is the invitation to the Holy Spirit to show us His world, in which nothing is justified but forgiveness. This enables us to see every situation as an opportunity for us to extend forgiveness so we can experience forgiveness for ourselves. This is how the Holy Spirit uses the law of perception that He adapted from Heaven's law to save us.

8. The Maker of the world of gentleness has perfect power to offset the world of violence and hate that <u>seems</u> to stand <u>between</u> you and His gentleness. It is not there in His forgiving eyes. And <u>therefore</u> it need not be there in yours. Sin is the fixed belief perception <u>cannot</u> change. What has been damned <u>is</u> damned and damned forever, <u>being forever unforgivable.</u> If, then, it <u>is</u> forgiven, sin's perception <u>must</u> have been wrong. And thus is change made possible. The Holy Spirit, too, sees what <u>He</u> sees as far beyond the chance of change. But on His vision sin cannot [Ur: can *not*] encroach, for sin <u>has been</u> corrected by His sight. And thus <u>it must have been an error, not</u> a sin. For what it

claimed could never be [change/correction], <u>has been</u>. Sin is <u>attacked</u> by punishment, and so <u>preserved</u>. But to <u>forgive</u> it is to change its state from error into truth.

As long as we believe in sin—in real attack that causes real harm—we will believe that what has happened is forever unchangeable and unforgivable. This is the big obstacle to forgiveness, right? "How can I forgive the man who killed my daughter? She's dead, and she's not coming back. What he's done can never be erased." We hope punishment of the offender will bring closure and a sense of relief, but all it does is cement the sin into place.

But the Holy Spirit sees beyond all this to something *truly* changeless: our eternal reality, totally unaffected by the "world of violence and hate" that seems to surround us. When the apparently unchangeable world of sin met His vision of our sinless reality, sin was corrected and undone. This proves that sin is not a real attack that causes real harm, but an unreal error with no effects. Only gentleness is real in His eyes. Therefore, we are not condemned to see a world of sin that can never change; the choice to see His world of gentleness is in our power to make. We have the power to forgive anything and anyone, even the man who killed our daughter. Isn't this great news?

> 9. The Son of God could <u>never</u> sin, but he <u>can</u> wish for what would hurt him. And he <u>has</u> the power to think he <u>can be</u> hurt. What could this be <u>except</u> a misperception of himself? Is this a sin or a mistake, forgivable or not? Does he need help or condemnation? Is it <u>your</u> purpose that he be saved or damned? Forgetting not that what he is to <u>you</u> will make this choice <u>your</u> future? For you <u>make it</u> *now*, the instant when <u>all</u> time becomes a means to reach a goal. Make, then, your choice. But recognize that in this choice the purpose of the world you see is chosen, and <u>will</u> be justified.

People can do crazy things. The world we see *is* a world of violence and hate. We are so bent on attacking others that we're blind to the fact that we're really trying to attack and destroy *ourselves*. But because of the law of perception—you see what you want to see—the choice of whether to see this as a mortal sin or a forgivable mistake is in our hands. Will we pursue specialness and see a world that justifies our attack, or will we listen to the Holy Spirit and see a world that justifies our forgiveness? The choice we make now will determine our goal, and will thus determine what is justified in our sight.

Application: Think of someone who has done something you find difficult to forgive. Now, make your choice with the following words:

> *Is what [name] has done a sin or a mistake, forgivable or not?*
> *Does he need help or condemnation?*
> *Do I want him to be saved or damned?*

> *Whichever choice I make will become my future as well.*
> *Are the things I regret doing sins or mistakes, forgivable or not?*
> *Do I need help or condemnation?*
> *Do I want to be saved or damned?*

> *I want to see the things I regret doing as forgivable mistakes.*
> *I need help.*
> *I want to be saved.*

> *So, Holy Spirit, I choose now to forgive [name].*
> *I choose now to see the world You made instead of mine,*
> *for thus will I experience forgiveness for myself.*

IV. The Light You Bring
Commentary by Greg Mackie

1. Minds that are joined <u>and recognize they are</u>, can feel no guilt. For they can<u>not</u> attack, and they <u>rejoice</u> that this is so, seeing their safety in this happy fact. Their joy is in the <u>innocence</u> they see. And thus they seek for it, because it is their <u>purpose</u> to behold it and rejoice. Everyone seeks for what will bring him joy as he defines it. It is <u>not</u> the aim, as such, that varies. Yet it <u>is</u> the way in which the aim is seen that makes the choice of means inevitable, and beyond the hope of change <u>unless the aim is changed</u>. And <u>then</u> the means are chosen once again, as what will bring rejoicing is defined <u>another</u> way and sought for differently.

We all seek for joy as we define it, and the means we choose to acquire it depend on how we define it. If joy for me is the heavenly taste of glazed donuts, I'm going to make a lot of trips to Krispy Kreme. According to the Course, one of the great sources of joy on our eyes is acquiring false "innocence" at others' expense, so we attack them for the "sins" we see in them. The actual effect of this is to acquire more guilt for ourselves, which is what brings the ego joy.

Those who recognize minds are joined, however, realize that precisely *because* minds are joined, they can't really attack at all—how can they attack without separation, without an "attacker" and an "attackee"? Therefore, they are innocent, as is everyone. What a joyous realization! They understand that only universal innocence brings joy, so with this new definition of joy, they now seek innocence instead of sin in the world. This is the real source of joy and safety.

2. Perception's basic law could thus be said, "You <u>will</u> rejoice at what you see <u>because</u> you see it <u>to</u> rejoice." And while you think that suffering and sin will bring you joy, so long will they be there for you to see. Nothing is harmful or beneficent <u>apart</u> from what you wish. It is your wish that <u>makes</u> it what it is in its effects on you. <u>Because</u> you chose it as a means to <u>gain</u> these same effects, believing them to be the bringers of rejoicing and of joy. Even in Heaven does this law obtain. The Son of God creates to bring him joy, sharing his Father's purpose

in his own creation, that his joy might be increased, and God's along with his.

In the last section, perception's basic law was defined this way: "You see what you believe is there, and you believe it there because you want it there" (T-25.III.1:3). The rephrasing here emphasizes that we want it there because we think it will bring us joy. As long as we are identified with the ego, we think sin and suffering bring us joy, so we project them from our minds out into the world. This is a truly twisted system, but the law behind it is actually an adapted form of Heaven's law of creation: We extend our minds in creation as God extended His when He created us, in order to experience *real* joy.

Application: Think of some example of sin or suffering you see in the world. Most likely, this does not bring you joy on the surface (though it may, especially if it happens to someone you don't like). Yet consider the possibility that even in those cases where you don't experience joy on the surface, deep down you really do find a perverse joy in it. Say, *"I will rejoice at this [example of sin and suffering]* **because** *I see it to rejoice."*

> 3. You maker [Ur: makers] of a world that is not so, take rest and comfort in another world where peace abides. This world you bring with you to all the weary eyes and tired hearts that look on sin and beat its sad refrain. From you can come their rest. From you can rise a world they will rejoice to look upon, and where their hearts are glad. In you there is a vision that extends to all of them, and covers them in gentleness and light. And in this widening world of light the darkness that they <u>thought</u> was there is pushed away, until it is but distant shadows, far away, not long to be remembered as the sun shines them to nothingness. And all their "evil" thoughts and "sinful" hopes, their dreams of guilt and merciless revenge, and every wish to hurt and kill and die, will disappear before the sun you bring.

Of course, we don't *really* want the world of sin and suffering we made. Far deeper than that perverse desire is our yearning for the world made by the other "Maker of the world" (T-25.III.4:1), the world of innocence and forgiveness and peace. We can rest in His world and bring it to all our brothers, who are as weary of the world of sin and suffering as we are. We bring it to them by looking upon them with the vision of Christ, the sun that rises and shines away the dark night of their souls. In this glorious sunrise that we bring, all of our brothers will recognize the source of real joy as their darkness disappears.

Application: This is a beautiful paragraph to read as a personal message to you. I recommend doing that now, inserting your name at appropriate points. Really see yourself, perhaps united with a partner (since this paragraph depicts two people walking the world together), bringing the sunshine of an innocent and peaceful world to those who suffer.

4. Would you not do this for the Love of God? And for *yourself?* For think what it would do for you. Your "evil" thoughts that haunt you now will seem increasingly remote and far away from you. And they go farther and farther off, because the sun in you has risen that they may be pushed away before the light. They linger for a while, a little while, in twisted forms too far away for recognition, and are gone forever. And in the sunlight you will stand in quiet, in innocence and wholly unafraid. And from you will the rest you found extend, so that your peace can never fall away and leave you homeless. Those who offer peace to everyone have found a home in Heaven the world cannot [Ur: can *not*] destroy. For it is large enough to hold the world within its peace.

The previous paragraph spoke of how the sunlight we bring will push our brothers' "evil" thoughts "far away." But it will do more than that: It will push *our* "evil" thoughts away as well. We see again a principle so often repeated in the Course: Giving what we have to others enables us to fully recognize that we have it. Think of some of the "evil" thoughts that haunt you. Do you not want to see them pushed away until they are gone forever and you bask in the sunlight, standing "in quiet, in innocence and wholly unafraid"? Offer peace to everyone—including that dirty, rotten so-and-so you just thought of—and you will find a home in Heaven so limitless that it will "hold the world within its peace."

5. In you is all of Heaven. Every leaf that falls is given life in you. Each bird that ever sang will sing again in you. And every flower that ever

185

bloomed has saved its perfume and its loveliness for you. What aim can supersede the Will of God and of His Son, that Heaven be restored to him for whom it was created as his <u>only</u> home? Nothing before and nothing after it. No other place; no other state nor time. Nothing beyond nor nearer. Nothing else. In <u>any</u> form. This can <u>you</u> bring to <u>all</u> the world, and <u>all</u> the thoughts that entered it and were mistaken for a little while. How better could your <u>own</u> mistakes be brought to truth than by your willingness to bring the light of Heaven with you, as you walk <u>beyond</u> the world of darkness into light?

Sometimes the Course says things that are so staggering it is easy to let them slide right by. Here's one: "In *you* is all of Heaven" (emphasis from Urtext). That's right, *you*. It's hard for me to imagine that in little old me, with all of my shortcomings and regrets and weaknesses and foibles, is the pure and radiant home of God's holy Son. Yet Jesus assures me—and all of us—that it's true. And the way to really experience this for ourselves is to bring Heaven to everyone, so our own mistakes can be corrected as the light we bring is given us.

Application: We cannot remind ourselves often enough of just how holy we really are. Repeat these words and really let them sink in:

> In **me**, *[name]*, is all of Heaven.
> Every leaf that falls is given life in me.
> Each bird that ever sang will sing again in me.
> And every flower that ever bloomed has saved its perfume and its loveliness for me.
> None of my petty aims and "evil" thoughts can obscure the fact that Heaven is my **only** home, and I share God's Will that it be restored to everyone.
> Let me bring Heaven to all the world, and thus remember that the heavenly light I bring is mine as well.

V. The State of Sinlessness
Commentary by Greg Mackie

1. The state of sinlessness is merely this: The whole desire to attack is gone, and so there is no reason to perceive the Son of God as other than he is. The need for guilt is gone because it has no purpose, and is meaningless without the goal of sin. Attack and sin are bound as one illusion, each the cause and aim and justifier of the other. Each is meaningless alone, but seems to draw a meaning from the other. Each depends upon the other for whatever sense it seems to have. And no one could believe in one unless the other were the truth, for each attests the other must be true.

Attack and sin are two sides of the same illusory coin, for attack perceived as real *is* sin. As an earlier passage told us: "To sin would be to violate reality, and to succeed. Sin is the proclamation that attack is real and guilt is justified" (T-19.II.2:2-3). Thus, each is inextricably bound with the other. Attack serves the goal of sin: We attack in order to accumulate sin. Sin, in turn, serves the goal of attack: The "sins" we see in others give us the perfect rationale to attack.

The state of sinlessness is the reversal of all this. Without the goal of sin, there is no need to attack anyone. Without the goal of attack, there is no need to see sin in anyone. As sin and attack are bound together, so they are undone together.

2. Attack makes Christ your enemy, and God along with Him. Must you not be afraid with "enemies" like these? And must you not be fearful of yourself? For you have hurt yourself, and made your Self your "enemy." And now you must believe you are not you, but something alien to yourself and "something else," a "something" to be feared instead of loved. Who would attack whatever he perceives as wholly innocent? And who, *because* he wishes to attack, can fail to think he must be guilty to maintain the wish, while wanting innocence [Ur: And who, *because* he wishes to attack, can *fail* to think it {whatever he perceives} *must* be guilty to *deserve* the wish and leave *him* innocent]? For who could see the Son of God as innocent and wish him dead? Christ stands before you [Ur: both], each time you look upon your brother [Ur: one

187

another]. He has <u>not</u> gone because your eyes are closed. But what is there to see by searching for your Savior, seeing Him through sightless eyes?

When we attack another person, we are attacking someone who is really Christ. This means that in our eyes, Christ is our "enemy," and His Father is as well. We will naturally be afraid of such formidable enemies. We will also be afraid of ourselves, because we have hurt ourselves with our attack and seemingly made our true Self (Christ) our enemy. Having detached from our true Self and made It into our enemy, we now believe we are "something else," an attacking ego to be feared.

We *have* to see Christ as our enemy if we want to attack our brother. How could we attack our brother if we really saw him as totally innocent? We couldn't, so to satisfy our desire to attack, we must see him as guilty and therefore deserving of attack, in order to make our attack seem innocent and just. That's why we focus so much on all the "terrible" things our brothers' bodies seem to be doing. That's why we see a guilty sinner instead of the holy Savior who really stands before us in each brother we meet.

> 3. It is <u>not</u> Christ you see by looking thus [through sightless eyes]. It is the "enemy," <u>confused</u> with Christ, you look upon. And <u>hate because</u> there is no sin in him for you to see. Nor do you hear his plaintive call, unchanged in content in <u>whatever</u> form the call is made, that you <u>unite</u> with him, and <u>join</u> with him in innocence and peace. And yet, beneath the ego's senseless shrieks, such <u>is</u> the call that God has given him, that <u>you</u> might hear in him His [God's] Call to <u>you</u>, and answer by returning unto God what is His Own.

When we see a brother as a guilty sinner, we are not seeing Christ in him. We are seeing him as an "enemy." There are two levels of seeing the enemy. On the surface, we see our brother as an enemy because we see so much sin in him. But on a deeper level, having identified with the ego, we see him as an enemy precisely because there is *no* sin in him. He is the innocent Christ, the ego's Public Enemy Number One. As the Course said earlier, "To the ego, *the guiltless are guilty*. Those who do not attack are its 'enemies'" (T-13.II.4:2-3). And the Christ does not attack.

This is why we don't want to join with our brothers. We tell ourselves that the reason is "the ego's senseless shrieks," all the rotten things our brothers' egos are doing. But in truth, we don't want to hear their underlying call to join in innocence because we don't want to hear *God's* Call to us, the call that would undo the ego for good.

> 4. The Son of God asks only this of you; that you return to him what is his due, that you may <u>share</u> in it with him. Alone does <u>neither</u> have it. So must it remain useless to both. Together, it will give to each an <u>equal</u> strength to save the other, and save himself along <u>with</u> him. <u>Forgiven</u> by you, your savior offers <u>you</u> salvation. <u>Condemned</u> by you, he offers death to you. In everyone you see but the reflection of what you choose to have <u>him</u> be to you. If you decide against his proper function, the <u>only</u> one he has in truth, you are depriving him of all the joy he <u>would</u> have found if he fulfilled the role God gave to him. But think not Heaven is lost to him alone. Nor can it be regained unless the way is shown to him through <u>you</u>, that <u>you</u> may find it, walking by his side.

Underneath whatever our brother is "shrieking," he is asking for *one* thing: that we forgive him, that we see the innocence that both of us share. In other words, as the Course tells us so many times, we must save our savior. We forgive our brother by seeing the innocent Christ in him, which saves him. This then frees him to fulfill the function that is his highest joy: the function of saving *us*, forgiving us by seeing the innocent Christ in us. The language here is very strong: If we don't save him, we are actually *depriving* him of the joy of saving us. The choice, then, is ours: Do we deny him Heaven and thus deny it to ourselves, or do we show him the way to Heaven and walk there together?

Application: As you go about your day today, you will probably have many occasions where someone will do something that upsets you. When this happens, use these words as a "response to temptation":

> *Forgiven by me, this person offers me salvation.*
> *Condemned by me, this person offers me death.*
> *Which of these do I really want?*

> 5. It is no sacrifice that he be saved, for <u>by</u> his freedom will you gain your own. To let <u>his</u> function be fulfilled is but the means to let <u>yours</u> be. And so you walk toward Heaven or toward hell, but <u>not</u> alone. How

189

beautiful his sinlessness will be when you perceive it! And how great will be your joy, when he is free to offer you the gift of sight God gave to him for you! He has no need but this; that you allow him freedom to complete the task God gave to him. Remembering but this; that what he does you do, along with him. And as you see him, so do you define the function he will have for you, until you see him differently and let him be what God appointed that he be to you.

When we see separate interests, we think that another's loss is our gain. Therefore, we must condemn another to save ourselves; her guilt is our innocence. If we can successfully point the finger at her, we're off the hook. In this scenario, forgiving her seems like a sacrifice. It seems that we're releasing our scapegoat without getting anything in return except perhaps the paltry satisfaction of doing the "noble" thing. But in truth, we have *common* interests; we gain or lose together. Therefore, saving another is the way we save ourselves; her innocence and freedom are ours.

We should thus devote each day to giving away the salvation we want for ourselves. We should wake up each day and think: "I'm going to forgive everyone I see today. I'm going to see sinlessness everywhere. How beautiful this sight will be! How joyous I will be when I save each person and thus set him loose to fulfill his joyous function of saving *me*!" Can you imagine what your life would be like if this were how you spent every day?

> 6. Against the hatred that the Son of God may cherish toward himself, is God believed to be without the power to save what He created from the pain of hell. But in the love he shows himself is God made free to let His Will be done. In your brother [Ur: each of you] you see the picture of your own belief in what the Will of God must be for you. In your forgiveness will you understand His Love for you; through your attack believe He hates you, thinking Heaven must be hell. Look once again upon your brother, not without the understanding that he is the way to Heaven or to hell, as you perceive him. But forget not this; the role you give to him is given you, and you will walk the way you pointed out to him because it is your judgment on [Ur made upon] yourself.

The last couple of paragraphs have said that we walk together with our brothers either to hell or to Heaven. When we choose hell as our destination, we hate ourselves and think God has condemned us to hell. Our hatred of ourselves takes the form of seeing our brothers as guilty sinners; our attacks on them make us think that God hates us as much as we do. By condemning our brothers to hell, we condemn ourselves to hell. But when we choose Heaven as our destination, we love ourselves and recognize that God loves us too. Our love for ourselves takes the form of forgiving our brothers. By freeing our brothers to return to Heaven, we return to Heaven with them.

Application: Think of someone against whom you're holding a grievance. Apply the following words to this person:

> *In [name], I see the picture of my own belief in what the Will of God must be for me.*
>
> *If I attack [name], I will think God hates me and condemns me to hell.*
>
> *If I forgive [name], I will know God loves me and embraces me in Heaven.*
>
> *Holy Spirit, let me help [name] find his way to Heaven instead condemning him to hell,*
>
> *And thus free him to show me the way to Heaven.*

VI. The Special Function
Commentary by Greg Mackie

1. The grace of God rests gently on forgiving eyes, and everything they look on speaks of Him to the beholder. He [the beholder] can see no evil; nothing in the world to fear, and no one who is different from himself. And as he loves them, so he looks upon <u>himself</u> with love and gentleness. He would no more condemn himself for <u>his</u> mistakes than damn another. He is not an arbiter of vengeance, nor a punisher of sin. The kindness of his sight rests on himself with all the tenderness it offers others. For he would <u>only</u> heal and <u>only</u> bless. And being <u>in accord</u> with what God wills, he <u>has</u> the power to heal and bless all those he looks on with the grace of God upon his sight.

This is a beautiful portrait of the person this course aims to produce: a miracle worker. The grace of God has enabled her to forgive the world, so all she sees in the world speaks of God. She loves everything she sees with the same pure, tender, limitless love that He does. She sees nothing evil, fearful, or deserving of condemnation. All she sees everywhere she looks is pure innocence, pure love, pure light. Because she sees the world this way, she sees herself this way as well—after all, she sees nothing different from herself. And because her only desire is to heal and bless everyone in accordance with God's Will, she has access to all the power of God to do exactly that. She has the power to work miracles.

Application: I recommend reading this paragraph in the first person, as a way of affirming the person you will become when you have "passed" this course. Give it a try. For instance, the first couple of sentences would go something like this: "The grace of God rests gently on my forgiving eyes, and everything they look on speaks of Him to me. I can see no evil; nothing in the world to fear, and no one who is different from myself."

2. Eyes become used to darkness, and the light of brilliant day seems painful to the eyes grown long accustomed to the dim effects perceived at twilight. And they turn away from sunlight and the clarity it brings

192

to what they look upon. Dimness seems better; easier to see, and better recognized. Somehow the vague and more obscure seems <u>easier</u> to look upon; <u>less</u> painful to the eyes than what is wholly clear and unambiguous. Yet this is <u>not</u> what eyes are <u>for</u>, and who can say that he <u>prefers</u> the darkness and maintain he <u>wants</u> to see?

We don't see the beautiful world of light depicted in the previous paragraph because we prefer the dim twilight of the world our body's eyes see. Though the specific image is different, this paragraph reminds me of Plato's Allegory of the Cave, in which the normal world we see is likened to dim shadows cast on the wall of a cave, and we are likened to prisoners who have never seen anything but those shadows. What happens when we are released from our chains and led into the light? Here is Plato's answer:

> If [the prisoner] is compelled to look straight at the light, will he not have a pain in his eyes which will make him turn away and take in the objects of vision which he can see [in the darkness], and which he will conceive to be in reality clearer than the things which are now being shown to him [in the light]?

This describes all of us. We are so familiar with the dark and shadowy world our physical eyes show us that we recoil from the clear radiance revealed by true vision. "Better the devil I know," we think. Yet who can really see in darkness? If we truly want to see, we must turn away from darkness and trust that however weird and scary it seems at first, we will grow to love the light of brilliant day and the clear and unambiguous vision it reveals.

> 3. The wish to see calls down the grace of God upon your eyes, and brings the gift of light that makes sight possible. Would you behold your brother? God is glad to have you look on him. He does not will your savior be unrecognized by you. Nor does He will that he remain without the function that He gave to him.

To see the light that reveals the world God would have us see, all we need to do is to *want* it as much as God wants us to have it. God wills that we see our brother in His light, which reveals him as the Christ, our savior from darkness. This will enable our brother to fulfill his function of *being* our savior, a function on which his happiness depends.

Let him no more be lonely, for the lonely ones are those who see no function in the world for them to fill; no place where they are needed, and no aim which <u>only</u> they can [Ur: undertake and] perfectly fulfill.

4. Such is the Holy Spirit's kind perception of specialness; His use of what you made, to heal <u>instead</u> of harm. To each He gives a special function in salvation he alone can fill; a part for <u>only</u> him. Nor is the plan complete until he finds his special function, and fulfills the part assigned to him, to make himself complete within a world where incompletion rules.

Jesus now introduces the concept of our *special function*. (It has been alluded to earlier, but here is where it is first spelled out clearly.) I think this is one of the Holy Spirit's most brilliant transformations of the ego's lemons into His lemonade. We made specialness to be unique: to set ourselves apart from and above our brothers. But the Holy Spirit takes our desire for specialness and turns it on its ear. In His eyes, instead of our unique way of standing apart from our brothers, specialness becomes our unique way of *serving* our brothers, our unique role in the Holy Spirit's plan of salvation *from* specialness.

I've always found the concept of the special function especially poignant, because I think it addresses a deep need. All of us have a deep yearning to make a difference, to be of service, to dedicate our lives to a goal that is larger and more meaningful than mere satisfaction of personal needs. In short, we need a meaningful function. Without it, we will be lonely and incomplete. All we will do with our lives is look out for number one, and what could be lonelier than that?

5. Here, where the laws of God do <u>not</u> prevail in perfect form, can he yet do *one* perfect thing and make *one* perfect choice. And <u>by</u> this act of special faithfulness to one perceived as <u>other</u> than himself, he learns the gift was given <u>to</u> himself, and so they <u>must</u> be one. Forgiveness is the <u>only</u> function meaningful in time. It is the means the Holy Spirit uses to <u>translate</u> specialness from sin into salvation. Forgiveness is for all. But when it <u>rests</u> on all it is complete, and every function of this world completed with it. Then is time no more. Yet [Ur: But] <u>while</u> in time, there is still much to do. And each must do what is allotted him, for on <u>his</u> part does <u>all</u> the plan depend. He *has* a special part in time for so he chose, and choosing it, he made it for himself. His wish was not denied but changed in form, to let it serve his brother <u>and</u> himself, and thus become a means to save <u>instead</u> of lose.

The content of our special function, whatever form it takes, is forgiveness. The *one* perfect thing we can do in this crazy world is to forgive those the Holy Spirit has especially called us to forgive, in particular our holy relationship partner (see T-20.IV.5:3). Our mad wish for specialness is thus converted by the Holy Spirit into an "act of special faithfulness" to a particular person, an act that will bless us as well, and thus prove that we and this other person are one. It is critical that we actually *do* this, "for on [our] part does all the plan depend." That plan is for global forgiveness, but our job, to paraphrase that old activist bumper sticker, is to "think globally, forgive locally."

> 6. Salvation is no more than a reminder this world is <u>not</u> your home. Its laws are <u>not</u> imposed on you, its values are <u>not</u> yours. And nothing that you <u>think</u> you see in it is <u>really</u> there at all. This is seen <u>and understood</u> as each one takes his part in its <u>undoing</u>, as he did in <u>making</u> it. He <u>has</u> the means for either, as he always did. The specialness he chose to <u>hurt</u> himself did God appoint to be the means for his salvation, from the very instant that the choice was made. His special sin was made his special grace. His special hate became his special love.

Way back at the beginning, we asked God for special favor (see T-13. III.10). When He refused us, we ran away from home like rebellious teenagers and set up a world where our specialness could reign supreme. This was a painful choice, but our Father loved us so much that He embedded healing balm in that very choice. Our special way of sinning was transformed into our unique grace (among other definitions, my dictionary defines "grace" as "a pleasing and admirable quality or characteristic" and "a capacity to tolerate, accommodate, or forgive people.") Our special way of hating was transformed into our unique way of loving. And as each of us takes our special function in time, we discover that the crazy world we made is not our real home at all. We were never capable of running away from home.

> 7. The Holy Spirit needs <u>your</u> special function, that <u>His</u> may be fulfilled. Think not you lack a special value here. You wanted it, and it <u>is</u> given you. <u>All</u> that you made can serve salvation easily and well. The Son of God can make <u>no</u> choice the Holy Spirit cannot employ on his <u>behalf</u>, and <u>not</u> against himself. Only in darkness does your specialness <u>appear</u> to be attack. In light, you see it as your <u>special function</u> in the plan to save the Son of God from <u>all</u> attack, and let him understand that he is

safe, as he has <u>always</u> been, and will remain in time and in eternity alike. This is the function given you for your brother [Ur: given each of you for one another]. Take it gently, then, from your brother's [Ur: one another's] hand, and let salvation be perfectly fulfilled in [Ur: *both* of] you. Do this *one* thing, that <u>everything</u> be given you.

Who among us does not desire to have a special value in this world? Of course, most of the time this desire takes the form of elevating ourselves above others, attacking them so we can be on the top of the heap. But remember the second paragraph's discussion of darkness and light? In the darkness of this world our specialness looks like attack. But in God's light we see the Holy Spirit's transformation of it into our special function in His plan to *save* us from attack, which enables us to learn that we have *always been* safe from attack.

But for all this to come about, as I said before, we have to really *do* it. The Holy Spirit needs each of us to fill the slot He has allotted us. As the section concludes, you can really hear Jesus pleading to Helen and Bill to accept their special function of forgiving each other, so they could find salvation together and receive the gift of everything.

What about us? Are we willing to commit to our special function? Do we want to receive the gift of everything?

Application: We may not be clear on what our special function is—in my experience, the discovery of it is a long-term process. But one thing we can do to open ourselves up to our special function is simply to commit ourselves to it. So, let's do that now. Say these words to the Holy Spirit:

> *Holy Spirit, I know You need **my** special function that **Yours** may be fulfilled.*
> *Your plan is not complete until I find my special function, and fulfill the part assigned to me, to make myself complete within a world where incompletion rules.*
> *I have a special value here.*
> *I wanted it, and it **is** given me.*
> *Therefore, I commit to finding and fulfilling my special function.*
> *I open my mind to You Who know what it is and will guide me in every aspect of it.*
> *I will do this **one** thing, that **everything** be given me.*

VII. The Rock of Salvation
Commentary by Greg Mackie

1. Yet [Ur: And,] if the Holy Spirit can commute each sentence that you laid upon yourself into a blessing, then it <u>cannot</u> be a sin. Sin is the only thing [Ur: Sin is *one* thing] in all the world that <u>cannot</u> change. It is immutable. And <u>on</u> its changelessness the world depends. The magic of the world can <u>seem</u> to hide the pain of sin from sinners, and deceive with glitter and with guile. Yet each one knows the cost of sin is death. And so it <u>is</u>. For sin is a <u>request</u> for death, a wish to make this world's foundation sure as love, dependable as Heaven, and as strong as God Himself. The world <u>is</u> safe from love to everyone who thinks sin possible. Nor <u>will</u> it change. Yet <u>is</u> it possible what God created <u>not</u> should <u>share</u> the attributes of His creation [specifically, the attribute of changelessness], when it <u>opposes</u> it in every way?

The previous section told us that when the Holy Spirit gave us our special function, "[our] special sin was made [our] special grace" (T-25.VI.6:7)—our sentence on ourselves was commuted into a blessing. Therefore, it must never have been a sin in the first place.

This totally reverses the world's belief that sin is changeless. It may not seem that we believe this, but it's really just another way of saying: "I have to attack in order to live in this world, and that's never going to change." Who among us doesn't live in a way that reflects this belief? We may disguise our attack in "attractive" forms, but we *do* attack, and deep down we know we're doomed to pay the ultimate price for it: "The wages of sin is death" (Rom. 6:23). Strangely, we believe in changeless sin precisely because we *want* death, because it "proves" this world of sin is real and thus keeps us away from the ego-dispelling Love of God. Yet does it really make sense that sin—the antithesis of God's creation—can be as changeless as the love He did create?

2. It <u>cannot</u> be the "sinner's" wish for death is just as strong as is God's Will for life. Nor <u>can</u> the basis of a world He did <u>not</u> make be firm and sure as Heaven. How <u>could</u> it be that hell and Heaven are the same? And is it possible that what He did <u>not</u> will cannot [Ur: can *not*] be

197

changed? What is immutable <u>besides</u> His Will? And what can share its attributes <u>except</u> itself? What wish can rise <u>against</u> His Will, and <u>be</u> immutable? If you could realize <u>nothing</u> is changeless <u>but</u> the Will of God, this course would not be difficult for you. For it is this that you do not believe. Yet there is nothing <u>else</u> you <u>could</u> believe, if you but looked at what it really <u>is</u>.

The point of this paragraph is simple but profound: Only God's Will is changeless, so anything that is not His Will must be changeable. Put another way: The only things that can share the attributes of God's Will—in this case, changelessness—are the things that *are* God's Will. Therefore, God's Will for life is changeless and our death wish is changeable. Innocence is changeless and the "sin" that forms the basis of our world is changeable. Heaven is changeless and the hell we made for ourselves is changeable.

"If you could realize *nothing* is changeless *but* the Will of God, this course would not be difficult for you" (Urtext version). Why? Because the whole problem the Course addresses is our false "will" and its effects, and the recognition that God's Will is changeless means that our problem doesn't even exist. Therefore, as the Workbook says, the idea that there is no will but God's "can be regarded as the central thought toward which all our exercises are directed" (W-pI.74.1:1).

> 3. Let us go back to what we said before, and think of it more carefully. It <u>must</u> be so that either God is mad, or is this world a place of madness. Not <u>one</u> Thought of His makes <u>any</u> sense at all within this world. And <u>nothing</u> that the world believes as true has <u>any</u> meaning in His Mind at all. What makes no sense and has no meaning <u>is</u> insanity. And what is madness <u>cannot</u> be the truth. If <u>one</u> belief so deeply valued here were true, then every Thought God ever had is an illusion. And if but <u>one</u> Thought of His is true, then <u>all</u> beliefs the world gives <u>any</u> meaning to are false, and make no sense at all. This <u>is</u> the choice you make. Do not attempt to see it differently, nor twist it into something it is not. For only <u>this</u> decision <u>can</u> you make. The rest is up to God, and <u>not</u> to you.

This paragraph makes another simple but profound point that is crucial to this section: Either God's Love is madness or the world of sin is madness. God's Love, which asks us to relinquish attack completely and love without limit, makes no sense at all from the perspective of a world where attack is necessary to survive. Conversely, this bloody battleground of a world makes no sense at all from the perspective of One Who is pure Love and literally incapable of attack. We try to mix love and attack together, but there is really no wiggle room here—it is an either/or choice. We must decide whether we believe God's Love is true or the world of sin is true. "This *is* the choice you make" (Urtext version) every day in every situation we encounter.

The idea that God's Love is madness because the world of sin is true is really quite common, though it is rarely put this way. For example, Sam Harris, the atheist author of a recent bestselling book called *The End of Faith*, dismisses pacifism (the commitment to total nonviolence) by saying that one man with a knife could kill an entire city of pacifists. This is his entire argument against pacifism; in his mind, it is self-evident that in a world of violent attackers, people who don't attack at all are hopelessly deluded and don't stand a chance. Jesus, however, wants us to go completely to the opposite side: to see that only God's laws of love are sane (something pacifist movements like Gandhi's have actually provided evidence for) and that the world of knife-wielders is the real place of madness.

> 4. To justify <u>one</u> value that the world upholds is to <u>deny</u> your Father's sanity <u>and yours</u>. For God and His beloved Son do <u>not</u> think differently. And it is the <u>agreement</u> of their thought that makes the Son a co-creator with the Mind Whose Thought created him. So [Ur: And] if he chooses to believe <u>one</u> thought <u>opposed</u> to truth, he has decided he is <u>not</u> his Father's Son because the Son is mad, and sanity must lie apart from both the Father <u>and</u> the Son. <u>This you believe.</u> Think not that this belief depends upon the form it takes. Who thinks the world is sane in any way, is justified in <u>anything</u> it thinks, or is maintained by <u>any</u> form of reason, believes this to be true. Sin is not real *because* the Father and the Son are <u>not</u> insane. This world is meaningless *because* it rests on sin. Who could create the changeless if it does <u>not</u> rest on truth?

We are again presented with the same choice, only with a twist: If we believe the world of sin is sane, we are believing not only that God is mad, but that *we* are mad as well. We think our true Self, which calls us to love just as our Father does, is as loony as He is—like Father, like Son. This leads to the conclusion of the fourth sentence: If we believe the world is sane, we believe that both the Father and the Son in Heaven are mad—love is mad and sin is sane. Therefore, we believe that we are not our Father's Son, because we are thinking differently from Them: What we think is sane They think is mad, and vice versa.

It seems strange to say that we believe that the Father and the Son are mad, but again, we *do* think that totally loving others and never attacking is an invitation to disaster, do we not? Jesus, whom the Western world has regarded as God's Son, was often seen as "mad" in his lifetime, and to this day his "hard sayings" about turning the other cheek and giving to anyone who asks seem so impractical (read: "crazy") that we think they can't possibly be taken literally. Yet his perspective, then and now, is entirely different: the Father and the Son are *not* insane, so the world of sin is meaningless and love is the only sane choice.

> 5. The Holy Spirit <u>has</u> the power to change the whole foundation of the world you see to something else; a basis <u>not</u> insane, on which a sane perception can be based, another world perceived. And one in which nothing is contradicted that would lead the Son of God to sanity and joy. Nothing attests to death and cruelty; to separation and to differences. For here is everything perceived as one, and no one loses that each one may gain.

This is the practical import of this entire discussion: The fact that the world is entirely insane and therefore false means that the foundation of the world—sin—*can be changed* by the Holy Spirit. He has made this change already through His making of the real world, a world based on the sane foundation of love. This world does not contradict the inherent sanity of the Father and the Son, but instead leads us back to awareness of it. Instead of sin and separation and differences, in the world He made "is everything perceived as one, and no one loses that each one may gain."

> 6. Test <u>everything</u> that you believe against this <u>one</u> requirement, and understand that everything that meets this <u>one</u> demand is worthy of your faith. But nothing else. What is not love is sin, and either one perceives the other as insane and meaningless. Love is the basis for a world perceived as wholly mad to sinners, who believe theirs is the way to sanity. But sin is equally insane within the sight of love, whose gentle eyes would look <u>beyond</u> the madness and rest peacefully on

200

truth. Each sees a world immutable, as each defines the changeless and eternal truth of what <u>you</u> are. And each reflects a view of what the Father and the Son <u>must</u> be [sane or insane], to make that viewpoint meaningful and sane.

As will become clear as the section proceeds, the "one requirement" is the previous paragraph's final sentence: "For here is everything perceived as one, and no one loses that each one may gain." This is the standard by which we should measure every belief we have. Any belief that says someone must lose for me to gain must be set aside.

The belief that someone must lose for me to gain is the essence of sin, for it means that we must *attack* in order to gain, and real attack is sin. Yet to us "sinners," this seems wholly sane, doesn't it? In this dog-eat-dog world, it seems we simply have to attack or we'll be crushed. We may find totally non-attacking love admirable, but again, a life based on it seems impractical—look at what happened to Jesus and Gandhi and Martin Luther King, Jr. In love's eyes, however, it is the belief that we can gain at another's expense that is insane. How can we gain by stealing from those who are one with us? Just as sin sees the constant warfare of this world as an eternal testament to the fact that the Love of God is insane, so love rests serenely above the battleground and attests to sanity and truth.

Application: Bring to mind some of the core beliefs you have about the world—not your highest spiritual ideals, but the beliefs that actually run your life on a day-to-day basis. Do these beliefs reflect the idea that everything is one so no one can gain at another's expense? With each belief that does not pass this test, say:

This belief is not worthy of my faith.
It is not love, so it is a false belief in sin.
Holy Spirit, help me to let it go.

7. Your special function is the special form in which the fact that God is <u>not</u> insane appears most sensible and meaningful to you. The <u>content</u> is the same. The <u>form</u> is suited to your special needs, and to the special time and place in which you think you find yourself, and where you

can be free of place and time, and all that you believe must limit you. The Son of God cannot [Ur: can *not*] be bound by time nor place nor anything God did not will. Yet if His Will is seen as madness, then the form of sanity which makes it most acceptable to those who are insane requires special choice. Nor can this choice be made by the insane, whose problem is their choices are not free, and made with reason in the light of sense.

Now Jesus ties the whole "Is God insane or is the world insane?" discussion to the last section's discussion of our special function. Remember, our special function is our particular part in the Holy Spirit's plan of salvation. Its *content* is forgiveness. Its *form* is designed by the Holy Spirit to fit our individual lives. It is designed to convince us that God is *not* insane—that love and forgiveness are sensible, not attack and sin—in some form that is so obvious to us that we can't possibly miss it.

We desperately need forms that convey this message. Think, for example, of how the Amish forgave the man who shot the children at the schoolhouse in Pennsylvania. I think the power of their example in such extreme circumstances has caused many people to wonder if forgiveness might be the most sane way of living in our world after all.

Our special function is our own unique form of the Amish demonstration. It is forgiving Joe for that unkind remark; extending healing to Sue, who has come to us for help; working a miracle for Mike, who feels trapped by his abused childhood. How better can we learn the sanity of love than by seeing its transforming effects in our own lives and in the lives of everyone we encounter?

> 8. It *would* be madness to entrust salvation to the insane. Because He is not mad has God appointed One as sane as He to raise a saner world to meet the sight of everyone who chose insanity as his salvation. To this One is given the choice of form most suitable to him; one which will not attack the world he sees, but enter into it in quietness and show him he is mad. This One but points to an alternative, another way of looking at what he has seen before, and recognizes as the world in which he lives, and thought he understood before.

The previous paragraph pointed out that we are too insane to design our own special function. That is why God, Who is perfectly sane, has appointed the Holy Spirit to design it for us. He who made the real world has crafted our special function to enable us to see the mad world we made in a new light that points to sanity. I love the emphasis here on Him giving us a form that will not attack the world we see. Our special function reveals an alternative world that still looks like the world in which we live, but with all the madness sifted out, leaving only the pure sanity He has placed there.

> 9. Now <u>must</u> he question this [his own understanding of the world], because the form of the alternative is one which he cannot [Ur: can *not*] deny, nor overlook, nor fail completely to perceive at all. To each his special function is designed to be perceived as possible, and more and more desired, as it <u>proves</u> to him that it is an alternative he really <u>wants</u>. From this position does his sinfulness, and <u>all</u> the sin he sees within the world, offer him less and less. Until he comes to understand it <u>cost</u> him his sanity, and stands <u>between</u> him and whatever hope he has of <u>being</u> sane. Nor is he left without <u>escape</u> from madness, for he has a special part in <u>everyone's</u> escape. He can no more be left outside, <u>without</u> a special function in the hope of peace, than could the Father overlook His Son, and pass him by in careless thoughtlessness.

Fulfilling our special function sets into motion a process in our mind. It enables us to see God's sanity in a way that is so obvious to us that we cannot overlook it. When we actually forgive and extend healing to Joe and Sue and Mike, we see results we cannot deny—results that offer us immense rewards. Thus, our special function becomes more and more desirable and our former commitment to sin less and less desirable, until we finally realize that our belief in sin has cost us everything and condemned us to madness. Fortunately, we also realize that there is an *escape* from madness: the very special function that has shown us the undesirability of madness in the first place. How could a loving God leave us without an escape hatch?

There's one line here that I don't want to let slip by: "To each his special function is designed to be perceived as possible." How reassuring! When we first hear about the idea of having a special function, we may think that it is some grand calling that will forever be beyond us. Well, it may well be grand, but it isn't beyond us. It's something that is truly *possible* for us, regardless of our apparent shortcomings or the seeming limitations of our life situation.

10. What is dependable <u>except</u> God's Love? And where does sanity abide <u>except</u> in Him? The One Who speaks for Him can show you this, in the alternative He chose especially for you. It is God's Will that you remember this, and so emerge from deepest mourning into perfect joy. Accept the function that has been assigned to you in God's Own plan to show His Son [Ur: Sons] that hell and Heaven are different, <u>not</u> the same. And [Ur: But] that in Heaven *They* are all the same, <u>without</u> the differences which <u>would</u> have made a hell of Heaven and a heaven of hell, had such insanity been possible.

Ultimately, fulfilling our special function reveals God's Love to us. We believe the hell we made is changeless. We believe Heaven has been permanently destroyed, and have even deluded ourselves into believing that the hell we live in now *is* Heaven. But none of this is so. Right now, we are in the real Heaven with the real God, resting in perfect sanity, at one with God and all our brothers.

Application: Accept your special function with the following words. Don't worry about whether or not you know the form of it yet—the Holy Spirit will reveal that to you. Right now, simply make the commitment to His role for you, as we did in the previous section:

> *Holy Spirit, I accept the function that has been assigned to me*
> *in God's plan for salvation.*
> *I accept the alternative You chose especially for me.*
> *My mind is open to whatever form You choose for me.*
> *It will reveal God's Love to me.*
> *It will help me emerge from deepest mourning into perfect joy.*
> *It will show me that I am the same as God and all my brothers.*
> *It will lead me to Heaven.*
> *What could I want but this?*

11. The whole belief that someone loses but reflects the underlying tenet God must be insane. For in this world it seems that one must gain *because* another lost [Ur: loses]. If <u>this</u> were true, then God is mad indeed! But what <u>is</u> this belief except a form of the more basic tenet, "Sin is real, and rules the world"? For every little gain must someone lose, and pay exact amount in blood and suffering. For otherwise would

evil triumph, and destruction be the total cost of any gain at all. You who believe that God is mad, look carefully at this, and understand that it <u>must</u> be <u>either</u> God <u>or</u> this must be insane, but hardly both.

The idea that sin is changeless—"Sin is real, and rules the world"— and the idea that someone must lose for me to gain are really different forms of the same idea. Sin means attack is real, and the idea that my gain equals your loss means that I must attack you to gain—I must sin. And since I sin when I gain at your expense, I must be punished through paying "exact amount in blood and suffering." Without this check on limitless greed, a check which the world calls "fairness" or "justice," evil would run rampant.

Is this bloody battle really sane, or is God's Love sane? This is the choice we face.

> 12. Salvation is rebirth of the idea no one <u>can</u> lose for <u>anyone</u> to gain. And everyone *must* gain, if anyone <u>would be</u> a gainer. Here is sanity restored. And on this single rock of truth can faith in God's eternal saneness rest in perfect confidence and perfect peace. Reason is satisfied, for <u>all</u> insane beliefs can be corrected here. And sin <u>must</u> be impossible, if <u>this</u> is true. This is the rock on which salvation rests, the vantage point from which the Holy Spirit gives meaning and direction to the plan in which your special function has a part. For here your special function is made whole, because it shares the <u>function</u> of the whole.

Here is the "rock of salvation" that gives this section its title: "no one *can* lose for *anyone* to gain" (Urtext version). We all gain or we all lose together. This one vital insight demonstrates that sin is not changeless— indeed, it is *impossible,* for gaining or losing together means we are all one, and how can you attack something that is one with you? This insight restores our own sanity and reawakens our awareness of God's sanity. This insight is at the heart of the Holy Spirit's plan for salvation, the plan our special function is meant to serve. It is what brings meaning and direction to the whole plan, allowing every aspect of it to come together into a harmonious whole.

> 13. Remember <u>all</u> temptation is but this; a mad belief that God's insanity would make <u>you</u> sane and <u>give</u> you what you want; that either God <u>or</u>

you must <u>lose</u> to madness because your aims can <u>not</u> be reconciled. Death demands life, but life is <u>not</u> maintained at <u>any</u> cost. No one <u>can</u> suffer for the Will of God to be fulfilled. Salvation <u>is</u> His Will *because* you share it. <u>Not</u> for you alone, but for the Self That <u>is</u> the Son of God. He <u>cannot</u> lose, for if he could the loss would be his Father's, and in Him <u>no</u> loss is possible. And this is sane <u>because</u> it is the truth.

All temptation to indulge the ego is rooted in this idea: We must make God's Love insane in order to preserve the world of sin that we want. Notice how this is a form of the central tenet of this insane world: someone must lose for me to gain. Here, *God* must lose His sanity for *us* to gain sanity. This must be so if God and we have truly different wills and we want our death wish to come true. But in truth, we actually share God's Will, so we gain or lose together. His sanity or insanity is ours, "for God and His beloved Son do not think differently." If we recognize this, we will choose His sanity, and realize that we cannot lose because *God* cannot lose. What could be saner than recognizing that the all-powerful Creator of everything is incapable of losing?

VIII. Justice Returned to Love
Commentary by Greg Mackie

1. The Holy Spirit can use <u>all</u> that you give to Him for your salvation. But He <u>cannot</u> use what you withhold, for He cannot [Ur: can *not*] take it from you <u>without</u> your willingness. For if He did, you would believe He wrested it from you <u>against</u> your will. And so you would not learn it *is* your will to be without it. You need not give it to Him <u>wholly</u> willingly, for if you could you had no need of Him. But this He needs; that you <u>prefer</u> He take it than that you keep it for yourself alone, and recognize that what brings loss to no one <u>you would not know</u>. This much is necessary to add to the idea no one <u>can</u> lose for you to gain. And nothing more.

In the last section, we learned that the "rock of salvation" is the idea that no one can lose for us to gain. Now we are given one more prerequisite for salvation: We must recognize our resistance to the idea that no one can lose, and become willing to let the Holy Spirit take our resistance away from us. He can't take this or *anything* we withhold from Him without our willingness, for if He did, we would never learn that our true will *is* to give it up.

How much willingness do we need? The Course speaks of "a little willingness" elsewhere, and here we find out how little it needs to be: Our desire to give our resistance to Him must be stronger than our desire to hold onto it. So, if I'm 51 percent willing and 49 percent unwilling, that's good enough.

2. Here is the <u>only</u> principle salvation needs. Nor is it necessary that your faith in it be strong, unswerving, and without attack from all beliefs opposed to it. You <u>have</u> no fixed allegiance. But remember salvation is not needed by the saved. You are <u>not</u> called upon to do what one divided still against himself <u>would</u> find impossible. Have little faith that wisdom <u>could</u> be found in such a state of mind. But be you thankful that only little faith is <u>asked</u> of you. What <u>but</u> a little faith remains to those who still believe in sin? What <u>could</u> they know of Heaven and the justice of the saved?

That 51 percent willingness to recognize that no one can lose for us to gain is all we need. Thank God! We aren't called to be spiritual giants here; we're only called to offer up our little faith to the Holy Spirit and let Him supply the rest.

Application: Think of some of the times you've thought, "This course asks so much of me. I'll never be willing enough or faithful enough to reach its goal." Now, read this paragraph as a personal message to you, inserting your name at appropriate points. You *will* make it, in spite of your imperfect faith.

> 3. There <u>is</u> a kind of justice in salvation of which the world knows nothing. To the world, justice and <u>vengeance</u> are the same, for sinners see justice <u>only</u> as their punishment, perhaps sustained by someone <u>else</u>, but <u>not</u> escaped. The laws of sin <u>demand</u> a victim. <u>Who</u> it may be makes little difference. But death <u>must</u> be the cost and <u>must</u> be paid. This is <u>not</u> justice, but insanity. Yet how could justice <u>be</u> defined <u>without</u> insanity where love means hate, and death is seen as victory and triumph over eternity and timelessness and life?

Now we come to the major theme of this section: justice. Justice is a principle of fairness that says everyone should get what he or she deserves. In a world where everyone sins, then, justice must be vengeance, for vengeance is what sinners deserve. As Paul famously said, "The wages of sin is death" (Rom 6:23). Perhaps someone can die in place of the sinner—like Jesus on the cross—but *someone* has to die. What else could justice be in an insane world that was designed for the very purpose of "proving" that death has defeated God's Will for life?

> 4. You who know not of justice still can ask, and learn the answer. Justice looks on all in the same way. It is <u>not</u> just that one should lack for what another has. For that is vengeance in <u>whatever</u> form it takes. Justice demands <u>no</u> sacrifice, for <u>any</u> sacrifice is made that sin <u>may be</u> <u>preserved</u> and <u>kept</u>. It is a payment offered for the cost of sin, <u>but not</u> <u>the total cost</u>. The rest is taken from another, to be laid beside your <u>little</u> payment, to "atone" for all that you would keep, and <u>not</u> give up. So is the victim seen as <u>partly</u> you, with someone <u>else</u> by far the greater part. And in the <u>total</u> cost, the greater his the less is yours. And justice, being blind, is satisfied by being paid, it matters not by whom.

The world's insane version of "justice" is based on the idea of payment for sin. All of our taking from others has made us sinners, and justice demands vengeance for our sin—we must sacrifice something, we must be punished. But as the last paragraph said, the punishment can be "sustained by someone else," so there is (we think) a way to get out of the punishment we deserve. If we can blame someone else for our sin and demand that *they* pay the bulk of the cost, then we can get away with paying less. This is a zero-sum game: the more the other pays, the less we do. And since justice is blind (a reference to the image of justice as a blindfolded woman holding a sword and scales), it doesn't matter who pays as long as she gets her due.

In the traditional image of justice, the blindfolded woman represents the idea that justice must impartially assess who is the sinner and who is innocent based on real evidence, being blind to any other factors that might bias the judgment. But true justice is blind to *sin itself*. It "looks on all in the same way." It is *totally* impartial, seeing no distinctions at all between people, not even the distinction of guilty and innocent. It sees no evidence of sin; it sees that we are all perfectly innocent, so no payment is required. Instead, everyone deserves everything: "no one should lack for what another has." We don't realize this now, but we can learn it if we ask the Holy Spirit.

> 5. Can this be justice? God knows not of this. But justice does He know, and knows it well. For He is wholly fair to everyone. Vengeance is alien to God's Mind *because* He knows of justice. To be just is to be fair, and not be vengeful. Fairness and vengeance are impossible, for each one contradicts the other and denies that it is real. It is impossible for you to share the Holy Spirit's justice with a mind that can conceive of specialness at all. Yet how could He be just if He condemns a sinner for the crimes he did not do, but thinks he did? And where would justice be if He demanded of the ones obsessed with the idea of punishment that they lay it aside, unaided, and perceive it is not true?

Again, justice is a principle of fairness in which everyone gets what he or she deserves. To a world rooted in the belief in sin, this takes the form of vengeance, punishment for sin. Such punishment seems to be the logical outcome of a fair and impartial assessment of the evidence. But it is anything but fair and impartial, for we judge "sinners" through the lens of our specialness, which is by definition unfair and biased.

God, however, sees justice entirely differently. He knows everyone is perfectly innocent, so vengeance is totally *unfair*. Therefore, the Holy Spirit won't punish us, no matter how much we think we have it coming. In fact, He's so fair that He won't even impose the unreasonable expectation that we give up our lust for punishment without His help.

> 6. It is extremely hard for those who still believe sin meaningful to understand the Holy Spirit's justice. They must believe He shares their <u>own</u> confusion, and cannot [Ur: can *not*] avoid the vengeance that their own belief in justice <u>must</u> entail. And so they fear the Holy Spirit, and perceive the "wrath" of God in Him. [Ur: They are unjust indeed to Him.] Nor can they trust Him <u>not</u> to strike them dead with lightning bolts torn from the "fires" of Heaven by God's Own angry Hand. They *do* believe that Heaven is hell, and *are* afraid of love. And deep suspicion and the chill of fear comes over them when they are told that they have <u>never</u> sinned. Their world <u>depends</u> on sin's stability. And they perceive the "threat" of what God <u>knows</u> as justice to be more destructive to themselves and to their world than vengeance, which they understand and love.

If you doubt the truth of the first sentence, just tell a "law and order" type that justice means punishing no one, and watch the sparks fly. "That's crazy! If we did that, evildoers would run amok!" This notion of justice is so firmly entrenched that it gets projected onto the Holy Spirit, Who then becomes an agent for the wrath of God. Yet oddly enough, what we fear the most is not His lightning bolts, but the nagging feeling that there *are* no lightning bolts. Identifying with the ego and its lust for sin, we're much more fearful of our sinlessness and God's true justice than of the "eye for an eye" approach we know so well.

> 7. So do they think the <u>loss</u> of sin a curse. And flee the Holy Spirit as if He were a messenger from hell, sent from above, in treachery and guile, to work God's vengeance on them in the guise of a deliverer and friend. What <u>could</u> He be to them except a devil, dressed to deceive within an angel's cloak? And what escape has He for them except a door to hell that <u>seems</u> to look like Heaven's gate?

We're so committed to justice as vengeance for sin that we just don't believe it when the Holy Spirit comes to us and says we haven't sinned.

Surely, we think, He can't be serious. He must be trying to deceive us into thinking He is our friend; His offers of deliverance are "deceptions which would cheat [us] of defenses, to ensure that when He strikes He will not fail to kill" (W-pI.197.1:5). I think this is a big reason we don't hear the Holy Spirit's guidance as much as we'd like. How willing will we be to hear Him if we think He is the devil in disguise?

Application: Think of some of the times you've asked the Holy Spirit for guidance and felt you didn't receive any (or felt you did but were reluctant to follow it). Could it be that part of the reason for this was that deep down, you thought He was your enemy bent on punishing you rather than a friend sent to deliver you?

> 8. Yet justice <u>cannot</u> punish those who ask for punishment, but have a Judge Who <u>knows</u> that they are wholly innocent in truth. In justice He is <u>bound</u> to set them free, and <u>give</u> them all the honor they deserve and have denied themselves because they are <u>not</u> fair, and <u>cannot</u> understand that they <u>are</u> innocent. Love is <u>not</u> understandable to sinners <u>because</u> they think that justice is <u>split off</u> from love, and stands for something else. And thus is love perceived as weak, and vengeance strong. For love has <u>lost</u> when judgment left its side, and is too weak to <u>save</u> from punishment. But vengeance <u>without</u> love has <u>gained</u> in strength by being separate and apart from love. And what <u>but</u> vengeance now can help and save, while love stands feebly by with helpless hands, bereft of justice and vitality, and powerless to save?

This paragraph is a commentary on a major issue in Christian theology: the relationship between God's justice and His Love. Traditionally, these two things are seen as complementary poles that are both necessary components of His nature. If He only had the love component, the theory goes, He would be weak: He would lack the ability to enforce morality and His creation would be lawless. But if He only had the justice component, He would be merciless, and we would all be doomed to destruction by His unbending standards, which we could never meet.

So, God has both love and justice in His nature, but they are not the same and they live in an uneasy tension—as this paragraph says, "justice is split off from love." His Love wants to save everyone from the consequences of sin, but His justice demands that sin be punished. The traditional resolution of this tension is in Jesus' death on the cross, which (in some Christian theories of Atonement) is said to satisfy both the love component (since Jesus' death saves everyone from the consequences of sin) and the justice component (since in Jesus our sin was punished).

Jesus says here: *Nonsense!* God's Love and justice are not two poles in tension, but two aspects of His nature that are in complete harmony. His Love wants to do nothing but bless us and honor us. His justice says that because we are perfectly innocent, we are *fully deserving* of blessing and honor. When justice and love are split, it seems that love is powerless to prevent the punishment meted out by merciless justice (as we see in the common view that Jesus simply *had* to be punished for our sins). But when justice and love are once again side by side, they are joined in the power to save us from the insane belief that we could ever sin.

> 9. What can Love ask of you who think that all of this is true? Could He, in justice <u>and</u> in love, believe in your confusion you <u>have</u> much to give? You are <u>not</u> asked to trust Him far. No more [Ur: no further] than what you <u>see</u> He offers you, and what you recognize you <u>could</u> not give yourself. In God's Own justice does He recognize all you deserve, but understands as well that you cannot [Ur: can *not*] accept it for yourself. It is His special function to hold out to you the gifts the innocent <u>deserve</u>. And every one that you accept brings joy to Him <u>as well</u> as you. He knows that Heaven is richer made by each one you accept. And God rejoices as His Son receives what loving justice <u>knows</u> to be his due. For love and justice are <u>not</u> different. *Because* they are the same does mercy stand at God's right Hand, and gives [Ur: *give*] the Son of God the power to forgive <u>himself</u> of sin.

As the last paragraph said, we believe justice is split off from love and has become the stronger of the two. In this view, justice mercilessly punishes us for our sins, while the love that would set us free is powerless to do anything about it. In truth, justice and love are the same, both offering us the gifts the innocent deserve. But it would not be loving or just of God to expect us to accept the gifts of loving justice without His help. As long as we're mired in our belief in sin, we're simply not capable of seeing just how deserving we are of pure love and forgiveness.

Therefore, all He asks is that we recognize we *can't* accept the gifts of loving justice without His help, and become willing (I assume with the 51 percent willingness paragraph 1 talked about) to accept whatever gifts we *can* see Him offering us, even if we can't see the full extent of how much we really deserve them. This willingness is enough to let in the gifts we really *do* deserve as perfectly innocent Sons of God—gifts God has always offered us, gifts that bring pure joy to the Giver and receiver alike. Mercy, not vengeance, stands at God's right Hand, giving us the power to forgive in place of our lust to condemn.

> 10. To him who merits <u>everything</u>, how can it be that <u>anything</u> be kept <u>from</u> him? For that would be injustice, and unfair indeed to all the holiness that <u>is</u> in him, however much he recognize it not. God knows of <u>no</u> injustice. He would not allow His Son be judged by those who seek his death, and <u>could</u> not see his worth at all. What honest witnesses could <u>they</u> call forth to speak on his behalf? And who would come to plead <u>for</u> him, and not <u>against</u> his life? No justice would be given him by you. Yet God ensured that justice <u>would</u> be done unto the Son He loves, and would protect from <u>all</u> unfairness you might seek to offer, believing vengeance <u>is</u> his proper due.

We administer "justice" the way the Sanhedrin did in the trial of Jesus: bent on the death of the innocent Son of God, we call false witnesses—like all those "terrible" things the body has done—to ensure the condemning verdict we want. But however much we believe in sin, the Son of God is wholly innocent. Therefore, however much we may think punishment is deserved, true justice dictates that everyone deserves only pure blessing, the gift of *everything*. Anything else would be unfair. We have set up a kangaroo court to deliver vengeance in the guise of "justice," but fortunately, God's Higher Court has the last word. He has protected His Son from the unfair verdict we have rendered upon him.

> 11. As specialness cares not who pays the cost of sin, so it <u>be</u> paid, the Holy Spirit heeds not who looks on innocence at last, provided it <u>is</u> seen and recognized. For just *one* witness is enough, if he sees truly. Simple justice asks no more. Of each one does the Holy Spirit ask if he will be that one, so justice may return to love and there be satisfied. Each special function He allots is but for this; that each one learn that love and justice are <u>not</u> separate. And both are strengthened by their union with each other. Without love is justice prejudiced and weak. And love <u>without</u> justice is impossible. For love <u>is</u> fair, and cannot chasten without cause. What cause can <u>be</u> to warrant an attack upon

213

the innocent? In justice, then, does love correct mistakes, but <u>not</u> in vengeance. For that would be unjust to innocence.

The world's "justice" doesn't care who gets punished for the guilty verdict it always renders. In like manner, the Holy Spirit doesn't care who renders the innocent verdict true justice dictates. It only takes one to do that, and the Holy Spirit asks each of us if we will be that one. Our special function—our particular role in the Holy Spirit's plan of forgiveness—is a call to be that one. Will *you* be that one?

Fulfilling our special function brings love and justice back together again, where they belong. When they are split apart, merciless justice seems strong and inexorable, while merciful love seems weak and ineffectual. But when they are reunited, each strengthens the other. The essence of this mutual reinforcement is that both love and justice are totally *fair* and *impartial*. Therefore, they can only give equal and total blessing to everyone, for the purely innocent deserve nothing else. Love does correct our mistakes, for that is just, but it never punishes us for them, for that would be unjust.

> 12. You can be perfect witness to the power of love <u>and</u> justice, if you understand it is impossible the Son of God <u>could</u> merit vengeance. You need <u>not</u> perceive, in every circumstance, that this is true. Nor need you look to your experience <u>within</u> the world, which is but shadows of all that is <u>really</u> happening within yourself. The understanding that you need comes <u>not</u> of you, but from a larger Self, so great and holy that He <u>could</u> not doubt His innocence. Your special function is a call to Him, that He may smile on you whose sinlessness He shares. <u>His</u> understanding will be <u>yours</u>. And so the Holy Spirit's special function has been fulfilled. God's Son has found a witness unto his sinlessness and <u>not</u> his sins [Ur: sin]. How <u>little</u> need you give the Holy Spirit that simple justice may be given <u>you</u>.

Again, we return to the theme of how little is asked of us. True, becoming a *perfect* witness to the power of love and justice and realizing that no one *ever* deserves vengeance sounds like a tall order. But we aren't asked to recognize this all the time or see it everywhere we look. All we are asked to do is realize that it *is* too tall an order for ourselves alone and turn to our true Self, Who will give us the understanding we need. And the way we turn to Him is to fulfill our special function, to forgive those whom the Holy Spirit has especially committed to our care. Thus we become that one witness to the Son of God's innocence, and thus we come to recognize our *own* innocence.

> 13. Without impartiality there is no justice. How can specialness be just? Judge not because you cannot, not because you are a miserable sinner too. How can the special really understand that justice is the same for everyone? To take from one to give another must be an injustice to them both, since they are equal in the Holy Spirit's sight. Their Father gave the same inheritance to both. Who would have more or less is not aware that he has everything. He is no judge of what must be another's due, because he thinks he is deprived. And so must he be envious, and try to take away from whom he judges. He is not impartial, and cannot fairly see another's rights because his own have been obscured to him.

We've seen several references in this section to the idea that specialness is incompatible with justice. Why? Because specialness is not impartial—it's all about me gaining at your expense. How can someone bent on inflating himself through deflating others understand the idea that justice treats everyone equally? How can someone who feels so deprived that she is envious of others and tries to take from them understand that everyone has everything? How can someone looking out for number one see another's rights and give him what is his due?

Therefore, if we want God's justice for ourselves, we must give up our addiction to specialness and the harsh judgment of others that it dictates. We should do so not out of a false humility that says, "I'm such a lowly sinner myself—who am I to judge him?" but out of the simple recognition that specialness by its very nature prevents us from being truly just to anyone.

> 14. You have the right to all the universe; to perfect peace, complete deliverance from all effects of sin, and to the life eternal, joyous and complete in every way, as God appointed for His holy Son. This is the only justice Heaven knows, and all the Holy Spirit brings to earth. Your special function shows you nothing else but perfect justice can prevail for you. And you are safe from vengeance in all forms. The world deceives, but it cannot [Ur: can *not*] replace God's justice with a version of its own. For only love is just, and can perceive what justice must accord the Son of God. Let love decide, and never fear that you, in

your unfairness, will deprive yourself of what <u>God's</u> justice has allotted
you.

I just want to jump into this paragraph and float in it. What a blessed
relief!

We're so convinced that we're sinners. We walk this world in
trepidation, waiting for our comeuppance. Sure enough, it comes, in the
form of all the pain and suffering that presses down upon us every day in
one form or another. But this all stems from our unfairness to ourselves,
and God's justice has *overruled* our unfairness to ourselves. He holds
out to us everything we have coming to us as innocent Sons of God: "the
right to all the universe; to perfect peace, complete deliverance from *all*
effects of sin, and to the life eternal, joyous and complete in *every* way,
as God appointed for His holy Son" (Urtext version). He holds out to us
our special function, the fulfilling of which will restore our awareness of
all that is truly our due. Why not accept the gift right now?

Application: This is a little exercise created by Robert. Apply these
lines to someone you would like to be loving toward, but see as meriting
something else:

In justice God is bound to set [name] free, and give him all the honor
he deserves and has denied himself because he is not fair, and
cannot understand that he is innocent.
To [name], who merits everything, how can it be that anything
[including my love] be kept from him?
For that would be injustice, and unfair indeed to all the holiness that
is in him, however much he recognize it not.
No justice would be given him by me.
Yet God ensured that justice would be done unto [name], the Son He
loves, and would protect from all unfairness I might seek to offer,
believing vengeance is [name's] proper due.
I can be perfect witness to the power of love and justice, if I understand
it is impossible that [name], the Son of God, could merit vengeance.
I need not perceive, in every circumstance, that this is true.
The understanding that I need comes not of me, but from my larger
Self,
so great and holy that He could not doubt His innocence.

[Name] has the right to all the universe;
to perfect peace, complete deliverance from all effects of sin, and to the
   life eternal, joyous and complete in every way, as God appointed
   for His holy Son.
This is the only justice Heaven knows.

IX. The Justice of Heaven
Commentary by Robert Perry

1. What can it be but arrogance to think your little errors <u>cannot</u> be undone by Heaven's justice? And what <u>could</u> this mean except that they are sins and <u>not</u> mistakes, forever uncorrectable, and to be met with vengeance, <u>not</u> with justice? <u>Are</u> you willing to be released from <u>all</u> effects of sin? You <u>cannot</u> answer this until you see all that the answer <u>must</u> entail. For if you answer "yes" it means you will forego <u>all</u> values of this world in favor of the peace of Heaven. Not one sin would you retain. <u>And not one doubt that this is possible</u> will you hold dear that sin be kept in place. You mean that truth has greater value now than <u>all</u> illusions. And you recognize that truth must be <u>revealed</u> to you, because <u>you</u> know not what it is.

Jesus addresses here a deep-seated belief of ours—that we are stuck in our sin. okay, perhaps we wouldn't call it sin; maybe ego, or lower self, or patterns. But we do feel stuck in it. Jesus' response is that this can only be arrogance. We are arrogantly assuming that our innocent mistakes are really mortal sins. As sins, they must be real; they must be our nature. And who can escape his or her nature? Yet all it takes to escape this false nature is our willingness to be released from all effects of sin.

Jesus asks us if we are willing to experience this release. We immediately want to shout "Yes!" But then he clarifies it. It means we have to forego all the values of the world. Why? Because all the world's values are just variations on the theme of sin. So then we think, "Oh God. That is too much for me. I can't let go of all the world's values." And that is the arrogance again. Who says you can't? Therefore, along with letting go of the world's sinful values, you also need to let go of all your doubts that this is possible.

2. To give reluctantly is not to gain the gift, <u>because you are reluctant to accept it</u>. It <u>is</u> saved for you until reluctance to receive it disappears, and you are <u>willing</u> it be given you. God's justice warrants gratitude, <u>not</u> fear. Nothing you give is lost to you or anyone, but cherished and preserved in Heaven, where all of the treasures given to God's Son

are kept for him, and offered anyone who but holds out his hand in willingness they be received. Nor is the treasure <u>less</u> as it is given out. Each gift but <u>adds</u> to the supply. For God <u>is</u> fair. He does not fight <u>against</u> His Son's reluctance to perceive salvation as a gift from Him. Yet would His justice not be satisfied until it is received by everyone.

We do engage in a great deal of reluctant giving, don't we? Yet if giving is receiving, what happens when we give reluctantly? Do we fail to qualify for receiving, because our giving wasn't wholehearted enough? This lovely paragraph gives an answer: Since giving is receiving, the reason we give reluctantly is that we are secretly reluctant to *receive*. And so our gift is laid up in God's treasure house, put in storage, waiting for the day when we are finally willing to receive it. God's justice will not be satisfied until the gift is in our hands, but God also is too respectful to fight against our reluctance. And so the gift we gave waits there in the treasure house, as long as it has to, until its true recipient is ready for it.

Application: Think of a place where you feel reluctant to give. Then consider that you are reluctant to give in this case because you are actually reluctant to *receive*.

3. Be certain any answer to a problem the Holy Spirit solves will <u>always</u> be one in which <u>no one</u> loses. And this <u>must</u> be true, <u>because</u> He asks no sacrifice of anyone. An answer which demands the slightest loss to <u>anyone</u> has not <u>resolved</u> the problem, but has added <u>to</u> it and made it greater, harder to resolve <u>and more unfair</u>. It is impossible the Holy Spirit could <u>see</u> unfairness as a resolution. To Him, what is unfair must be corrected *because* it is unfair. And <u>every</u> error is a perception in which one, at least, is seen unfairly. Thus is justice <u>not</u> accorded to the Son of God. When <u>anyone</u> is seen as losing, <u>he has been condemned</u>. And punishment becomes his due <u>instead</u> of justice.

To the Holy Spirit, the very nature of "problem" is that someone is losing. Someone is being seen unfairly, through eyes of condemnation, and thus being punished. Since someone losing is what defines a problem as a problem, the only real solution must be one in which no one loses. The problem can't just shift from me losing to you losing. The problem can't just move from one place to another. This sounds obvious, but this *is* how we try to resolve problems. If the landfill is not in my backyard, but is moved to someone else's backyard, I consider the problem solved. In the Holy Spirit's eyes, however, this "has not *resolved* the problem, but has added *to* it and made it greater, harder to resolve *and more unfair*" (Urtext version). When He solves problems, He *really* solves them.

> 4. The sight of innocence makes punishment impossible, and justice sure. The Holy Spirit's perception leaves no ground [Ur: *grounds*] for an attack. Only a <u>loss</u> could justify attack, and loss of <u>any</u> kind He cannot see. The world solves problems in another way. <u>It</u> sees a resolution as a state in which it is <u>decided</u> who shall win and who shall lose; <u>how much</u> the one shall take, and <u>how much</u> can the loser still defend. Yet does the problem still remain unsolved, for <u>only</u> justice can set up a state in which there <u>is</u> no loser; no one left unfairly treated and deprived, and thus with grounds for vengeance. Problem <u>solving</u> can<u>not</u> be vengeance, which at best can bring another problem <u>added</u> to the first, in which the murder is not obvious.

Jesus here seems to have in mind interpersonal problems. There, the resolution we generally hope for looks like something out of Judge Judy, where some third party decides who the guilty party is and how much that party owes his victim. The guilty one loses so that his victim can gain restitution. When I'm in a conflict, I often hope for a Judge Judy to stride onto the scene, render a verdict, and get me my compensation.

Yet from the Holy Spirit's standpoint, this is no resolution at all, because *someone has lost*. He looks at things completely differently. The reason the guilty party seems guilty is because he caused his victim to lose. But the Holy Spirit *sees* no loss, ever. This means that there is nothing to make the defendant guilty. He must, therefore, be innocent. And being innocent, he deserves no punishment. Punishment would only make things worse. It would only add a second murder onto the first.

> 5. The Holy Spirit's problem solving is the way in which the problem <u>ends</u>. It has been solved <u>because</u> it has been met with justice. <u>Until</u> it has it will recur, because it has <u>not</u> yet been solved. The principle that justice <u>means</u> no one can lose is crucial to this course. For miracles <u>depend</u> on justice. <u>Not</u> as it is seen through this world's eyes, but as God knows it and as knowledge is reflected in the sight the Holy Spirit gives.

Only when the Holy Spirit solves the problem so that no one loses, only when everyone gets the blessing he in truth deserves, only then is the problem over. Until then, it will keep rearing its ugly head in different forms and different places, like a vampire that travels down the ages, appearing in new places under new identities, without anyone connecting the dots.

"The principle that justice *means* no one can lose is crucial to this course." Why? Because this is a course in miracles, and how can we give a miracle if we think the person in front of us really deserves condemnation instead? We can only give him a miracle when we honestly believe that this is his just due.

> 6. No one deserves to lose. And what would be unjust to him cannot occur. Healing must be for everyone, because he does not merit an attack of any kind. What order can there be in miracles, unless someone deserves to suffer more and others less? And is this justice to the wholly innocent? A miracle *is* justice. It is not a special gift to some, to be withheld from others as less worthy, more condemned, and thus apart from healing. Who is there who can be separate from salvation, if its purpose is the end of specialness? Where is salvation's justice if some errors are unforgivable, and warrant vengeance in place of healing and return of peace?
>
> 7. Salvation cannot seek to help God's Son be more unfair than he has sought to be. If miracles, the Holy Spirit's gift, were given specially to an elect and special group, and kept apart from others as less deserving, then is He ally to specialness. What He cannot perceive [specialness] He bears no witness to. And everyone is equally entitled to His gift of healing and deliverance and peace.

These paragraphs expand on the connection between miracles and justice. Jesus says that the first principle of miracles—that there is no order of difficulty in miracles—is intimately related to the idea that miracles are everyone's just due. At first that sounds odd, but when you think about it, it makes perfect sense. If it is harder to give a miracle to certain people, that implies that they are less deserving, "less worthy, more condemned, and thus apart from healing." But if everyone is equally deserving of a miracle, then it must be just as easy to give miracles to one person as another.

Otherwise, God is trafficking in specialness. Just like we humans, He looks down and holds certain people in greater favor. They are His Elect, His in-crowd, and He reserves His really special treats—miracles—for them. Admittedly, this is how history has tended to see God. Yet how can this be true when the whole purpose of salvation is "the end of specialness"?

> To give a problem to the Holy Spirit to solve <u>for</u> you means that you *want* it solved. To keep it for yourself to solve <u>without</u> His help is to decide it should remain <u>un</u>settled, <u>un</u>resolved, and lasting in its power of injustice and attack. No one can <u>be</u> unjust to you, unless you have decided first to *be* unjust. And then <u>must</u> problems rise to block your way, and peace be scattered by the winds of hate.

We so often try to solve our problems on our own. And yet we caused the problem. So solving it ourselves means that it doesn't leave the state of mind that produced it. That state of mind was one in which I decided to be unjust to someone else. I decided to cause him loss in an attempt to gain something for myself. The guilt that resulted then dreamt into my experience problems to block my way, because they were my idea of what I deserved.

Application: Think of a problem currently facing you, and say the following to yourself:

> *The root of this problem is that I decided to try to gain from someone else's loss.*
> *My guilt over this then dreamt this problem into my experience, as my idea of my just deserts.*
> *That is why I need to give it to the Holy Spirit.*
> *It must be solved from outside the state of mind that produced it.*
> *Trying to solve it myself is a statement that I don't want it solved.*
> *Holy Spirit, I give this problem to You.*
> *Solve it for me.*
> *I trust You to solve it in a way that no one loses.*

8. Unless you think that <u>all</u> your brothers have an equal right to miracles with you, you will not claim <u>your</u> right to them because you were unjust

to one with <u>equal</u> rights. Seek to deny and you <u>will</u> feel denied. Seek to deprive, and you <u>have been</u> deprived. A miracle can <u>never</u> be received because another could receive it <u>not</u>. Only forgiveness <u>offers</u> miracles. And pardon <u>must</u> be just to everyone.

Both this paragraph and the previous one imply that our minds innately operate by a principle of fairness, even if it is not God's fairness. When we deprive someone, we then dream deprivation into our own lives, as our kind of vigilante justice. If we withhold a miracle from someone, we won't let ourselves accept the miracle that we need to solve our own problem.

Application: Is there a problem in your life that seems intractable, that seems impervious to the miracle? Then ask yourself, "Do I feel undeserving of the miracle here because there is someone (maybe even someone who seems unconnected to this problem) that I am being loveless toward?" If you get a sense that there is such a person, then say to the Holy Spirit,

> *Holy Spirit, I acknowledge that he (or she) has as much right to a miracle as I do, as much right to a miracle as Jesus did, as much right as any of God's Sons does.*

9. The little problems that you keep and hide become your secret sins, <u>because</u> you did not choose to let them be removed <u>for</u> you. And so they gather dust and grow, until they cover <u>everything</u> that you perceive and leave you fair to no one. Not <u>one</u> right do <u>you</u> believe you have. And bitterness, with vengeance justified and mercy lost, condemns you as <u>unworthy</u> of forgiveness. The unforgiven <u>have</u> no mercy to bestow upon another. That is why your sole responsibility <u>must</u> be to take forgiveness for yourself.

With so many of our problems, we say to the Holy Spirit, "No thanks, I can deal with this one." Little do we realize that this is because we want to hang onto the lump of hate that lies at the heart of each one. We are like the politician who engages in a cover-up because he wants to keep repeating the crime that he is covering up. That lump of hate we refused to expose to the Holy Spirit then becomes our secret sin. And like all secret sins, it refuses to stay in the closet. From its dark hiding place, its ghostly tendrils reach out until they cover everything. Haunted by this secret sin, we end up feeling that we have no rights at all, especially no right to a miracle. And feeling that *we* have no rights leaves us with no mercy to give to others.

In the end, our only choice will be to give the problem to the Holy Spirit. This requires opening the closet in which we have stashed the skeleton of our hate. Only when He has cleansed us of our hidden hate will we feel deserving of mercy, and only then will we have mercy to give to someone else.

> 10. The miracle that you receive, you <u>give</u>. Each one becomes an illustration of the law on which salvation rests; that justice <u>must</u> be done to all, if <u>anyone</u> is to be healed. No one can lose, and everyone <u>must</u> benefit. Each miracle is an example of what justice can accomplish when it is offered to everyone alike. It is received and <u>given</u> equally. It <u>is</u> awareness that giving and receiving <u>are</u> the same. <u>Because</u> it does not make the same unlike, it sees no differences where none exists. And thus it is the <u>same</u> for everyone, because it sees no differences in <u>them</u>. Its offering is universal, and it teaches but one message:

> *What is God's <u>belongs</u> to everyone, and **is** his due.*

What an interesting (and subtle) chain of reasoning. When we keep our problems to solve on our own, we are keeping the hate at the heart of each one. By keeping that hate, we don't feel we deserve a miracle. By thinking that we don't deserve a miracle, we have no access to miracles and can't give them to others.

See how this is the opposite of the sole responsibility of the miracle worker? We *won't* accept Atonement for ourselves, so we *can't* give miracles to others. Therefore, we need to reverse this whole chain: give our problems to the Holy Spirit, so that He can heal our own hidden hate, so that we feel deserving of miracles, so that we can *give* miracles.

Based of all this, we have to ask ourselves: If I feel powerless to heal someone else's problem, could that be because I don't feel deserving of miracles myself? And could that be because I refused to give certain problems to the Holy Spirit, because I wanted to hang onto the hidden hate at the core of them?

IX. The Justice of Heaven

If we will just let Him in, we will learn one of the greatest truths there is, that wherever a miracle is received, it blesses everyone. It doesn't matter who receives it; everyone receives it, because everyone deserves it. The miracle is like an executor of an estate who has been searching for a family for years, so that he can give all family members the inheritance they have coming to them. When he finally finds their ramshackle house, it doesn't matter who lets him in the front door. Once he sets foot inside, everyone is going to get a check.

Commentaries on Chapter 26

THE TRANSITION

I. The 'Sacrifice' of Oneness
Commentary by Robert Perry

1. In the "dynamics" of attack is sacrifice a key idea. It is the pivot upon which all compromise, all desperate attempts to strike a bargain, and all conflicts achieve a seeming balance. It is the symbol of the central theme that *somebody must lose*. Its focus on the body is apparent, for it is always an attempt to limit loss. The body is itself a sacrifice; a giving up of power in the name of saving just a little for yourself. To see a brother in another body, separate from yours, is the expression of a wish to see a little part of him and sacrifice the rest.

In the interpersonal dynamics around attack, sacrifice is the valve that keeps the war from getting totally out of control. To reach a compromise, to strike a bargain, to bring enough balance into the picture for both of us to lay down our arms, there needs to be sacrifice. I give up some of what I want, you give up some of what you want, we meet in the middle and call a truce. We each do this to keep the war from taking everything. If I can give you some of the outlying provinces, I can keep my nation's capital.

Jesus then takes this familiar principle and gives it an utterly surprising application. This, he says, is what we have done with limitless reality. We have given away all the provinces, stretching to infinity, to keep a tiny capital—our body. We have done this not only with ourselves, but with everyone we look upon. With each person, we have sacrificed all the rest of him, and kept just that tiny body we see in front of us.

My dad once told me, "Son, when I left your mom, I took a carload of my things and I took the marlin [a seven-foot long stuffed marlin he caught off Catalina, winning the trophy for that year]. When I left my second wife, I took a carload of things, and left the marlin." This is not unlike what we said in the beginning: "When I left God, I left it all behind, and just took the body."

Look at the world, and you will see nothing attached to anything beyond itself. All seeming entities can come a little nearer, or go a little farther off, but cannot join.

2. The world you see is based on "sacrifice" [Ur: *sacrifice*] of oneness. It

is a picture of <u>complete</u> disunity and total <u>lack</u> of joining. Around each entity is built a wall so seeming solid that it looks as if what is inside can never reach without, and what is out can never reach and join with what is locked away within the wall. Each part must <u>sacrifice</u> the other part, to keep itself complete. For if they joined each one would <u>lose</u> its own identity, and <u>by</u> their separation are their selves maintained.

It doesn't take much to look around and see that Jesus is right. Everyone here is inside a wall that seems so solid that real, true joining appears to be impossible. We accept this as the way things are, and yet this is the source of our loneliness, as well as a deep frustration about our apparent inability to transcend that loneliness.

Jesus then again applies the principles of sacrifice to this. Remember how I said that we give up some of what we have in order to keep from losing everything? That applies here, too. We gave up Heaven in order to keep from losing our identity completely. We believed that without the boundary of the body, we would no longer be ourselves. We would be dispersed in some endless, undifferentiated mush. That is why we gave up the outer provinces—to keep from losing our very existence.

> 3. The little that the body fences off <u>becomes</u> the self, preserved through sacrifice of all the rest. And all the rest must <u>lose</u> this little part, remaining incomplete to keep its [the rest's] own identity intact. In <u>this</u> perception of yourself the <u>body's</u> loss would be a sacrifice indeed. For sight of bodies becomes the sign that sacrifice <u>is</u> limited, and something still remains for you alone. And <u>for</u> this little to belong to you are limits placed on <u>everything</u> outside, just as they are on everything you think is <u>yours</u>. For giving and receiving <u>are</u> the same. And to <u>accept</u> the limits of a body is to <u>impose</u> these limits on each brother whom you see. For you <u>must</u> see him as you see yourself.

Let's go back to our country analogy. Imagine a country so proud of its unique cultural history and identity that it wouldn't want to transcend being one country and become the whole world. For then it would lose that unique identity. So instead it gives away the entire world, all of the outlying provinces, in order to keep its tiny capital city, the home of its unique cultural heritage. Now if it loses that capital city, it has truly lost everything. There is nothing left. It is absolutely crucial, therefore, to hang onto that city.

That is how we feel about our body. The body is that tiny capital city that we still have left. If we lose it, we lose everything (or so it seems). And so we not only hang onto our own body, we see everyone else as holed up inside their bodies. How could we convince ourselves that our wall actually contained us if no one else was contained in a wall?

> 4. The body *is* a loss, and *can* be made to sacrifice. And while you see your brother as a body, <u>apart</u> from you and separate in his cell, you are demanding sacrifice of him <u>and</u> you. What greater sacrifice could be demanded than that God's Son perceive himself without his Father? And his Father be without His Son? Yet <u>every</u> sacrifice demands that they be separate and without the other. The memory of God <u>must</u> be denied if <u>any</u> sacrifice is asked of <u>anyone</u>. What witness to the wholeness of God's Son is seen within a world of separate bodies, however much he [the Son of God as he really is] witnesses to truth? He is <u>invisible</u> in such a world. Nor can his song of union and of love be heard at all. Yet is it given him to make the world recede before his song, and sight of him <u>replace</u> the body's eyes.

Application: Choose the person nearest you right now and repeat the following:

> *If I see you as a body, I am demanding that you sacrifice Heaven and your Father.*
> *And if I demand that you sacrifice, I am making that same demand of myself.*

In a world of bodies, there is no witness to the wholeness of God's Son. Everything we see tells us that God's Son is carved up into tiny pieces. Nothing even hints at his true wholeness. We cannot see his real magnitude. We cannot hear "his song of love and union." Or can we?

> 5. Those who would see the witnesses to truth [to the wholeness of God's Son] <u>instead</u> of to illusion merely ask that they might see a <u>purpose</u> in the world that gives it sense and makes it meaningful. <u>Without</u> your special function <u>has</u> this world no meaning for you. Yet it can become a treasure house as rich and limitless as Heaven itself. No instant passes

here in which your brother's holiness ca<u>nn</u>ot be seen, to add a limitless supply to every meager scrap and tiny crumb of happiness that you allot yourself.

We dearly want to see in this world the witnesses to the truth of who we are. But in order to do this, it would help if we could see a purpose here, a purpose that gives the world meaning. That purpose is our special function. Once we set about fulfilling that purpose, the world becomes a treasure house filled with "silver miracles and golden dreams of happiness" (T-28.III.7:1). Now it is our function to look on our brother's holiness as often as we can. Doing this reveals to us that we have been standing right outside a storehouse full of treasure, while we have been starving, nibbling on the tiny crumbs of happiness that we allotted ourselves.

> 6. You <u>can</u> lose sight of oneness, but can <u>not</u> make sacrifice of its reality. Nor can you <u>lose</u> what you would sacrifice, nor keep the Holy Spirit from His task of showing you that it has <u>not</u> been lost. Hear, then, the song your brother sings to you, and <u>let</u> the world recede, and <u>take</u> the rest his witness offers on behalf of peace. But judge him not, for you will hear no song of liberation for yourself, nor see what it is given him to witness to, that <u>you</u> may see it and rejoice <u>with</u> him. Make not his holiness a sacrifice to your belief in sin. You sacrifice <u>your</u> innocence with his, and die each time you see in him a sin deserving death.

We cannot really throw oneness away. We can't even keep the Holy Spirit from showing us that it has not been thrown away. Why not, then, just admit defeat in this endeavor, and instead hear the song of love and unity our brother sings to us, beneath the din of battle? And why not see the witness he offers on behalf of truth and peace? If we do, the world will recede from us, and we will enter a state of rest, rest from all the strategizing and fighting of a world at war.

Application: Think of someone you have been battling with, and say:

> *I want to hear your song of love and union.*
> *I want to see the witness you give to God's Son.*
> *How can I do so?*

I must simply refuse to judge you.
Each time I judge you as guilty and deserving of death, I die.
Instead, let me hear and let me see.

7. Yet every instant can you be reborn, and given life again. His holiness gives life to you, who <u>cannot</u> die because his sinlessness is known to God; and can no more be sacrificed by you than can the light in you be blotted out because he sees it not. You who would make a sacrifice of life, and make your eyes and ears bear witness to the death of God and of His holy Son, think not that you have power to make of Them what God willed not They be. In Heaven, God's Son is <u>not</u> imprisoned in a body, nor is sacrificed in solitude to sin. And as he is in Heaven, so <u>must</u> he be eternally and everywhere. He is the same forever. Born again each instant, untouched by time, and <u>far</u> beyond the reach of <u>any</u> sacrifice of life <u>or</u> death. For neither did he make, and only <u>one</u> was given him by One Who <u>knows</u> His gifts can <u>never</u> suffer sacrifice and loss.

Application: Think of someone you know, and dwell on the following lines, trying to let them sink in:

I think I can see this person as a sinning body, deserving of death.
I think I can see him as a witness to the sacrifice of oneness and
    the death of God and His Son.
Each time I see him this way, I die.
Yet in every instant I can be reborn.
*I can be given life again because **his** holiness gives life to me.*
And his holiness can never die.
In Heaven, he is not imprisoned in a body.
And as he is in Heaven, so must he be eternally and everywhere.
He is the same forever.
He is born again each instant, untouched by time, and far beyond
    the reach of any sacrifice of life or death.
Let me look upon his holiness, and be reborn.

8. God's justice rests in gentleness upon His Son, and keeps him safe from <u>all</u> injustice the world would lay upon him. <u>Could</u> it be that <u>you</u> could make his sins reality, and sacrifice his Father's Will for him? Condemn him not by seeing him within the rotting prison where he sees himself. It is your special function to ensure the door be opened, that he may come forth to shine on you, and give you back the gift of freedom by receiving it of you. What is the Holy Spirit's special function but to release the holy Son of God from the imprisonment he made to <u>keep</u> himself from justice? Could <u>your</u> function be a task apart and <u>separate</u> from His Own?

Application: Choose a person to focus on and then go through the following visualization:

Picture this person standing before you.
See his face, his build, his clothing.
Now realize that merely by seeing him this way, you have locked him up in prison.
You have locked him away in the rotting prison of his body.
You have condemned him to death, out of a misplaced sense of justice.
Now realize that your special function, the reason you are here, is to set him free.
Picture yourself opening the door of his prison.
You might imagine the body as a door that you cause to swing open on invisible hinges.
As it swings, a light from behind it blazes forth.
Out of this light steps a radiant being, with Great Rays streaming off of him.
The first thing he does is shine on you in love and gratitude.
Feel the rays penetrating your heart and causing something deep within you to awaken.
As a result, the door of *your* body now swings open.
And now you step out of your solitary confinement.
Returned to your original condition as pure light.
Free at last.
The two of you haven't escaped God's justice.
You have just *experienced* God's justice.

II. Many Forms; One Correction
Commentary by Robert Perry

This section revisits the issue introduced in "The Justice of Heaven" (T-25.IX)—the real nature of our problems and our need to give them to the Holy Spirit.

> 1. It is not difficult to understand the reasons why you do not ask the Holy Spirit to solve all problems for you. He has not greater difficulty in resolving some than others. Every problem is the same to Him, because each one is solved in just the same respect and through the same approach. The aspects that need solving do not change, whatever form the problem seems to take. A problem can appear in many forms, and it will do so while the problem lasts. It serves no purpose to attempt to solve it in a special form. It will recur and then recur again and yet again, until it has been answered for all time and will not rise again in any form. And only then are you released from it.

We think of a problem as defined by the outer form of it. Jesus, however, says that underneath that form is the real core of it, the real problem. This can appear in all sorts of different forms. If we solve the outer form while leaving the core untouched, then that core will simply appear again in a new form.

While we focus on the outer form, the Holy Spirit looks on the core. He sees the core of every problem as exactly the same, equally vacuous and equally easy to solve. And *that* is why we are reluctant to give our problems to Him.

> 2. The Holy Spirit offers you release from every problem that you think you have. They are the same to Him because each one, regardless of the form it seems to take, is a demand that someone suffer loss and make a sacrifice that you might gain. And when the situation is worked out so no one loses is the problem gone, because it was an error in perception that now has been corrected. One mistake is not more difficult for Him to bring to truth than is another. For there *is* but one mistake; the whole idea that loss is possible, and could result in gain for anyone. If this

were true, then God <u>would</u> be unfair; sin <u>would</u> be possible, attack be justified and vengeance fair.

Now Jesus tells us what the core of each problem is. At the heart of each one is "a demand that someone else suffer loss and make a sacrifice that you might gain." Is this how we think of our problems? When we look at our problems, we see something pressing on us from the outside, causing us loss. That, however, is the effect. Underneath that form lies the cause: our attempt to cause someone else loss, so that we can gain.

Application: Think of a problem you are experiencing. Notice how it seems to come from the outside, causing you loss. To dispel this myth, repeat the following words to yourself:

> *The appearance that the problem is causing me loss from without*
> *is just a symptom.*
> *The underlying cause is within me.*
> *It is my demand that someone else suffer loss that I might gain.*

> *Now ask the Holy Spirit, "Whom am I demanding suffer loss*
> *that I might gain?" Perhaps an answer comes immediately, or*
> *perhaps one does not come. Either way, continue with these*
> *words:*

> *This demand is not a sin; it is just a mistake.*
> *For no one can lose.*
> *Nor could I gain from their loss.*
> *Holy Spirit, release me from this demand for sacrifice.*
> *I trust that when I have been released, this problem will not rise*
> *again in any form.*

3. This <u>one</u> mistake, in <u>any</u> form, has <u>one</u> correction. There <u>is</u> no loss; to think there <u>is</u>, is a mistake. You <u>have</u> no problems, though you <u>think</u> you have. And yet you <u>could</u> not think so if you saw them vanish one by one, <u>without</u> regard to size, complexity, or place and time, or <u>any</u> attribute which you perceive that makes each one seem different from the rest. Think not the limits <u>you</u> impose on what you see can limit God in <u>any</u> way.

The single truth that solves all our problems is this: There is no such thing as loss. I cannot cause another loss. I cannot suffer loss myself. Since the nature of problems is to cause loss, then I cannot have any real problems. And this is what I will realize when I see all of my problems miraculously vanish, regardless of what I see as their level of difficulty.

Application: Think of a list of problems you have, maybe three or four. Try to pick both big and small ones. Now imagine that one of them simply vanished. How would that feel? Then imagine that another vanished, just as quickly and effortlessly. Then imagine that another vanished, and so on. Note that they are vanishing without any regard for their level of difficulty as you see it. Big ones vanish as quickly as small ones. Note further that this implies that they have no real substance, that behind their forms they are vacuous, empty. Finally, draw the inevitable conclusion: All your problems are empty of substance. They have no reality. Therefore, you have no real problems. You have no problems at all.

4. The miracle of justice can correct all errors. Every problem is an error. It does injustice to the Son of God, and therefore is not true. The Holy Spirit does not evaluate injustices as great or small, or more or less. They have no properties to Him. They are mistakes from which the Son of God is suffering, but needlessly. And so He takes the thorns and nails away. He does not pause to judge whether the hurt be large or little. He makes but one judgment; that to hurt God's Son must be unfair and therefore is not so.

A problem is an injustice because it causes hurt; it causes loss. Its core is our attempt to cause someone else loss. Its outer shell is the world's attempt to cause *us* loss. We look at such a situation and immediately want to evaluate its details. We want to know how much loss is being caused. We especially want to know how fair it is. Did we do something to deserve the loss we are experiencing? Did the person we want to lose do something to deserve our spite? The Holy Spirit, however, doesn't regard the details. All He sees is that this problem is causing hurt. And hurt, no matter what the circumstances, is unfair. It does injustice to God's Son. And therefore it cannot be.

5. You who believe it safe to give but <u>some</u> mistakes to be corrected while you keep the others to yourself, remember this: Justice is total. There <u>is</u> no such thing as partial justice. If the Son of God is guilty then is he condemned, and he <u>deserves</u> no mercy from the God of justice. But ask not God to punish him because *you* find him guilty and would have him die. God <u>offers</u> you the means to see his innocence. Would it be fair to punish him because you will not <u>look</u> at what is there to see? Each time you keep a problem for <u>yourself</u> to solve, or judge that it is one that <u>has</u> no resolution, <u>you</u> have made it great, and past the hope of healing. <u>You</u> deny the miracle of justice *can* be fair.

Jesus is acutely aware of how selective we are in giving our problems to the Holy Spirit. We want to surrender some to Him, and hold back others. But remember, the ones we hold back have at their core our belief that someone else deserves to suffer. This implies an entire concept of justice, in which everyone deserves to suffer for their sins. And since we know that justice is total, we cannot limit this concept of justice. It will spread out and cover everything, turning our attempts to be loving into weird inconsistencies, groundless exceptions, strange eccentricities. And this will make *our* problems, in which we suffer for *our* sins, seem beyond the hope of healing. For justice is total.

We need to realize that all of this is a demand that the perfectly innocent Son of God suffer because we arranged a kangaroo court in which we are the prosecutor, judge, and jury. Is that fair?

6. If God is just, then <u>can</u> there be <u>no</u> problems that justice cannot solve. But <u>you</u> believe that some injustices <u>are</u> fair and good, and necessary to preserve yourself. It is <u>these</u> problems that you think are great and cannot <u>be</u> resolved. For there are those you <u>want</u> to suffer loss, and <u>no one</u> whom you wish to be preserved from sacrifice entirely. Consider once again your special function. <u>One</u> is given you to see in him his perfect sinlessness. And you will <u>ask</u> no sacrifice of him because you could not will he suffer loss. The miracle of justice you call forth will rest on you as surely as on him. Nor will the Holy Spirit be content until it is received by everyone. For what you give to Him <u>is</u> everyone's, and <u>by</u> your giving it can He ensure that everyone receives it equally.

God would solve all of our problems, and all of them with equal ease. Why, then, do some problems seems so impossible to solve? It is not because they are actually larger, because they aren't. It is because we are more attached to their unjust core. We think, "*This* demand that someone sacrifice is fair and good, and necessary to preserve myself." The tightness of our grip on this demand is what determines the intractability of the resulting problem. We can be hell-bent on hanging onto this demand even if it means that, for consistency's sake, it makes us see everyone as deserving of suffering, even ourselves.

Our special function is the reversal of this entire picture. Rather than hanging onto one key grudge that makes us unfair to everyone, we forgive one key person, and thereby release everyone. In talking about this "one," I'm sure that Jesus has our holy relationship partner in mind here. Our function is to forgive that one central person, the person that we probably hold uniquely responsible for our pain. When we finally see her as perfectly sinless, when we ask no sacrifice of her because we could not wish that she suffer loss, then the release that we gave her will return and rest on us. And then it will generalize to everyone.

> 7. Think, then, how great your <u>own</u> release will be when you are willing to receive correction for <u>all</u> your problems. You will not keep <u>one</u>, for pain in <u>any</u> form you will not <u>want</u>. And you will see each little hurt resolved before the Holy Spirit's gentle sight. For all of them *are* little in His sight, and worth no more than just a tiny sigh before they disappear, to be forever undone and unremembered. What seemed once to be a <u>special</u> problem, a mistake <u>without</u> a remedy, or an affliction <u>without</u> a cure, has been transformed into a universal blessing. Sacrifice is gone. And in its place the Love of God can be remembered, and will shine away all memory of sacrifice and loss.

This paragraph depicts the incredible desirability of giving over all of our problems. When we understand the cost of holding onto our demands that others sacrifice (the core of our problems), we will not keep even one. Then we will see all our problems disappear. As they go, we will realize that what seemed so huge in our eyes was quite small in the Holy Spirit's sight. We will see each stubborn demand that someone suffer "transformed into a universal blessing." As our desire to inflict sacrifice and loss goes, all of our *experience* of sacrifice and loss will go with it. And then the memory of God will rise in our mind, and will replace even the memory of sacrifice and loss.

8. God cannot <u>be</u> remembered until justice is loved <u>instead</u> of feared. He cannot be unjust to anyone or anything, because He knows that <u>everything</u> that is belongs to Him, and will forever be as He created it. Nothing He loves but <u>must</u> be sinless and beyond attack. Your special function opens wide the door beyond which is the memory of His Love kept perfectly intact and undefiled. And all you need to do is but to wish that Heaven be given you instead of hell, and every bolt and barrier that seems to hold the door securely barred and locked will merely fall away and disappear. For it is <u>not</u> your Father's Will that you should offer or receive <u>less</u> than He gave, when He created you in perfect love.

From where we stand, it seems that the memory of God (the final awakening to God) lies on the other side of a thick, massive door, which is bolted and "securely barred and locked." Doesn't it seem at times as if that door will never open? The problem is that on the other side of the door is a God Who knows only justice, which means that all He knows is giving Himself to all of His Sons, without reservation, for He knows that only this is what they deserve. In contrast, on this side of the door is us, stuck in our dedication to being unjust to His Sons.

Our special function is what opens the door. Through it we learn to bless and free the brothers whom we had wrapped in the chains of our demands. Through our special function, then, we learn of justice, and thus we become like the One on the other side of the door. And as we become like Him, the bolts and locks and barriers simply fall away, and the door swings silently open. Then the light blazes forth from behind the door, and we forget all the injustices, all the drama surrounding them, and even the self we saw at the center of that drama. All we know is that we are in God, where we have always been.

III. The Borderland
Commentary by Robert Perry

1. Complexity is not of God. How <u>could</u> it be, when all He knows is one? He knows of <u>one</u> creation, <u>one</u> reality, <u>one</u> truth and but <u>one</u> Son. Nothing <u>conflicts</u> with oneness. How, then, <u>could</u> there be complexity in Him? What <u>is</u> there to decide? For it is <u>conflict</u> that makes choice possible [Ur: it is <u>conflict</u> that makes choice complex]. The truth is simple; it is one, <u>without</u> an opposite. And how could strife enter in its simple presence, and bring complexity where oneness is? The truth makes <u>no</u> decisions, for there is nothing to decide *between*. And <u>only</u> if there were could choosing be a necessary step in the advance toward oneness. What is everything leaves room for <u>nothing else</u>. Yet is this magnitude beyond the scope of this curriculum. Nor is it necessary we dwell on anything that cannot be immediately grasped.

In God, there is nothing to decide, no choices to make. Why? Because in God there is no complexity and no conflict. This is so completely different from our experience here. Our world is a jumble of different, conflicting alternatives. That is why we have to make choices. We have to decide to go right or left, to marry Bill or Bob, to hate or to love. But how would you make choices if there were no alternatives? How would you make decisions if there were only oneness? Obviously, you couldn't. Yet this is not the focus of the Course. As long as we are in this world, the illusion of choice will seem real, and thus there will be choices to make.

2. There is a borderland of thought that stands between this world and Heaven. It is not a place, and <u>when</u> you reach it is <u>apart</u> from time. Here is the meeting place where thoughts are brought <u>together</u>; where conflicting values <u>meet</u> and <u>all</u> illusions are laid down beside the truth, where they are judged to be untrue. This borderland is just beyond [this side of] the gate of Heaven. Here is every thought made pure and wholly simple. Here is sin denied, and everything that *is* received instead.

This paragraph introduces the section's main topic: the real world. The real world is a strange sort of borderland, "a borderland of thought."

It is a middle ground between this world, with its conflicting alternatives, and Heaven, with its simple oneness. In this borderland, the two big alternatives meet: Heaven's truth and the world's illusions. And as they meet, illusions are revealed to be illusory, and nothing else, and so only truth remains. In the real world, then, our thoughts are no longer complex mixtures of light and dark. Instead, they are "pure and wholly simple," because they contain only the unitary truth.

> 3. This is the journey's end. We have referred to it as the real world. And yet there is a contradiction here, in that the words imply a <u>limited</u> reality, a <u>partial</u> truth, a <u>segment</u> of the universe made true. This is because knowledge makes <u>no</u> attack upon perception. They are brought together, and only <u>one</u> continues past the gate where Oneness is. Salvation <u>is</u> a borderland where place and time and choice have meaning still, and yet it can be seen that they are temporary, <u>out</u> of place, and <u>every</u> choice has been <u>already</u> made.

How could there be a borderland between nothing and everything? That is the conundrum this paragraph addresses. Just think about the term "real world." In Course language, that is the same as saying "the real illusion." It seems to make no sense. And yet there is an explanation. The real world is a place where "real" and "illusion" meet. "They are brought together and only *one* continues past the gate where Oneness is" (Urtext version). Two men go into the room, but these two men are so totally incompatible, that only one comes out. The other one has vanished.

The real world is the "room," then, where illusions are in the process of vanishing. There, you still relate to the concept of place, but can see that the very concept is out of place. You still think that time governs things, but you can see that time itself is temporary. You still think there are choices to make, yet you realize that "every choice has been already made."

> 4. Nothing the Son of God believes can be destroyed. But what is truth to him must be brought to the last comparison that he will ever make; the last evaluation that will be possible, the final judgment upon this world. It is the judgment of the truth upon illusion, of knowledge on perception: <u>"It has no meaning, and does not exist."</u> This is <u>not</u> your decision. It is but a simple statement of a simple fact. But in this world

there are no simple facts, because what is the same and what is different
remain unclear. The one essential thing [needed] to make a choice at all
is this distinction. And herein lies the difference between the worlds.
In this one, choice is made impossible. In the real world is choosing
simplified.

According to the preceding paragraphs, what takes place in the real
world sounds exactly like the Last Judgment, which is the process whereby
our illusions are compared with the truth and as a result disappear. It is
no surprise, then, that Jesus directly mentions the Last Judgment here.

The process embodied in the Last Judgment is one that we are
supposed to be engaged in all the time. Yet now we are not very good at
it. Now when we set illusions and truth side by side and ask ourselves
which is true, we often think, "Give me a minute here. It's just not that
simple." In the meantime, we vaguely suspect that it's our job to crown
one of them true, rather than acknowledge which one is *already* true.

In the real world, however, the choice is simple and obvious. It's
as plain as day, and we realize it was decided by God long ago. What
wouldn't we give to be in that place now?

> 5. Salvation stops just short of Heaven, for only perception needs
> salvation. Heaven was never lost, and so cannot be saved. Yet who can
> make a choice between the wish for Heaven and the wish for hell unless
> he recognizes they are not the same? This difference is the learning
> goal this course has set. It will not go beyond this aim. Its only purpose
> is to teach what is the same and what is different, leaving room to make
> the only choice that can be made.

This paragraph explains why we find the choice between truth and
illusion so hard: We have a very hard time telling them apart. For us, it's
like telling the difference between a real diamond and a cubic zirconium
when you're not a diamond expert, and when the lights are out. Saying
we can't distinguish between truth and illusion is the same as saying that
we can't distinguish between the wish for Heaven and the wish for hell.
We are like the alcoholic who is convinced that the thirst for the bottle is
really the wish for Heaven, when everyone around him knows otherwise.

That is why the Course's only purpose is to teach us the difference
between the two. Once you learn that one impulse in you is the wish for

Heaven and the other is actually the wish for *hell*, that's all you need to learn. The rest will happen naturally.

> 6. There is no basis <u>for</u> a choice in this complex and over-complicated world. For no one understands what is the same, and seems to choose where no choice really is. The real world is the area of choice made real, <u>not</u> in the outcome, but in the perception of alternatives <u>for</u> choice. That there <u>is</u> choice is an illusion. Yet within this <u>one</u> [illusion—the illusion of choice] lies the undoing of every illusion, <u>not</u> excepting this.

Choosing in this world is like an absurd shell game. There are fifty walnut shells, and you have no idea which one the pea is under. All the shells look the same. In the real world, however, things are simplified. There are only two shells—truth and illusion—and they are made of clear glass. You can instantly see which one the pea is under. And when you choose that one, you realize that the other shell was a hallucination. It was never there in the first place. For truth is all there is.

Choice, then, is an illusion, for there are no alternatives. Only one thing is real. Yet we should not begrudge the illusion of choice. It will get us out of all illusions, including the illusion of choice. It is like a hand that erases everything on the blackboard and then erases itself.

> 7. Is not this like your special function, where the separation is undone by change of <u>purpose</u> in what once was specialness, and now <u>is</u> union? All illusions are but one. And in the recognition this is so lies the ability to give up <u>all</u> attempts to choose <u>between</u> them, and to make them different. How simple is the choice between two things so clearly <u>un</u>alike. There <u>is</u> no conflict here. No sacrifice is possible in the relinquishment of an illusion <u>recognized</u> as such. Where <u>all</u> reality has been withdrawn from what was <u>never</u> true, can it <u>be</u> hard to give it up, and choose what *must* be true?

What Jesus is saying about choice is like what he said about our special function (see T-25.VI.4). Specialness was made as the ultimate separation device. Yet the Holy Spirit places it into the service of union and thus uses it to undo all separation. It's the same with choice. Choice is an illusion that was made to decide between illusions. Yet the Holy Spirit uses it to decide for truth, and thus undo all illusions. This is another example of the Holy Spirit using for truth what we made for illusion.

Using choice in this way would be so easy, if only we recognized that illusions are illusions. That is what makes all of our choosing so hard. We don't realize that there's nothing under the walnut shell. If we could just see that, choosing would be a breeze.

IV. Where Sin Has Left
Commentary by Robert Perry

1. Forgiveness is this world's equivalent of Heaven's justice. It translates the world of sin into a simple world, where justice can be reflected from <u>beyond</u> the gate behind which total lack of limits lies. Nothing in boundless love could <u>need</u> forgiveness. And what is charity <u>within</u> the world gives way to simple justice past the gate that opens into Heaven. No one forgives unless he has believed in sin, and <u>still</u> believes that he has much to be forgiven. Forgiveness thus becomes the means by which he learns <u>he</u> has done nothing to forgive. Forgiveness always rests upon the one who offers it, until he sees <u>himself</u> as needing it no more. And thus is he returned to his <u>real</u> function of creating, which his forgiveness offers him again.

Forgiveness is a borderland concept, just like the real world and just like choice. It is an illusion that undoes all illusions, including itself. In Heaven, God's justice says, "You are My Son, and all I have is yours." In the world, this translates to, "You didn't do all those bad things you thought you did. You have done nothing that needs forgiveness." Forgiveness, then, is the letting go of crimes that never occurred. It is the erasure of words that were never written. What can it be but an illusion to erase an illusion? Yet in this world, forgiveness is a necessary illusion. It is the illusion that ends all illusions, including itself.

There is one more layer to this. It seems that in forgiveness we are saying to another, "You have done nothing that needs forgiveness." And we are saying that, but saying that is the way that we learn that *we* have done nothing to forgive. It is the way in which justice catches up with us at last.

2. Forgiveness turns the world of sin into a world of glory, wonderful to see. Each flower shines in light, and every bird sings of the joy of Heaven. There is no sadness and there is no parting here, for everything is <u>totally</u> forgiven. And what has been forgiven <u>must</u> join, for nothing stands <u>between</u> to keep them separate and apart. The sinless <u>must</u> perceive that they are one, for nothing stands between to push the other

off. And in the space that sin left vacant do they <u>join</u> as one, in gladness recognizing what is part of them has <u>not</u> been kept apart and separate.

It is sin that weighs this world down and tears it apart. It is the sin that seems to live in us that makes us push others away. It is the sin that two people see in each other that makes them part company. Sin stands between us all like an invisible force field. Just imagine, then, a world in which sin had been replaced by forgiveness. It would be a world in which everyone would naturally join. It would be a world of universal reconciliation. It would be a world in which every flower would shine in light, and every bird sing of the joy of Heaven. The people of that world would truly beat their swords into plowshares and they would study war no more.

Application: Think of someone with whom you have parted company. Now imagine that all the sin that seems to stand between you, all the desire to attack each other for private gain, all the history that built walls of hate between you, is gone. All the bricks of sin that built that wall between you are gone. Can you imagine that at this point your only natural, spontaneous desire would be to join?

3. The holy place on which you stand is but the space that sin has left. And here you see the face of Christ, arising in its place. Who could behold the face of Christ and <u>not</u> recall His Father as He really is? Who could fear love, and stand upon the ground where sin has left a place for Heaven's altar to rise and tower far above the world, and reach beyond the universe to touch the Heart of <u>all</u> creation? What <u>is</u> Heaven but a song of gratitude and love and praise by everything created to the Source of its creation? The holiest of altars is set where once sin was believed to be. And here does every light of Heaven come, to be rekindled and increased in joy. For here is what was lost restored to them, and all their radiance made whole again.

What a beautiful vision of "the space that sin has left." When all the sin that stood between you and this other person is gone, you will find yourself standing on holy ground. Out of this ground will rise the face of Christ, in place of the wall of sin. Out of this ground will rise a holy

247

altar, before which you and your brother will kneel together. Around this altar will gather all the lights of Heaven, "to be rekindled and increased in joy." And this altar will "rise and tower far above the universe to touch the Heart of all creation," to touch the Heart of God Himself.

> 4. Forgiveness brings no little miracles to lay before the gate of Heaven. Here the Son of God Himself comes to receive each gift that brings him nearer to his home. Not one is lost, and none is cherished more than any other. Each reminds him of his Father's Love as surely as the rest. And each one teaches him that what he feared he loves the most. What <u>but</u> a miracle could change his mind, so that he understands that love cannot <u>be</u> feared? What other miracle is there <u>but</u> this? And what else <u>need</u> there be to make the space between you disappear?

"Forgiveness brings no little miracles." It is not a little thing to suddenly believe that God actually loves us. It is not a little thing to learn that the brother we feared we actually love the most. It is not a little thing to realize that we want to love so much that we are no longer willing to let the slightest anger darken our minds. And most of all, it is not a little thing to see the wall of resentment that kept us apart from a dear brother come tumbling down.

> 5. Where sin once was perceived will rise a world that will become an altar to the truth, and <u>you</u> will join the lights of Heaven there, and sing their song of gratitude and praise. And as they come to <u>you</u> to be complete, so will you go with them. For no one hears the song of Heaven and remains without a voice that adds its power to the song, and makes it sweeter still. And each one joins the singing at the altar that was raised within the tiny spot that sin proclaimed to be its own. And what <u>was</u> tiny then has soared into a magnitude of song in which the universe has joined with but a single voice.
> 6. This tiny spot of sin that stands between you and your brother [Ur: between you] still is holding back the happy opening of Heaven's gate. How <u>little</u> is the hindrance that withholds the wealth of Heaven from you. And how <u>great</u> will be the joy in Heaven when you join the mighty chorus to the Love of God!

Application: This section is so full of beautiful imagery that it would be a shame not to do a visualization. Further, the section is really all of a piece, laying out a single process that results from forgiveness. To pull it all together, let's do the following visualization:

> Think of a relationship in which the two of you are separated by mutual condemnation, bitterness, and blame.
> See the space between you filled with a dark cloud of sin, blocking each other from clear sight.
> Now repeat this line to yourself as a prayer of forgiveness and reconciliation:
> "Let our grievances be replaced by miracles, [name]."
> Say it over and over, and as you do, picture it actually happening:
> the grievances on both sides are replaced by miracles.
> The cloud of sin between you evaporates. The air between you clears up.
> You and this person are filled with a sense of being one, "for nothing stands between to push the other off."
> And now the two of you "join as one, in gladness recognizing what is part of [you] has not been kept apart and separate."
>
> As you join, the place around you begins to transform.
> The ground on which you stand becomes holy ground.
> The sun comes out; you see the flowers shine in light and hear the birds sing a love song to God.
> In front of the two of you arises an altar to the Holy One, shining with purity and sparkling with the lilies of forgiveness that you gave each other.
> The world of sin has been transformed into a world of glory, wonderful to see.
> Spend a moment taking this in and realizing that all this came from your forgiveness.
>
> Then the two of you look up and see countless radiant lights from Heaven coming to this altar as if completing a pilgrimage.
> They gather round it and hover above it.
> They begin to sing a song of love to God, a song of indescribable sweetness and power,
> of beauty beyond what you could have imagined.

Without thinking, you and your brother are drawn to join in this song.

You find that you actually can harmonize with this song, that you fit into it, that you *belong* in this song.

Indeed, with your voice, the song becomes somehow even more sweet and powerful.

Now that you have added your voice, literally every voice in the universe joins in, and the song soars into an incomprehensible magnitude.

The altar begins to rise higher and higher, and as it does, you go with it.

The lights of Heaven are taking you with them.

You are now part of them.

And you and they continue to rise as one, past the world, past the stars,

until you touch and enter the formless Heart of God Himself, the One to Whom you have all been singing.

There you remain, to join your voice to the endless, timeless, boundless chorus to the Love of God, forever and ever.

This is what your forgiveness of your brother offers you.

V. The Little Hindrance
Commentary by Robert Perry

1. A little hindrance can seem large indeed to those who do not understand that miracles are all the same. Yet teaching that is what this course is <u>for</u>. This is its only purpose, for only that is all there is to learn. And you can learn it in many different ways. All learning is a help or hindrance to the gate of Heaven. Nothing in between is possible. There are <u>two</u> teachers only, who point in different ways. And you will go along the way your chosen teacher leads. There are but <u>two</u> directions you can take, while time remains and choice is meaningful. For never will another road be made except the way to Heaven. You but choose whether to go <u>toward</u> Heaven, or away to nowhere. There is nothing else to choose.

The little hindrance is the "tiny spot of sin that stands between you and your brother" (T-26.IV.6:1). We don't usually think of the sin that stands between us and another as little or tiny. Yet we would, if we only recognized that every miracle, big or small, is equally effortless. We don't know that yet, but learning that is why we are studying the Course.

Indeed, everything we learn either contributes to or hinders learning this one lesson, which is the gateway to Heaven. For there are only two teachers, and they lead us in opposite ways. One leads us to Heaven and the other leads us away from Heaven, to nowhere. It's as if we are on a vast ocean with one island—a true paradise—in the middle of it. One teacher leads us straight to this island, whereas the other speaks of a tantalizing, nonexistent island, and leads us out into the middle of the ocean.

2. Nothing is ever lost but time, which in the end <u>is</u> meaningless [Ur: nothing]. For it is but a little hindrance to eternity, quite meaningless to the real Teacher of the world. Yet since you <u>do</u> believe in it, why should you waste it going nowhere, when it <u>can</u> be used to reach a goal as high as learning can achieve? Think not the way to Heaven's gate is difficult at all. Nothing you undertake with certain purpose and high resolve and happy confidence, holding your brother's [Ur: each other's] hand and

keeping step to Heaven's song, is difficult to do. But it is hard indeed to wander off, alone and miserable, down a road that leads to nothing and that <u>has</u> no purpose.

Yes, time is meaningless. It is nothing. But while you believe in it, you are in it. And while you are in it, you can use it in two ways. You can walk along the road to Heaven, filled with happy confidence and enthusiastic resolve, "holding your brother's hand and keeping step to Heaven's song." The image of Dorothy and her companions on the yellow brick road comes to mind. Or you can "wander off, alone and miserable, down a road that leads to nothing and that has no purpose." You're by yourself, feeling miserable and aimless, because as the landscape becomes increasingly lifeless and bleak, you realize that you are wandering off to nowhere. True, one way involves mustering that confidence and resolve. It means keeping hold of our brother's hand. It means keeping step to Heaven's song. But all things considered, which way is truly harder?

> 3. God gave His Teacher to <u>replace</u> the one you made, <u>not</u> to <u>conflict</u> with it. And what He would replace <u>has been</u> replaced. Time lasted but an instant in your mind, with <u>no</u> effect upon eternity. And so is <u>all</u> time past [Ur: passed], and everything <u>exactly</u> as it was before the way to nothingness was made. The tiny tick of time in which the first mistake was made, and <u>all</u> of them within that <u>one</u> mistake, held also the Correction for that one, and <u>all</u> of them that came within the first. And in that tiny instant time was gone, for that was all it ever was. What God gave answer to <u>is</u> answered and <u>is</u> gone.

This paragraph contains the famous reference to the "tiny tick of time." We think of time as an interminable march of events. In fact, all of time is contained inside one tiny tick. That tiny tick is composed of a single mistake, a mistake which instantly splintered into trillions of fractured versions of itself, trillions of variations on its single theme. These fractured versions are the events of time. Each one is a snapshot of the error of separation, taken from a slightly different angle. Though they seem to comprise a long succession, they are in fact simultaneous.

Yet in that same instant, God gave His Teacher, the one Correction for the single mistake. This Correction instantly adapted Itself to every single fractured version of the error. In every one of time's events, therefore, the Correction is there, standing off to the side. It is the silent alternative, the unnoticed doorway out of the mistake.

The Correction cancels out the mistake. It's as if the lights went out in a room, and someone who already stood ready with match in hand instantly lit a lamp. And so, in the same instant in which the tiny tick occurred, it was cancelled out and was gone. There wasn't even time for a tock.

> 4. To you who still believe you live in time and know not it is gone, the Holy Spirit still guides you through the infinitely small and senseless maze you still perceive in time, though it has long since gone. You think you live in what is past. Each thing you look upon you saw but for an instant, long ago, before its unreality gave way to truth. Not one illusion still remains unanswered in your mind. Uncertainty was brought to certainty so long ago that it is hard indeed to hold it to your heart, as if it were before you still.

All of the fractured versions of the mistake, each accompanied by a specific version of the Correction, make up what appears to be a vast and intricate maze. In fact, this maze is "infinitely small and senseless." We seem to be trapped inside this maze, trying to find our way out. We wander around, running into dead ends. We keep thinking, "I could swear I have been at this corner before."

What we don't realize is that the maze "has long since gone." Not only is the past gone, but what we see as the present is gone, too. Even the apparently distant future is actually the past. The whole saga of time, stretching billions of years into the "future," was over a long, long time ago.

Application: Look upon the scene in front of you right now. Realize that the sense you have of it being here and now is supplied by you. Realize that you are actually watching an ancient newsreel of a prehistoric past. The things you see now have long since fossilized and turned to dust and then vanished completely. It's been over and done with for an eternity. Try to get that sense as you look at what's in front of you. How does it feel?

5. The tiny instant you would keep and make eternal, passed away in Heaven too soon for anything to notice it had come. What disappeared too quickly to affect the simple knowledge of the Son of God can hardly still be there, for you to choose to be your teacher. Only in the past,—an ancient past, too short to make a world in answer to creation,—did this world <u>appear</u> to rise. So <u>very</u> long ago, for such a tiny interval of time, that not one note in Heaven's song was missed. Yet in each unforgiving act or thought, in every judgment and in all belief in sin, is that one instant still called back, as if it could be made again in time. You keep an ancient memory before your eyes. And he who lives in memories alone is unaware of where he <u>is</u>.

Imagine that you had a magic video camera that would allow you to peer back in time hundreds of millions of years. Imagine that you spent hours a day at it, watching the dance of tiny one-celled creatures in the prehistoric sea. You saw one slowly engulf another. You saw them divide. Now imagine that you became so absorbed in their tiny drama that you responded to it emotionally as if it were now. Imagine that this drama became your whole reality. It became your teacher. Family members tried to coax you away from the video camera, but you no longer heard them.

That, sadly enough, is the situation we are in now. By identifying with the drama of what seems like our life, we have chosen an ancient past as our reality and our teacher. We are identifying with a microscopic dance in an ancient sea. We are, in other words, unbelievably senile. We make Granny, with her constant reminiscing about the thirties, seem like the model of sanity.

6. Forgiveness is the great release from time. It is the key to learning that the past is over. Madness speaks no more. There <u>is</u> no <u>other</u> teacher and no <u>other</u> way. For what has been undone no longer is. And who can stand upon a distant shore, and dream himself across an ocean, to a place and time that have long since gone by? How <u>real</u> a hindrance can this dream be to where he really <u>is</u>? For this is fact, and does <u>not</u> change whatever dreams he has. Yet can he still <u>imagine</u> he is elsewhere, and in another time. In the extreme, he can delude himself that this is true, and pass from mere imagining into belief and into madness, quite convinced that where he would prefer to be, he <u>is</u>.

V. The Little Hindrance

I love the image from the sixth sentence, however chilling it is. There is someone on a beach, dreaming about a romantic time and place that has long since passed into history. Maybe he is dreaming about the days of chivalry, days that lie on the other side of centuries and on the other side of the ocean. He dreams that he is a knight in those days, jousting in tournaments and rescuing fair maidens. He enjoys this fantasy. In fact, he becomes so deeply absorbed in it that he goes beyond simply imagining it. Now, while still standing on the beach, he actually believes he is there. He passes "from mere imagining into belief and into madness, quite convinced that where he would prefer to be, he *is*."

This is a picture of us. Only instead of believing we are back in the days of chivalry, we believe we are back in the days of the twenty-first century, a long ago and faraway time that disappeared ages ago. To the extent we really believe we are here in this time, we have gone completely mad.

The way to sanity is forgiveness. It doesn't just teach us that what we think of as the past is gone. It teaches us that even the "present" and "future" are gone, for they are really the past.

> 7. Is this a hindrance to the place whereon he stands? Is any echo from the past that he may hear a fact in what is there to hear where he is now? And how much can his own illusions about time and place effect a change in where he really is?

Does the man's dream that he is back in the days of chivalry actually transport him off of that beach? In the same way, does our dream that we are back in the days of the twenty-first century actually change where *we* really are? We are standing on the shores of Heaven, lost in our fantasy of a bygone era. The fantasy is what we see in front of us, but that doesn't mean that we are really *in* this scene. We cannot make our madness true. We are in Heaven, right this instant.

> 8. The unforgiven is a voice that calls from out a past forevermore gone by. And everything that points to it as real is but a wish that what is gone could be made real again and seen as here and now, in place of what is *really* now and here. Is this a hindrance to the truth the past is gone, and cannot be returned to you? And do you want that fearful instant kept, when Heaven seemed to disappear and God was feared and made a symbol of your hate?

255

Jesus keeps talking about refusing to forgive this one brother in the "present" as a way of hanging onto the whole tiny tick—the entirety of time. To understand this rather counter-intuitive connection, we need to remember two things. First, unforgiveness is a way in which one hangs onto a past that is over and gone. We can readily see this with other people who are hanging onto old grudges. Second, each little event and situation in our lives is really the whole tiny tick in miniature.

Therefore, when you hang onto an injustice being done to you in the "present," you are hanging onto a miniature version of the tiny tick. You are thus hanging onto the whole thing. And you are hanging onto it because you sense that the whole thing is really past, but *you* want to keep it present.

> 9. Forget the time of terror that has been so long ago corrected and undone. Can sin withstand the Will of God? Can it be up to you to see the past and put it in the present? You can *not* go back. And everything that points the way in the direction of the past but sets you on a mission whose accomplishment can <u>only</u> be unreal. Such is the justice your All-Loving Father has ensured <u>must</u> come to you. And from your own unfairness to yourself has He protected you. You <u>cannot</u> lose your way because there is no way but His, and nowhere <u>can</u> you go except to Him.

Now Jesus brings back the theme of going to Heaven or going nowhere. When we are trying to hang onto the past (which is the whole of time) through unforgiveness, we are trying to go back to something that is gone. But, he says, "You can *not* go back." How can you go back to what's not there anymore? We are trying to travel to an island that sank beneath the waves eons ago. Aren't we lucky that God sank that island? Otherwise, we could actually arrive there and choose to stay forever.

Let's say that your child as an adult wanted to go back to his preschool because he desperately wanted to spend the rest of his days in a fantasy of revenge on the kids that mistreated him there. Wouldn't the kindest thing to him be that, when he went there, the building was gone and all that was left was a vacant lot?

> 10. Would God allow His Son to lose his way along a road long since a memory of time gone by? This course will teach you <u>only</u> what is

now. A dreadful instant in a distant past, now perfectly corrected, is of no concern nor value. Let the dead and gone be peacefully forgotten. Resurrection has come to take its place. And now you are a part of resurrection, <u>not</u> of death. No past illusions have the power to keep you in a place of death, a vault God's Son entered an instant, to be instantly restored unto his Father's perfect Love. And how can he be kept in chains long since removed and gone forever from his mind?

For an instant, we, the Sons of God, locked ourselves up in a vault and wrapped ourselves in chains. Yet just as soon as we closed the door, God opened it, and gently removed our chains. We left the tomb and were resurrected.

Now we are taking a trip down memory lane. We are sitting where the vault used to be and visualizing our long-ago experience inside of it. We are such vivid visualizers that we actually experience ourselves back inside. That is why we feel so imprisoned and entombed in our situation right now. That is why we feel we are in chains. It's all just a very engrossing memory. Yet just as we wouldn't have been left in the vault, so we won't be left in this memory. "Would God allow His Son to lose his way along a road long since a memory of time gone by?"

11. The Son whom God created is as free as God created him. He was reborn the instant that he chose to die instead of live. And will you not forgive him now, because he made an error in the past that God remembers not, and is not there? Now you are shifting back and forth between the past and present. Sometimes the past seems real, as if it *were* the present. Voices <u>from</u> the past are heard and then are doubted. You are like to one who still hallucinates, but lacks conviction in what he perceives. This is the borderland between the worlds, the bridge between the past and present. Here the shadow of the past remains, but still a present light is dimly recognized. Once it is seen, this light can never be forgotten. It <u>must</u> draw you from the past into the present, where you really <u>are</u>.

Now we are like an insane person who is slowly coming out of it. We stand before our brother, vacillating between our memory of him in that ancient vault and the reality of him now, as the resurrected Son of God. Sometimes we look at him and see before us only the long-ago brother in the tomb. We hear the things he said back in that tomb, and think he is saying them now. Yet even when we do, we doubt the reality of these hallucinatory memories. We dimly sense the light of his resurrected reality, and suspect that *it* might be the real present. And the more we sense it, the more frequently our mind turns in its direction.

Application: Think of a brother whom you want to forgive but you feel conflicted about it. Realize that as you see him do those selfish things, you are really seeing ancient films of a time that was over long ago. Realize that as you hear him say those unkind things, you are hearing echoes from that same long ago time. On the other hand, realize that as you feel more forgiving, you are like an insane person who is at last doubting his hallucinations. You are dimly sensing this brother as he is *now*, resurrected and standing in light. It is only a matter of time before you regain your sanity in full.

> 12. The shadow voices do not <u>change</u> the laws of time nor of eternity. They come from what is past and gone, and hinder not the true existence of the here and now. The real world is the second part of the hallucination time and death are real, and have existence that can be perceived. This terrible illusion was denied in but the time it took for God to give His Answer to illusion for <u>all</u> time and <u>every</u> circumstance. And then it was no more to be experienced as there.

Just think: When you hear someone say attacking things, you are hearing "shadow voices"—ghost voices. You are hearing an echo from the distant past. Can such shadow voices, such echoes, actually change the here and now?

The real world is the place where the shadow voices meet reality, where the single-but-fractured error meets the unified-but-specified Correction. How long can we stand here before we let the Correction do its work and erase the past completely?

> 13. Each day, and every minute in each day, and every instant that each minute holds, you but relive the single instant when the time of terror took the place of love [Ur: was replaced by Love]. And so you die each day to live again, until you cross the gap between the past and present, which is <u>not</u> a gap at all. Such is each life; a seeming interval from birth

258

to death and on to life again, a repetition of an instant gone by long ago that <u>cannot</u> be relived. And <u>all</u> of time is but the mad belief that what is over is still here and now.

Remember, every event, every situation, is a microcosm of the tiny tick. We are forever engaged in reliving that tiny tick. This sounds weird, but we can actually see this if we look closely. First, let's look at the tiny tick itself. Before the tiny tick, God created us in boundless life. Then, in the tiny tick, we tried to die—we closed ourselves up in that vault. But then God raised us back to life. So the tiny tick contains the pattern of birth, death, birth.

Second, let's look at the nature of time. Time is composed of cycles, and each cycle has an upstroke and a downstroke, followed by a new upstroke. Each begins with life and ends in death, to be followed again with life. Time's cycles, then, are composed of birth/death/birth. Every breath, every day, every year, every lifetime, starts with a birth and ends with a death. But this death is not final. It is not a real end. And so after every exhale, every night, every winter, every funeral, we are born again, and given another chance to choose differently.

And so we can see in time's cycles exactly what Jesus is saying: Each one is a miniature reflection of "the single instant when the time of terror was replaced by Love" (Urtext version).

Application: Look out at the daylight or the darkness, depending on what time of day it is. If darkness is falling or has fallen, realize this is literally the repetition of the ancient instant in which you tried to die (by separating from God). If it is morning, realize that this is the reflection of God raising you to life because you cannot die. And so you have a new chance to choose again.

14. Forgive the past and let it go, for it *is* gone. You stand no longer on the ground that lies between the worlds. You <u>have</u> gone on, and reached the world that lies at Heaven's gate. There <u>is</u> no hindrance to the Will of God, nor any need that you repeat again a journey that was over long ago. Look gently on your brother [Ur: each other], and behold the world in which perception of your hate has been transformed into a world of love.

It is easy to focus on the metaphysics of this section, which are indeed mind-boggling. But notice that Jesus takes pains to yoke those lofty metaphysics to some very immediate practicalities. We let go of the tiny tick and realize that all of time is past by *forgiving our brother*.

Part of us has already done that, and so that part stands at the very gate of Heaven, ready to walk in. Now the rest of us has to catch up. We need to stop believing the voices that seem present but are really just echoes from a distant past. We need to doubt our hallucinations, sincerely and repeatedly, until they have no hold on us whatsoever. We need to look gently on our brother. If we do, we will behold the real world, the world of the real present, in which our perception of "hate has been transformed into a world of love."

VI. The Appointed Friend
Commentary by Robert Perry

1. Anything in this world that you believe is good and valuable and worth striving for can hurt you, and will do so. Not because it has the power to hurt, but just because you have denied it is but an illusion, and made it real. And it is real to you. It is not nothing. And through its perceived reality has entered all the world of sick illusions. All belief in sin, in power of attack, in hurt and harm, in sacrifice and death, has come to you. For no one can make one illusion real, and still escape the rest. For who can choose to keep the ones that he prefers, and find the safety that the truth alone can give? Who can believe illusions are the same, and still maintain that even one is best?

Application: Pick a favorite illusion of yours. Maybe it's a worldly goal. Maybe it's a special location. Maybe it's a favorite food. "Anything in this world that you believe is good and valuable and worth striving for." Now say to yourself:

This will hurt me.
Not because it has the power to hurt, but just because I have denied it is but an illusion.
I have made it real.
And through its perceived reality has entered all the world of sick illusions.
All belief in sin, in power of attack, in hurt and harm, in sacrifice and death, has come to me.
For I cannot make one illusion real, and still escape the rest.
How can I believe illusions are the same, and still maintain that even one is best?

2. Lead not your little life in solitude, with one illusion as your only friend. This is no friendship worthy of God's Son, nor one with which he could remain content. Yet God has given him a better Friend, in

Whom [Ur: whom] all power in earth and Heaven rests. The one illusion that you <u>think</u> is friend obscures His [Ur: *his*] grace and majesty from you, and keeps His [Ur: his] friendship and forgiveness from your welcoming embrace. Without Him [Ur: him] you are friendless. Seek not another friend to take His [Ur: his] place. There *is* no other friend. What God appointed <u>has</u> no substitute, for what illusion <u>can</u> replace the truth?

Who is the "appointed Friend"? I have concluded in the past that it must be Christ, our true Self. However, now that I have seen that "he" is not capitalized in the Urtext, I have a whole new view. Now I think the friend is our brother, for a number of reasons (which I don't have space to go into here).

Application: Use the same illusion that you used in the previous exercise. Now think of a person to whom you should have given the friendship that you gave to this illusion instead.

> *I will not lead my little life in solitude, with one illusion as my only friend.*
> *God has given me a better friend, [name], in whom all power in earth and Heaven rests.*
> *The one illusion that I think is friend obscures [name's] grace and majesty from me, and keeps [name's] friendship and forgiveness from my welcoming embrace.*
> *Without [name] I am friendless.*
> *I will not seek another friend to take [name's] place.*
> *For there is no other friend.*
> *What illusion can replace the truth?*

3. Who dwells with shadows is alone indeed, and loneliness is <u>not</u> the Will of God. Would you allow one shadow to usurp the throne that God appointed for your Friend, if you but realized <u>its</u> emptiness has left <u>yours</u> empty and unoccupied? Make <u>no</u> illusion friend, for if you do, it <u>can</u> but take the place of Him Whom [Ur: him whom] God has called your Friend. And it is He Who [Ur: he who] is your <u>only</u> Friend in truth. He brings you gifts that are not of this world, and only He [Ur:

he] to Whom [Ur: whom] they have been given <u>can</u> make sure that you receive them. He will place them on <u>your</u> throne, when you make room for Him on His [Ur: him on his].

Application: Continue applying these lines to the same illusion and the same person:

> *By valuing this illusion, I dwell with shadows.*
> *And who dwells with shadows is alone indeed.*
> *Yet loneliness is not the Will of God.*
> *Would I allow one shadow to usurp the throne that God appointed*
> *   for my friend, [name], especially when I realized that leaving*
> *   [name's] throne empty has left mine empty?*
> *I will make no illusion, including this one, my friend.*
> *For if I do, it can only take the place of the one whom God has*
> *   called my friend.*
> *[Name] is my only friend in truth.*
> *[Name] brings me gifts that are not of this world.*
> *And only [name] can make sure that I receive them.*
> *[Name] will place them on my throne, when I make room for him*
> *   on his.*

VII. The Laws of Healing
Commentary by Robert Perry

> 1. This is a course in miracles. As such, the laws of healing must be understood before the purpose of the course can be accomplished. Let us review the principles that we have covered, and arrange them in a way that summarizes all that must occur for healing to be possible. For when it once is possible it <u>must</u> occur.

This is a course in working miracles. To accomplish the purpose of the Course, then, you must give miracles. You must heal others. And before you can give healing, you must understand the laws of healing. Jesus, therefore, is going to review these laws now. This is clearly a very important section. It doesn't say anything new. In fact, you will probably recognize the ideas from particular sections we have covered. But it does give us an idea of the principles that Jesus considers necessary to miracle working.

> 2. <u>All</u> sickness comes from separation. When the separation is denied, it goes. For it <u>is</u> gone as soon as the idea that brought it has been healed, and been replaced by sanity. Sickness and sin are seen as consequence and cause, in a relationship kept hidden from awareness that it may be carefully preserved from reason's light.
> 3. Guilt <u>asks for</u> punishment, and its request is granted. <u>Not</u> in truth, but in the world of shadows and illusions <u>built</u> on sin.

He is talking about physical illness here. He says that all of it—from cancer, to heart attacks, to colds and flu—is the projection of the idea of separation, which is a sick (or insane) idea. A sick idea, of course, would naturally project a sick picture.

Jesus, however, doesn't leave it at that general level. More specifically, the act of separating is an attack. This attack makes us believe that we are sinners. We then feel guilty, and this guilt automatically calls for punishment. It actively asks for punishment. This request is not answered by truth, but by ourselves. To satisfy the lie of guilt, we project the shadow of illness. As the *Psychotherapy* supplement says, "Illness can

264

be but guilt's shadow" (P-2.IV.2:6).

It certainly does not seem that illness comes from guilt, and that's because we have purposefully hidden this fact. The cause and effect relationship between sin and sickness is "kept hidden from awareness that it may be carefully preserved from reason's light." If it was out in the light, we could undo it, and we don't want that.

> The Son of God perceived what he would [wants to] see because perception is a wish fulfilled. Perception changes, made to take the place of changeless knowledge. Yet is truth unchanged. It cannot be perceived, but only known. What is perceived takes many forms, but none has meaning. Brought to truth, its senselessness is quite apparent. Kept apart from truth, it seems to have a meaning and be real.

When we perceive, we think we are looking out upon the truth, but we are actually seeing only what we want to see. We are seeing the projection of our own wishes. What we see is constantly changing, because we made perception to take the place of changeless knowledge. What we see takes a great many forms, because we are trying to use the form to hide what lies beneath it: our own senseless wish. If we would only bring the wish to light, we would see how senseless it is and let it go.

> 4. Perception's laws are opposite to truth, and what is true of knowledge is not true of anything that is apart from it. Yet has God given answer [Ur: Answer] to the world of sickness, which applies to all its forms. God's answer [Ur: Answer] is eternal, though it [Ur: It] works [Ur: operates] in time, where it [Ur: It] is needed. Yet because it [Ur: It] is of God, the laws of time do not affect its [Ur: Its] workings. It is in this world, but not a part of it. For it [Ur: It] is real, and dwells where all reality must be. Ideas leave not their source, and their effects but seem to be apart from them. Ideas are of the mind. What is projected out, and seems to be external to the mind, is not outside at all, but an effect of what is in, and has not left its source.
> 5. God's answer [Ur: Answer] lies where the belief in sin must be, for only there can its effects be utterly undone and without cause. Perception's laws must be reversed, because they *are* reversals of the laws of truth. The laws of truth forever will be true, and cannot be reversed; yet can be seen as upside down. And this must be corrected where the illusion of reversal lies.

Perception works in ways that are directly opposite to knowledge. Rather than *knowing* the love that is forever real, we *perceive* our own insane wishes projected outward. Now those wishes seem to be outside our mind. Now they seem to be independently real, requiring us to bow to their reality. Yet in fact they are still inside us, still no more than a demented fantasy. In viewing our body's illnesses, for instance, we are simply viewing certain thoughts *as if* they were external images. There is no illness, because there is no body.

This is why God gave us His Answer, the Holy Spirit. The Holy Spirit dwells in God, in eternity, yet from there He reaches down into the world of time. His workings reflect the laws of eternity and knowledge, and so are not bound by the laws of time and perception. His whole job is to bring the workings of higher laws down into our belief in the upside-down laws of perception. We need His sanity to come right down into the heart of our insanity. That is how He heals.

To apply this to sickness: He brings a reflection of the knowledge of who we are right down into our belief that we are sinful and deserve to bear the punishment for that in our flesh. That belief is a reversal of the truth, yet He is the only One Who truly knows that. We have to borrow His certainty, so that with His help, we can reverse our reversal. We can set our mind right-side-up again.

> 6. It is impossible that one illusion be <u>less</u> amenable to truth than are the rest. But it <u>is</u> possible that some are given greater <u>value</u>, and less willingly <u>offered</u> to truth for healing and for help. <u>No</u> illusion has <u>any</u> truth in it. Yet it appears some are <u>more</u> true than others, although this clearly makes no sense at all. All that a hierarchy of illusions can show is <u>preference, not</u> reality. What relevance has preference to the truth? Illusions are illusions and are false. Your preference gives them <u>no</u> reality. Not one is true in <u>any</u> way, and all must yield with equal ease to what God gave as answer to them all. God's Will is one. And <u>any</u> wish that <u>seems</u> to go <u>against</u> His Will has <u>no</u> foundation in the truth.

This paragraph is about the first principle of miracles, that there is no order of difficulty in miracles. This means, of course, that every sickness, no matter how seemingly extreme, can be healed by a miracle with equal ease. That obviously doesn't seem to be the case. Some illnesses seem bigger and more intractable. Yet according to Jesus, this is not because they are actually bigger. They seem bigger for one reason, and one reason only: At the heart of them is something we are more attached to, some wish that we will not let go. The result is that they "are given greater value, and less willingly offered to truth for healing and for help."

Application: Think of some problem, perhaps even a physical illness, that you want solved, but that seems too big for a miracle to heal. Now ask yourself,

> *Is it possible that at the core of this problem is some wish I am hanging onto, which makes me unwilling to truly place this problem in the Holy Spirit's hands?*
> *Holy Spirit, what is that wish?*

7. Sin is not error, for it goes <u>beyond</u> correction to impossibility. Yet the belief that it is real has made some errors seem forever <u>past</u> the hope of healing, and the lasting grounds for hell. If this were so, would Heaven be opposed by its own opposite, as real as it. Then would God's Will be split in two, and all creation be subjected to the laws of two opposing powers, until God becomes impatient, splits the world apart, and relegates attack unto Himself. Thus has He lost His Mind, proclaiming sin has taken His reality from Him and brought His Love at last to vengeance's heels. For such an insane picture an insane defense can be expected, but can <u>not</u> establish that the picture must be true.

We tend to divide things into errors (mistakes) and sins. The former are seen as innocent and as correctable. We may hit ourselves for them, but we don't see them as permanent marks on our soul. Sins, however, are a whole different matter. We see them as justified, necessary, yet evil. Because of this, and because of the harm they cause, they cannot be corrected, but are instead "lasting grounds for hell"—for our own residence in hell.

Yet before we simply accept this idea, we must be willing to look on its implications. If sin is real, then there is an opposite to Heaven, an opposite as real as Heaven. Now the world must become a battleground between "two opposing powers," good and evil. And on and on the battle must rage, down the ages, until finally, God becomes impatient and steps in to end the battle Himself. He defeats evil by bringing vengeance down upon it. Thus, God Himself has been taken over by the power of sin. The evil He sought to defeat has possessed Him. "Thus has He lost His Mind, proclaiming sin has taken His reality from Him and brought His Love at last to vengeance's heels."

This is an apt description of the worldview of Western religion, going all the way back to Zoroastrianism (which introduced the whole concept of the Last Judgment). Yet what a crazy picture. Are we really willing to accept this? Yet if we will *not* accept it, then we also cannot accept the idea of sin. We cannot accept that any of our errors are actual sins. To be consistent, then, we must reject any notion of sinfulness in ourselves, anything that is not perfect holiness. Are we willing to do that?

> 8. Nothing <u>gives</u> meaning where no meaning <u>is</u>. And truth needs <u>no</u> defense to make it true. Illusions <u>have</u> no witnesses and no effects. Who looks on them is but deceived. Forgiveness is the only function here, and serves to bring the joy this world denies to every aspect of God's Son [every Son] where sin was thought to rule. Perhaps you do not see the role forgiveness plays in ending death and <u>all</u> beliefs that rise from mists of guilt. Sins are beliefs that you impose between your brother and yourself. They limit you to time and place, and give a little space to you, <u>another</u> little space to him. This separating off is symbolized, in your perception, by a body which is clearly separate and a thing apart. Yet what this symbol <u>represents</u> is but your wish to *be* apart and separate.

He keeps talking about defense of illusion. "For such an insane picture an insane defense can be expected." The insane picture is the picture of sin and separation, and the insane defense is the external witnesses to this picture, the external conditions that "prove" the picture is true. One such witness, of course, is physical illness. It seems to prove that we have done something wrong, as you can see by the fact that we so often ask, "What did I do to deserve this?"

Forgiveness is the solution for all of this. Forgiveness wipes away the sense of guilt that manifests in the form of illness. Forgiveness wipes away the belief in sin that claims we are separate from our brother and that manifests as us being locked up in a body.

9. Forgiveness <u>takes</u> <u>away</u> what stands between your brother and yourself. It is the wish that you be <u>joined</u> with him, and <u>not</u> apart. We call it "wish" because it still conceives of other choices, and has not yet reached beyond the world of choice entirely. Yet is this wish in line with Heaven's state, and not in <u>opposition</u> to God's Will. Although it falls far short of giving you your full inheritance, it <u>does</u> remove the obstacles that <u>you</u> have placed between the Heaven where you are, and <u>recognition</u> of where and what you are. Facts are unchanged. Yet facts can be denied and thus unknown, though they were known <u>before</u> they were denied.

Look at your body. Realize this body is not real. It is just a dream symbol. And like all dream symbols, it reflects something going on within your psyche. Look at it and realize that it is the picture of your wish to be separate and apart.

At the heart of this wish is the belief in sin. Sin says two things: "I don't want to join with that rotten sinner over there," and "I am justified in taking advantage of him (which makes me a sinner myself)." Both statements put a wall up between me and my brother. And that wall is my body.

Forgiveness is the opposite wish. "It is the wish that you be joined with him, and not apart." It says, "All those things you did to me didn't matter," and "All those ways I wanted to take advantage of you were crazy." What are these statements but the prerequisite for joining? Indeed, what are they but the *wish* to join? This wish is not the heavenly state, but it sweeps away all the obstacles to that state. Therefore, this is our function now.

Application: Think of someone you need to forgive. Say to this person:

All those things I thought you did to me didn't matter.
They didn't even really happen.
All those ways I wanted you to lose for my sake were crazy.
They were my mistake.
I do not wish to be apart and separate anymore.
I wish to join.

Realize that if you made this wish with all your mind and heart, your body would disappear, and your mind and this person's mind would be one.

> 10. Salvation, perfect and complete, asks but a <u>little</u> wish that what is true be true; a <u>little</u> willingness to overlook what is not there; a <u>little</u> sigh that speaks for Heaven as a preference to this world that death and desolation seem to rule. In joyous answer will creation rise within you, to <u>replace</u> the world you see with Heaven, wholly perfect and complete. What is forgiveness but a willingness that truth be true? What can remain unhealed and broken from a Unity Which holds all things within Itself? There is <u>no</u> sin. And <u>every</u> miracle is possible the <u>instant</u> that the Son of God perceives his wishes and the Will of God are one.

This is forgiveness: "a little wish that what is true be true." How can we not have that little wish? It is "a little willingness to overlook what is not there." Surely this is not asking too much of us. It is "a little sigh that speaks for Heaven as a preference to this world that death and desolation seem to rule." How hard can it be to slightly prefer Heaven to death and desolation? Forgiveness, then, is not what we think it is. It is not a Herculean act of undeserved charity. It is a slight acknowledgment of what is already true, a tiny nod in the direction of what our brother really deserves. And once we make this tiny nod, everything will be given us—every miracle along with Heaven itself.

> 11. What is the Will of God? He wills His Son have everything. And this He guaranteed when He created him *as* everything. It is impossible that anything be lost, if what you *have* is what you *are*. This is the miracle by which creation became <u>your</u> function, sharing it with God. It is not understood <u>apart</u> from Him, and therefore has no meaning in this world. Here does the Son of God ask <u>not</u> too much, but <u>far</u> too little. He would sacrifice his own identity <u>with</u> everything, to find a <u>little</u> treasure of his own. And this he cannot do without a sense of isolation, loss and loneliness. This <u>is</u> the treasure he has sought to find. And he <u>could</u> only be afraid of it. Is fear a treasure? Can uncertainty be what you want? Or is it a mistake about your will, and what you <u>really</u> are?

All we have to do is wish for ourselves what God wills for us. What, then, does He will for us? He wills us to *have* everything, and so He created us *as* everything. That way, since what we *have* is what we *are*, we could never lose what we have. This is what we should wish for—everything.

This is why Jesus says that we do not ask too much, "but far too little." Rather than asking for everything, which is our right, we sacrifice our identification with everything, so we can keep a little treasure of our own. This little treasure is probably a reference to the body (see T-26.I.1-3). Giving up everything to hang onto the body makes us feel lonely and deprived—and afraid. What kind of treasure is that? Throwing away everything to keep fear and loneliness shows that we clearly don't understand what we really want, nor what we really are.

> 12. Let us consider what the error is, so it can be corrected, not protected. Sin is belief attack can be projected outside the mind where the belief arose. Here is the firm conviction that ideas can leave their source made real and meaningful. And from this error does the world of sin and sacrifice arise. This world is an attempt to prove your innocence, while cherishing attack. Its failure lies in that you still feel guilty, though without understanding why. Effects are seen as separate [Ur: Effects are *separated*] from their source, and seem [Ur: They *seem*] to be beyond you to control or to prevent. What is thus kept apart can never join.

Here is the error that starts it all: We think we can project our attack outside our mind. We are horrified at all the attack inside of us, and so we throw it out there. As a result, we see ourselves ringed by attackers. We tiptoe through a world full of sin and war, full of demands for sacrifice. We think we are innocent, since all the attack is out there. We can't control the attack that swirls around us. It is not ours. Yet we still feel guilty, and can't figure out why. Couldn't our guilt be testament to the fact that all the attack we see out there is really *in here*?

> 13. Cause and effect are one, not separate. God wills you learn what always has been true: That He created you as part of Him, and this must still be true because ideas leave not their source. Such is creation's law; that each idea the mind conceives but adds to its abundance, never takes away. This is as true of what is idly wished as what is truly willed, because the mind can wish to be deceived, but cannot make it [what the

mind wishes to be deceived about?] be what it is not. And to believe ideas can leave their source is to invite illusions to be true, <u>without success</u>. For never will success <u>be</u> possible in trying to deceive the Son of God.

The world we see is an idea that has not left its source: our mind. In just the same way, we are an idea that has not left our Source: God's Mind. No idea leaves the mind that thought it. When we try to project ideas outside our minds, we simply add to the total number of ideas *within* the mind. We can try to deceive ourselves about this, but we will never truly succeed. Somewhere deep down we will understand that the attack we see in the world is really a projection of what is within, and we will feel guilty.

14. The miracle is possible when cause and consequence are brought together, <u>not</u> kept separate. The healing of effect <u>without</u> the cause can merely shift effects to other forms. And this is <u>not</u> release. God's Son could never be content with <u>less</u> than full salvation and <u>escape</u> from guilt. For otherwise he still demands that he must make <u>some</u> sacrifice, and thus denies that <u>everything</u> is his, unlimited by loss of any kind. A tiny sacrifice is just the same in its <u>effects</u> as is the <u>whole</u> idea of sacrifice. If loss in <u>any</u> form is possible, then is God's Son made incomplete and not himself. Nor will he know himself, nor recognize his will. He has forsworn his Father <u>and</u> himself, and made Them both his enemies in hate.

Now we come back to miracles. The miracle is made possible by bringing together the cause (the attack within) and the effect (the attack coming from without). The miracle heals the attack within, and thereby heals the attack coming from without (which, of course, may take the form of physical illness). If we just heal the outer problem, the real inner cause will simply manifest new effects, which, if solved, will be replaced by even newer effects. The process is never-ending.

Healing the outer effects, then, is simply not good enough. We want *total* release, "full salvation and escape from guilt." If we have to sacrifice even a little bit of the everything that is our birthright, then we have been made incomplete and not ourselves. We simply cannot settle for anything less than everything.

15. Illusions serve the purpose they were <u>made</u> to serve. And <u>from</u> their purpose they derive whatever meaning that they seem to have. God gave to <u>all</u> illusions that were made <u>another</u> purpose that would justify a miracle <u>whatever</u> form they took. In every miracle <u>all</u> healing lies, for God gave answer to them all [all illusions] as one. And what is one to Him must <u>be</u> the same. If you believe what is the same is different you but deceive yourself. What God calls one will be forever one, <u>not</u> separate. His Kingdom <u>is</u> united; thus it was created, and thus will it ever be.

The illusions of this world were made for a purpose, a hidden purpose. That purpose is not specified here, but we can say that, generally speaking, their purpose is to imprison us. The effect they have on us derives not from how pleasant or unpleasant their form is, but from that underlying purpose. God, on the other hand, gave them all a different purpose. If we see them in light of His purpose, then they all become justifications for a miracle, regardless of their form. And the miracle can heal all of them with equal ease, for each miracle contains all healing, while each illusion is just the same nothingness dressed up in different clothes.

Application: Think of some imprisoning form in your life, and say,

I can see this not as justification to feel imprisoned, but as justification for a miracle.
That is the purpose God assigned to this form, when He answered all of this world's illusions as one.

16. The miracle but calls your ancient Name, which you <u>will</u> recognize because the truth is in your memory. And to this Name your brother calls for his release and yours. Heaven is shining on the Son of God [your brother]. Deny him not, that <u>you</u> may be released. Each instant is the Son of God reborn until he chooses <u>not</u> to die again. In every wish to hurt he chooses death instead of what his Father wills for him. Yet every instant offers life to him because his Father wills that he should live.

Application: Think of someone who recently seemed to attack you, and say,

You are calling my ancient Name, the Name of my true Identity.
You are calling for mercy and for release.
I will deny not your call, that I may be released.
In your wish to hurt, you are choosing death.
Yet in my forgiveness, I offer you life.
I offer you a miracle.
For God's Will for you is life, and only life.

17. In crucifixion is redemption laid, for healing is not needed where there is no pain or suffering. Forgiveness is the <u>answer</u> to attack of any kind. So is attack <u>deprived</u> of its effects, and hate is answered in the name of love. To you to whom it has been given to save the Son of God from crucifixion and from hell and death, all glory be forever. For you <u>have</u> power to save the Son of God because his Father willed that it be so. And in your hands does <u>all</u> salvation lie, to be both offered and received as one.

Application: Continue applying to this same person the following lines:

Forgiveness is my answer to [name's] attack, and to any attack.
I answer his hate in the name of love.
I therefore deprive his attack of effects, so it cannot hurt him.
It has been given me to save [name] from crucifixion.
For God willed that [name] be resurrected.
In my hands does all salvation lie, to be given and received as one.
All glory be to me forever.

18. To use the power God has given you as He would have it used is natural. It is <u>not</u> arrogant to be as He created you, nor to make use of what He gave to answer <u>all</u> His Son's mistakes and set him free. But it <u>is</u> arrogant to <u>lay aside</u> the power that He gave, and choose a little senseless wish instead of what He wills. The gift of God to you is limitless. There is <u>no</u> circumstance it cannot answer, and <u>no</u> problem which is not resolved within its gracious light.

Did it feel arrogant in that exercise to say, "All glory be to me forever"? Did it feel arrogant to say that all salvation lies in your hands? Jesus assumes that it did, so he addresses that in this paragraph. He says that to use this power is not arrogant, it is only natural. Indeed, what is arrogant is *laying aside* this power; refusing to use His gift to you to heal your brothers and solve the world's problems.

Application: Say to yourself,

> *It is not arrogant to use the power God gave me to heal my brothers.*
> *It is arrogant to lay it aside unused.*

> 19. Abide in peace, where God would have you be. And be the means whereby your brother finds the peace in which your wishes are fulfilled. Let us unite in bringing blessing to the world of sin and death. For what can save each one of us can save us all. There is no difference among the Sons of God. The unity that specialness denies will save them all, for what is one can have no specialness. And everything belongs to each of them. No wishes lie between a brother and his own. To get from one is to deprive them all. And yet to bless but one gives blessing to them all as one.

It is easy to miss that here, at the end of the section, all of the talk is about miracle working. He has given us the principles behind miracles; now he is urging us to do them. Let us read the paragraph again with some explanatory comments inserted:

> "And be the means—through giving miracles—whereby your brother finds the peace in which your wishes—for joining, for everything—are fulfilled. Let us unite in bringing blessing—through our miracles—to the world of sin and death. For the miracles that can save each one of us can save us all. There is no difference among the Sons of God. The unity that specialness denies will save them all, for what is one can have no specialness. And everything belongs to each of them. No wishes lie between a brother and his own—his brother. To get from one is to deprive them all. And yet to bless but one—with a miracle—gives blessing to them all as one."

Jesus is once again calling us to be miracle workers. Since we are all one, as we give a miracle to one brother, everyone is blessed, including ourselves.

> 20. Your ancient Name belongs to everyone, as theirs to you. Call on your brother's name and God will answer, for on Him you call. Could He refuse to answer when He has <u>already</u> answered all who call on Him? A miracle can make no change at all. But it <u>can</u> make what always has been true be <u>recognized</u> by those who know it not; and by this little gift of truth but let to be itself, the Son of God [is] allowed to be himself, and all creation [is] freed to call upon the Name of God as one.

When you give a miracle, you call on your brother's ancient Name, the Name he forgot when he closed his eyes in Heaven and the saga of the universe began. When you call on his Name (by giving a miracle), you also call on your own Name, for you and he share the same name.

This call will be answered by God Himself. Yet this answer is not something new, something that just happened, even though it seems like it is. You will simply be tapping into the answer that God gave everyone a long time ago. You will simply be recognizing the truth that has always been there, and sparking this same recognition in your brother. This frees all of creation to call upon the Name of God as one.

VIII. The Immediacy of Salvation
Commentary by Robert Perry

You can really see the contrast between this section and the last. The last one was a review. Nearly every paragraph was condensed from some previous discussion. Now Jesus is back to introducing new themes. This section deals with a crucial question: If forgiveness, once given, is meant to be returned, so that it results in a *mutual* reconciliation and joining, why does it seem that we can't count on that?

> 1. The one remaining problem that you have is that you see an interval between the <u>time</u> when you forgive, and will receive the benefits of [Ur: trust.] trusting in your brother. This but reflects the little you would keep between you and your brother [Ur: *yourselves*], that you and he [Ur: *that you*] might be a <u>little</u> separate. For time and space are <u>one</u> illusion, which takes different forms. If it has been projected <u>beyond</u> your mind [Ur: minds] you think of it as time. The nearer it is brought to where it <u>is,</u> the more you think of it in terms of space.

We are afraid of forgiving our brother. It would be so much easier if we thought he would instantly say, "Thank you! And I let go of everything I've been holding against you, too. Let's let bygones be bygones and embrace as friends." But we suspect that this rosy scenario will not play out. According to Jesus, we suspect this because we want to keep *space* between this brother and ourselves. Space, Jesus explains is the primary illusion. Space, after all, is separation. They are one and the same. When we project space beyond ourselves, it becomes *time*. In other words, if we want to keep some *space* between ourselves and someone else, this produces the illusion that it will take a long *time* before the two of us can join. Separation translates directly into *procrastination*.

> 2. There is a <u>distance</u> you would keep apart from your brother [Ur: one another], and this space you perceive as time because you still believe you are <u>external</u> to him [Ur: each other]. This makes trust impossible. And you can<u>not</u> believe that trust would settle every problem <u>now</u>. Thus do you think it <u>safer</u> to remain a <u>little</u> careful and a <u>little</u> watchful

of interests perceived as separate. From this perception you cannot conceive of gaining what forgiveness offers *now*. The interval you think lies in between the giving and receiving of the gift <u>seems</u> to be one in which you sacrifice and suffer loss. You see <u>eventual</u> salvation, not <u>immediate</u> results.

This paragraph elaborates on the same scenario. First, we have an internal wish for space between us and this brother. Being internal, it's in our hands; we have power over it. Second, we project this internal wish from our mind onto our brother. Now the wish that resided in us is seen as residing in him. Once we see it as in him, as external, the desire for space turns into objective time, time that we can't control. It goes from "I want some space between me and him" to "he will take a long time before he's willing to join with me."

Expecting that this interval will be there means that we assume we can't trust this guy. We thus withhold the trust that "would settle every problem now." And so we are left sitting in this interval, the interval between giving and receiving. It is an interval in which we feel we did our part but he won't do his. We reached out, made a sacrifice, but he left us hanging. We leapt from our trapeze, hoping he would catch us, but instead he let us fall.

3. Salvation *is* immediate. Unless you so perceive it, you <u>will</u> be afraid of it, believing that the risk of loss is great between the time its <u>purpose</u> is made yours and its <u>effects</u> will come to you. In this form is the error still obscured that is the <u>source</u> of fear. Salvation *would* wipe out the space you see between you still, and let you <u>instantly</u> become as one. And it is <u>here</u> you fear the loss would lie. Do not project this fear to time, for time is <u>not</u> the enemy that you perceive. Time is as neutral as the body is, except in terms of what you see it <u>for</u>. If you would keep a little <u>space</u> between you and your brother still, you then would want [Ur: you want] a little <u>time</u> in which forgiveness is withheld a little while. And this but makes the interval <u>between</u> the time in which forgiveness is withheld from you [by your brother] and given [to you] seem dangerous, with terror justified.

Cause and effect are not separated by time. This means that forgiveness (cause) and joining (effect) cannot be separated by time (we'll see how this is so later). We, however, are afraid that they are. It's as if we are asked to give away our car and promised that we'll get an even better one back—maybe in an hour, or a day, or a week, or a year, or a decade. That makes giving away our car a pretty fearful prospect.

Jesus, however, says that this fear is a smokescreen for our real fear. Our real fear is that the results *will* be immediate. We are afraid that salvation *will* "wipe out the space you see between you still, and let you *instantly* become as one" (Urtext version). This is what scares us, and so we essentially arrange for that interval to be there. We make sure that our gift arrives in our mail after a comfortable four to six weeks (or longer). And then we say, "Oh why isn't it here? This whole forgiveness thing is a scam."

> 4. Yet <u>space</u> between you and your brother is apparent only in the present, *now*, [Ur: Yet *space* between you is apparent *now*,] and cannot <u>be</u> perceived in future time. No more can it be <u>overlooked</u> except within the present. <u>Future</u> loss is not your fear. But <u>present</u> joining <u>is</u> your dread. Who can feel desolation except <u>now</u>? A <u>future</u> cause as yet <u>has</u> no effects. And therefore <u>must</u> it be that if you fear, there is a <u>present</u> cause. And it is *this* that needs correction, <u>not</u> a future state.

Jesus has a good point. The future isn't here yet. This lingering future gap that you foresee does not yet exist. How, then, can it be the cause of your fear? A cause must exist before it has effects. Therefore, the real cause of your fear must be something in the present. It must, in fact, be your present fear of real joining. The next paragraph will elaborate on this entire picture.

> 5. The plans <u>you</u> make for safety all are laid within the future, where you <u>cannot</u> plan. No purpose has been <u>given</u> it as yet, and what <u>will</u> happen has as yet no cause. Who can predict effects without a cause? And who could fear effects <u>unless</u> he thought they had <u>been</u> caused, and judged disastrous *now*? Belief in sin arouses fear, and like its cause [the mind and its power of choice?], is looking forward, looking back, but <u>overlooking</u> what is here and now. Yet <u>only</u> here and now its [sin's] cause must be, if its [sin's] effects <u>already</u> have been judged as fearful. And in overlooking <u>this,</u> is it [sin] protected and kept separate from healing. For a miracle is *now*. It stands <u>already</u> here [Ur: there], in present grace, within the only interval of time that sin and fear have overlooked, but which is all there <u>is</u> to time.

This is a hard paragraph to decipher. Here is my best attempt to do so. The future, being free and open, can't be known, *unless* you have already dedicated it to a certain purpose, unless it already has a present cause. Therefore, if you are projecting a *fearful* future, it can only be because you have already dedicated that future to a *sinful* purpose. You are thinking, "I want to stay separate from my brother for a while yet." That is a thought of sin. However, you deny that thought, which then surfaces as a different thought: "My brother is going to refuse to join with me for a long time." That is a thought of fear. The first thought is the cause, the second is the effect. By overlooking the first, you see no need to heal it. What needs healing, you think, is the length of time your brother is going to take before he joins with you. You thus keep the real cause apart from the miracle, which would heal it where it exists, in the present.

> 6. The working out of <u>all</u> correction takes no time at all. Yet the <u>acceptance</u> of the working out can <u>seem</u> to take forever. The change of purpose the Holy Spirit brought to your relationship has <u>in</u> it all effects that you will see. They can be looked at *now*. Why wait till they unfold in time and fear they may <u>not</u> come, although already <u>there</u>? You have been told that everything brings good that comes from God. And yet it <u>seems</u> as if this is not so. Good in disaster's form is difficult to credit in advance. Nor is there really <u>sense</u> in this idea.

The way Jesus has been talking, it sounds as if, when you forgive your brother totally, with no hidden wish to keep him at arm's length, he will immediately and wholeheartedly reciprocate. But to think that would be naïve, wouldn't it? This paragraph clarifies things. It is speaking directly to Helen and Bill's holy relationship, so let's paraphrase things in those terms.

"When you forgave each other, the Holy Spirit didn't wait to give you the benefits of that. He made your relationship completely holy right at that instant. On some level, He brought the two of you together in a state of perfect union. All the effects—the joining—that will someday play out on the surface were made present at that moment. Thus, if you forgive your brother now without any ambivalence, you can see past the surface and experience your union now, even before it manifests on the surface."

To put this in more general terms, when you forgive someone, if your forgiveness is completely pure, even if the other person does not reciprocate, you will see through to a place where he *is* reciprocating and the two of you *are* joined. As Lesson 197 says, "It does not matter if another thinks your gifts unworthy. In his mind there is a part that joins with yours in thanking you" (W-pI.197.4:1-2).

> 7. Why <u>should</u> the good appear in evil's form? And is it not deception if it does? Its <u>cause</u> is here, if it appears at all. Why are not its effects apparent, then? Why in the future? And you seek to be content with sighing, and with "reasoning" you do not understand it now, but <u>will</u> some day. And <u>then</u> its meaning will be clear. This is <u>not</u> reason, for it is unjust, and clearly hints at punishment until the time of liberation is at hand. Given a change of purpose for the good, there is <u>no</u> reason for an interval in which disaster strikes, to be perceived as "good" some day but now in form of pain. This is a <u>sacrifice</u> of *now*, which <u>could</u> not be the cost the Holy Spirit asks for what He gave <u>without</u> a cost at all.
> 8. Yet this illusion has a cause which, though untrue, must be <u>already</u> in your mind. And <u>this</u> illusion is but one effect that it engenders, and one form in which its outcome is perceived. This interval in time, when retribution is perceived to be the form in which the "good" appears, is but one aspect of the little space that lies between you, unforgiven still.

We don't just project our desire for space onto our brother. We also project it onto the Holy Spirit. We think, "He's given me this gift, and I accepted it. I did my part. But even though I'm sure this gift is really a good thing, for now it looks like disaster. It will probably be a long time before it actually looks like a blessing. But I know that the Lord works in mysterious ways. Maybe I don't deserve the full gift right now. Hopefully, some day I'll understand it all."

We have probably all said something like this. But this is not the way the Holy Spirit works. He gives us everything for free the instant we accept it. His gifts are not like savings bonds that mature in twenty years. If the blessing is taking a long time to unfold its petals, it's because we are afraid of the flower. We are afraid of really joining with our brother.

> 9. Be not content with future happiness. It has <u>no</u> meaning, and is <u>not</u> your just reward. For you have cause for freedom *now*. What profits freedom in a prisoner's form? Why <u>should</u> deliverance be disguised

as death? Delay is senseless, and the "reasoning" that would maintain effects of <u>present</u> cause must be delayed until a <u>future</u> time, is merely a denial of the fact that consequence and cause <u>must</u> come as one. Look not to time, but to the little space between you still, to be delivered <u>from</u>. And do not let it be <u>disguised</u> as time, and so preserved <u>because</u> its form is changed and what it <u>is</u> cannot be recognized. The Holy Spirit's purpose <u>now</u> is yours. Should not His happiness be yours as well?

Jesus now summarizes his message to Helen and Bill, "You have accepted the Holy Spirit's purpose (in that original moment of joining) and so the benefits of that purpose are now yours. Cause and effect always come together. You should therefore be experiencing His freedom and happiness now. You should be basking in your union now. Don't think that a long delay is being forced on you, and that it is from this that you must be delivered. Instead, realize that the real problem is the space you want to keep between you. That is what you need to be delivered from. If you disguise this space as time, you will hide it and so keep it beyond the reach of healing."

Application: Choose someone with whom you have some sort of rift, someone you have perhaps wanted to forgive, but have had difficulty really forgiving. You still find yourself holding back your love and desire to join.

Imagine this scenario: You completely forgive this person for everything she's done, and she receives your gift totally appropriately, just like you wanted, and responds in kind, returning forgiveness to you, so that the relationship is reconciled and healed.

If you really trusted that this would happen, wouldn't forgiving this person be easy?

If so, doesn't that mean that your lack of forgiveness is about not trusting that your gift will be properly returned to you? What *do* you imagine will happen when you think of giving this person the gift of your forgiveness?

If you imagine that you will love and forgive in the face of her continuing resentment, and that this will go on for a while until she returns your gift, doesn't it seem like, in that interval, you made a sacrifice for the sake of being good?

And doesn't this make it seem "safer to remain a little careful and a little watchful of interests perceived as separate"—a little watchful of your interests so that you aren't left hanging out to dry?

If yes, then, in other words, you are saying, "I am afraid to forgive this person now, for I know there will be this time lag in between me forgiving her and her forgiving and joining with me." How do you know this future? Are you some kind of prophet? Do you really know that this is what's going to happen?

The Course is saying that, since you don't know what this person will choose in the future, there must be something else causing your fear. If you are so sure that this is what the future holds, then your mind must have actually assigned this purpose to the future. Is that possible?

But why would you assign to the future the purpose of delaying this person's forgiveness of you and joining with you?

The reason, says the Course, is that you don't really *want* to join with this person. And so you want to delay the joining, put it off. When you think of joining with this person, how do you feel? Is it a totally welcome idea, or not?

Try these lines on for size:

> *In regard to my fear that [name] will not return my forgiveness,*
> *future loss is not my fear.*
> *Present joining is my dread.*
> *My prediction that [name] will not forgive and join with me in*
>   *the future,*
> *is just a projection of my present wish that [name] doesn't.*

What's really going on is this: You want to keep a space, a distance between you and this person. This exists in the present moment, inside you, where you have a choice about it. But then you project this "desire for space" onto the other person, where it becomes outside you, outside your control. Now it becomes translated into time, into a time lag imposed on you from without, from the other person.

This reflects a belief that things that come from God are good in the long run, but demand sacrifice on your part in the short run. But that is not how God works.

But what if you gave total forgiveness? Would this person really receive it, return it and join with you? Didn't Jesus give total forgiveness to the whole world, and haven't we still failed to really receive the gift? The answer lies in the sixth paragraph of this section. Try telling yourself:

> *If I completely forgive [name] and trust [name]*
> *then I can look upon the holy effects of that now.*
> *I can experience the return of my gift now,*
> *And I can experience our joining now even if those things have*
>   *not yet taken place on the visible level.*

IX. For They Have Come
Commentary by Robert Perry

This is such a beautiful section, perhaps the most beautiful in the entire Course. In honor of this, I am going to comment on it in a somewhat different way. I am going to lay the section out in iambic pentameter (which, remember, has five pairs of syllables per line, with the accent on the second syllable in each pair). Then I'll intersperse comments that are simply intended to guide you through a quiet, slow, contemplative reading of the section. Before you start, please pick a particular person and apply all the talk about "your brother" to this person. Again, read slowly. Visualize the images. Savor every line.

1. Think but how holy you must be from whom
the Voice for God calls lovingly unto
your brother, that you may awake in him
the Voice that answers to <u>your</u> call!
(Do this. Think how holy you must be.
For the Holy Spirit calls lovingly through you to your brother,
to awaken His Own Voice in that brother.)
                              And think
how holy <u>he</u> must be when in him sleeps
your <u>own</u> salvation, with <u>his</u> freedom joined!
(Again do this. Think how holy this brother must be.
For in him sleeps your salvation.
That's what you're trying to awaken in him.
And when it does awaken and he gives it to you, he will find his own freedom.)
However much you wish he be condemned,
(Reflect on how you have wished for him to be condemned,
how much you have wanted events to reveal just how rotten he has been.)
God is in him. And never will you know
He is in <u>you</u> as well while you attack
His chosen home, and battle with His host.
(Think about this: God is in this brother, unheeding of your

condemnation.

This is God's home, His host.

And while you attack His home, you will never see His home in *you*.)

Regard him gently. Look with loving eyes

on him who carries Christ within him, that

you may behold his glory and rejoice

that Heaven is <u>not</u> separate from you.

(Feel yourself regarding this brother gently,

looking on him lovingly.

For he carries Christ in him.

Then feel yourself rejoice at what this means.

It means that Heaven is not separate from you.)

2. Is it too much to ask a little trust

for him who carries Christ to you, that you

may be forgiven <u>all</u> your sins, and left

without a single one you cherish still?

(Ask yourself this.

Is it really too much to ask that you trust this brother a little,

when he not only carries Christ in him,

but carries Christ *to you*?

Especially considering that when you trust him,

the Christ in him will forgive you all your sins,

and wipe away every last bit of your attachment to them?)

Forget not that a shadow held between

your brother and yourself obscures the face

of Christ and memory of God.

(Think about the dark shadow of resentment that lies between you and

this brother.

Realize that this is what obscures Christ and God from your awareness.)

And would you trade Them for an ancient hate?

(Really ask this question deeply.

Would you trade Christ and God for this shadow, this ancient hate?)

The ground whereon you stand is holy ground

<u>because</u> of Them Who, standing there with you,

have blessed it with <u>Their</u> innocence and peace.

(Now you have forgiven this brother, and everything else flows from

this.

Now the ground on which the two of you stand is holy ground.

For They—God and Christ—have joined you,

and blessed this space with Their innocence and peace.
Just imagine this.)

3. The blood of hatred fades to let the grass
grow green again, and let the flowers be
all white and sparkling in the summer sun.
(Picture the pain from your battles with this person
as blood staining the ground.
But now you see that blood fade before your eyes.
In its place grass grows up, new and green,
and white flowers spring up that sparkle in the warm summer sun.)
What was a place of death has now become
a living temple in a world of light.
(The ground on which you stand used to be a battleground,
dark and blood-stained.
But now the plants that have sprung up
have formed themselves into a living temple,
to reflect the sanctity of the forgiveness that has taken place there.)
Because of Them. It is Their Presence which
has lifted holiness again to take
its ancient place upon an ancient throne.
(It is Their Presence, invited by your forgiveness,
that has sanctified this ground where battle used to rule.
Now holiness occupies the throne instead,
as it used to, long, long ago, before the battle first began.)
Because of Them have miracles sprung up
as grass and flowers on the barren ground
that hate had scorched and rendered desolate.
(The ground had been scorched by the heat of your hate.
But Their life-giving Presence has reversed that.
The grass and flowers spoken of are just symbols.
They symbolize the miracles that are now springing up all around you.
Because of Them.)
What hate has wrought have They undone. And now
you stand on ground so holy Heaven leans
to join with it, and make it like itself.
The shadow of an ancient hate has gone,
and all the blight and withering have passed
forever from the land where They have come.
(Before, you stood on a scorched landscape,

with barren ground and a few diseased and withered plants,
and dark clouds hanging perpetually overhead.
But all that has changed forever,
now that They have come.)

4. What is a hundred or a thousand years
to Them, or tens of thousands? When They come,
time's purpose is fulfilled. What never <u>was</u>
passes to nothingness when They have come.
(It doesn't matter how long hate had ruled the earth.
It doesn't matter how many tens of thousands of years
had gone by while They were shut out.
When They come, the rule of hate is over.
Time itself is over.)
What hatred claimed is given up to love,
and freedom lights up every living thing
and lifts it into Heaven, where the lights
grow ever brighter as each one comes home.
(Watch as each living thing that had been held captive by hate
is lit up with the light of freedom.
And what does it do with this freedom?
What does a bird do when set free?
It flies home, to Heaven,
where there is great rejoicing at its return.)
The incomplete is made complete again,
and Heaven's joy has been increased because
what is its own has been restored to it.
The bloodied earth is cleansed, and the insane
have shed their garments of insanity
to join Them on the ground whereon you stand.
(As this blood-soaked earth is cleansed,
see the insane shed the various uniforms that announced their insanity
and caused the blood to spill.
See them come from all over to stand on your holy ground,
clad in pure white robes.)

5. Heaven is grateful for this gift of what
has been withheld so long. For They have come
to gather in Their Own. What has been locked
is opened; what was held <u>apart</u> from light

is given up, that light may shine on it
and leave no space nor distance lingering
between the light of Heaven and the world.
(God and Christ have not just come to transform the earth.
"They have come to gather in Their Own."
Their Own have been scattered, locked away from love,
held apart from light.
But that is all changing.
Now the formerly insane are gathering where They have set down,
to be taken home again.)

6. The holiest of all the spots on earth
is where an ancient hatred has become
a present love.
(This spot on which you stand,
this place in which you forgave this one brother,
is now the holiest spot on earth,
holier than Jerusalem.)
                    And They come quickly to
the living temple, where a home for Them
has been set up. There is no place
in Heaven holier. And They <u>have</u> come
to dwell within the temple offered Them,
to be <u>Their</u> resting place as well as <u>yours</u>.
(By forgiving this brother, you set up a temple for Them,
a holy resting place that mirrors Their heavenly home.
And They come instantly to rest in this temple, along with you.)
What hatred has released to love becomes
the brightest light in Heaven's radiance.
And all the lights in Heaven brighter grow,
in gratitude for what has been restored.
(Your relationship with this brother was full of hate.
But now it has been released to love.
Picture it becoming the brightest light in Heaven's radiance.
Picture it causing all the lights of Heaven to grow brighter.
They grow brighter because they are eternally grateful
for what was lost being restored to them.)

7. Around you angels hover lovingly,
to keep away all darkened thoughts of sin,

and <u>keep</u> the light where it has entered in.
(Again, picture this.
Imagine angels hovering all around you,
protecting the beautiful light of forgiveness that now shines in you and
your brother,
keeping it safe from all dark thoughts of sin.)
Your footprints lighten up the world, for where
you walk forgiveness gladly goes with you.
(Imagine that wherever you and your brother now go
you leave shining footprints behind you,
pointing the way home.)
No one on earth but offers thanks to one
who has restored his home, and sheltered him
from bitter winter and the freezing cold.
And shall the Lord of Heaven and His Son
give <u>less</u> in gratitude for so much <u>more</u>?
(You know very well the gratitude you would receive
if a man's home burned down,
leaving him homeless and exposed to the elements,
and you rebuilt his home for him.
Realize that by forgiving your brother,
this is exactly what you have done for God and Christ, and even *more*.
Try to imagine Their gratitude.)

8. Now is the temple of the living God
rebuilt as host again to Him by Whom
it was created. Where He dwells, His Son
dwells with Him, <u>never</u> separate. And They
give thanks that They are welcome made at last.
(There is an ancient belief that a temple
is the earthly dwelling place of the deity,
and that when the temple is destroyed,
it must be rebuilt if He is to have a home again on earth.
This is true in a sense, but the temple is not a building.
It is the love between you and your brother.
This is the temple you have rebuilt.)
Where stood a cross stands now the risen Christ,
and ancient scars are healed within His sight.
(On your battleground stood a cross, ready for use whenever needed.
Now in its place stands the Christ Himself.

And every scar within the range of His sight, however old and ugly, is
healed.)
An ancient miracle has come to bless
and to <u>replace</u> an ancient enmity
(between you and your brother)
that came to kill. In gentle gratitude
do God the Father <u>and</u> the Son return
to what is Theirs, and will forever be.
Now is the Holy Spirit's purpose done.
(He has worked for eons just to prepare the way for Them.)
For They have come! For They have come at last!
(Feel the celebration, the exultation in these final lines.
Feel your own deep desire to set that temple up for Them,
to let Them come,
by forgiving your brother.)

X. The End of Injustice
Commentary by Robert Perry

1. What, then, remains to be undone for you to <u>realize</u> Their Presence? Only this; you have a <u>differential</u> view of <u>when</u> attack is justified, and <u>when</u> you think it is unfair and <u>not</u> to be allowed. When you perceive it <u>as</u> unfair, you think that a response of anger now is just. And thus you see what <u>is</u> the same as <u>different</u>. Confusion is not limited. If it occurs at all it <u>will</u> be total. And its presence, in <u>whatever</u> form, will hide Their Presence. They are known with clarity or not at all. Confused perception will block knowledge. It is <u>not</u> a question of the <u>size</u> of the confusion, or <u>how much</u> it interferes. Its simple <u>presence</u> shuts the door to <u>Theirs,</u> and keeps Them there unknown.

After reading the last section, what could we want but to let Them come? But we still hold back from doing so, by holding back from forgiving our brother. Why? Because we think that sometimes his attack on us is fair (because of what we have done) and sometimes is unfair. When we judge it fair, we think we have no right to attack back. But when we judge it unfair, we think our retaliation is simple justice.

This means that we see these two attacks, which are really the same, as different. It's as if we are responding to identical twins as if they were opposites. We are, in other words, deeply confused. And the presence of this confusion blocks from our awareness the Presence of God and Christ. We can only have one in our mind: the presence of confusion or the Presence of Father and Son.

2. What does it <u>mean</u> if you perceive attack in certain <u>forms</u> to be unfair to you? It means that there <u>must</u> be some forms in which <u>you think</u> <u>it fair</u>. For otherwise, how could some be evaluated as <u>unfair</u>? Some, then, are <u>given</u> meaning and perceived as sensible. And only <u>some</u> are seen as meaning<u>less</u>. And this <u>denies</u> the fact that *all* are senseless, <u>equally</u> without a cause or consequence, and <u>cannot</u> have effects of <u>any</u> kind. Their Presence is obscured by <u>any</u> veil that stands between Their shining innocence, and your awareness that it [Their innocence] is your own and <u>equally</u> belongs to every living thing along with you. God limits not. And what is limited can<u>not</u> be Heaven. So it <u>must</u> be hell.

Our confusion means that, in our eyes, some attacks are crazy, senseless, while others are just and sensible. This blocks us from understanding that *all* attacks are senseless; so senseless that they have no substance, no power, and no effects.

Seeing different attacks as being actually different means that we dole out innocence very selectively. Those who attack unjustly are guilty, while those who attack justly are innocent. Yet God doesn't dole out innocence like this. He doesn't give limited gifts. What He gives one, He gives to all. Thus, the limited innocence that we dole out can't be God's. It can't be Heaven. "So it must be hell." And how can doling out hell to our brothers open the door of awareness to Their heavenly Presence? It cannot. Our selective innocence, then, is a veil. It *hides* Their Presence from us.

> 3. Unfairness and attack are <u>one</u> mistake, so firmly joined that where one is perceived the other <u>must</u> be seen. You <u>cannot</u> be unfairly treated. The belief you <u>are</u> is but another form of the idea you are deprived by someone <u>not</u> yourself. <u>Projection</u> of the cause of sacrifice is at the root of everything perceived to be unfair and <u>not</u> your just deserts. Yet it is <u>you</u> who ask this [sacrifice] of yourself, in deep injustice to the Son of God [your brother]. You <u>have</u> no enemy except yourself, and you are enemy indeed to him because you do not know him *as* yourself. What <u>could</u> be more unjust than that he be deprived of what he <u>is</u>, denied the right to be himself, and asked to sacrifice his Father's Love and yours as <u>not</u> his due?

All attack is unfair, no matter what the circumstances. Attack and unfairness are the same thing. And so, just as you cannot be attacked, so you cannot be treated unfairly. Whenever someone causes you loss, you have actually caused this loss of yourself. Then you projected the causation onto that other person. First you shot yourself in the foot, and then, while the gun was still smoking, you placed the gun in your brother's hand. You thus made him appear to be your enemy. This deprived him of his right to be himself (he is God's Son) and asked him to sacrifice his Father's Love along with yours. You did all of this by framing him for your own attack on yourself.

> 4. Beware of the temptation to perceive yourself unfairly treated. In this view, you seek to find an innocence that is <u>not</u> Theirs but yours alone,

and at the cost of someone else's guilt. Can innocence be purchased by the giving of your guilt to someone else? And *is* it innocence that your attack on him attempts to get? Is it not retribution for your own attack upon the Son of God [your brother] you seek? Is it not safer to believe that you are innocent of this, and victimized despite your innocence? Whatever way the game of guilt is played, there must be loss. Someone must lose his innocence that someone else can take it from him, making it his own.

We perceive ourselves to be unfairly treated so readily! Yet Jesus says we should beware of this tendency; we should regard it as a temptation. For we are trying to find an innocence for ourselves that is not the inclusive innocence of God and Christ. It is an exclusive innocence, which we purchase for ourselves by giving our guilt to our brother. Once we place the gun in his hands, he is the guilty one and we the innocent victim.

If I understand the fifth sentence correctly, when we blame our brother, we are really trying to get back at him for our attack on him. How strange! It's as if we kick our dog in his hind leg, and when we see him limping, we say, "Stupid dog! Now what've you done to yourself?" And then we kick him again for his stupidity.

> 5. You think your brother is unfair to you because you think that one must be unfair to make the other innocent. And in this game do you perceive one purpose for your whole relationship. And this you seek to add unto the purpose given it. The Holy Spirit's purpose [for the relationship] is to let the Presence of your holy Guests be known to you. And to this purpose nothing can be added, for the world is purposeless except for this. To add or take away from this one goal is but to take away all purpose from the world and from yourself. And each unfairness that the world appears to lay upon you, you have laid on it by rendering it purposeless, without the function that the Holy Spirit sees. And simple justice has been thus denied to every living thing upon the earth.

In our relationships, we are playing the game of guilt. And in this game, someone has to win and someone has to lose. One has to be guilty so that the other can be innocent. According to Jesus, winning at this game is our whole purpose in the relationship. What an unpleasant idea!

He says that we have added this unholy purpose onto the holy purpose that the Holy Spirit gave to our relationship. His purpose is that we forgive each other, so that the Presence of our holy Guests can be made known to us. Every time that we obscure this holy purpose, we drain the world of purpose. This is exactly what we are doing when we see ourselves being unfairly treated by someone. We are seeing him as guilty, so that we can feel innocent. And by doing so, we have taken his true purpose away from him, so that now he feels purposeless, functionless.

If you ever want to help someone find a sense of purpose, then, don't see him or her as treating you unfairly.

> 6. What this injustice does to you who judge unfairly, and who see as you have judged, you cannot calculate. The world grows dim and threatening, not a trace of all the happy sparkle that salvation brings can you perceive to lighten up your way. And so you see <u>yourself</u> deprived of light, abandoned to the dark, unfairly left without a purpose in a futile world. The world is fair <u>because</u> the Holy Spirit has brought injustice to the light within, and there has <u>all</u> unfairness been resolved and been <u>replaced</u> with justice and with love. If you perceive injustice anywhere, you need but say:

> *By this do I **deny** the Presence of the Father and the Son.*
> *And I would rather know of Them than see injustice, which Their Presence shines away.*

Discarding the Holy Spirit's purpose does more than deprive our brother of a sense of purpose. It deprives us as well. We see ourselves walking through a purposeless world, a dim and threatening world. Futility surrounds us on all sides. In such a world, our lives seem futile as well.

Yet we can walk through a different world, a world that is *fair*. How can Jesus tell us that the world is fair, after telling us that it's full of attack, and that all attack is unfair? The world is fair because somewhere beneath the surface, the Holy Spirit has brought all the world's unfairness to the light within, where it has been undone and replaced with love. Beneath all the world's unfair surfaces is shining pure justice.

Application: Think of someone you see as treating you unfairly. Realize that the loss you see this person as causing you, you caused yourself. And then you blamed this person (for what was essentially your attack on you), so that you could feel innocent by making him or her guilty. Then, thinking again of the injustice you were seeing, say:

> *By this do I **deny** the Presence of the Father and the Son.*
> *And I would rather know of Them than see injustice,*
> *which Their Presence shines away.*

About the Circle's
TEXT READING PROGRAM

An Unforgettable Journey through the Text in One Year

The Text is the foundation of *A Course in Miracles*, yet many students find it hard going. This program is designed to guide you through the Text, paragraph by paragraph, in one year.

Each weekday, you will receive an e-mail containing that day's Text section, along with commentary on each paragraph, written by Robert Perry or Greg Mackie. The readings contain material edited out of the published Course as well as exercises for practical application. This is the material that has been presented now in book format in our series *The Illuminated Text*.

By signing up for our online program, you will also receive:

- Weekly one-hour class recordings led by Robert Perry and Greg Mackie that summarize that week's sections and answer students' questions
- An online forum for sharing with others in the program
- Related articles on key Text sections e-mailed directly to you
- Your personal web archive, with access to all your commentaries and class recordings
- An unlimited "pause feature" for pausing your program while you're away

Want to learn more? Call us today on 1-888-357-7520, or go to www.circleofa.org, the largest online resource for *A Course in Miracles*!

We hope that you will join us for this truly enlightening program!

ABOUT THE AUTHORS

 Robert Perry has been a student of *A Course in Miracles* (ACIM) since 1981. He taught at Miracle Distribution Center in California from 1986 to 1989, and in 1993 founded the Circle of Atonement in Sedona, Arizona. The Circle is an organization composed of several teachers dedicated to helping establish the Course as an authentic spiritual tradition.

One of the most respected voices on ACIM, Robert has traveled extensively, speaking throughout the U.S. and internationally. In addition to contributing scores of articles to various Course publications, he is the author or co-author of nineteen books and booklets, including the hugely popular *An Introduction to A Course in Miracles*. Robert's goal has always been to provide a complete picture of what the Course is—as a thought system and as a path meant to be lived in the world on a daily basis—and to support students in walking along that path.

Robert has recently authored his first non-ACIM book, *Signs: A New Approach to Coincidence, Synchronicity, Guidance, Life Purpose, and God's Plan*, available on Amazon sites internationally.

 Greg Mackie has been a student of *A Course in Miracles* since 1991. He has been teaching and writing for the Circle of Atonement since 1999, and has written scores of articles for A Better Way, the newsletter of the Circle of Atonement, as well as other ACIM publications. He is the author of *How Can We Forgive Murderers?* and co-taught, along with Robert Perry, the Text Reading Program and the Daily Workbook Program, which consisted of 365 recordings.

CPSIA information can be obtained
at www.ICGtesting.com
Printed in the USA
LVOW08s0155120117
520671LV00001B/34/P